# the hip girl's guide
## to the
# kitchen

# the hip girl's guide
## to the
# kitchen

### A Hit-the-Ground-Running Approach
### to Stocking Up and Cooking Delicious,
### Nutritious, and Affordable Meals

# Kate Payne

#### Foreword by Eugenia Bone

**HARPER** DESIGN
*An Imprint of HarperCollins Publishers*

THE HIP GIRL'S GUIDE TO THE KITCHEN: A HIT-THE-GROUND-RUNNING APPROACH TO STOCKING UP AND COOKING DELICIOUS, NUTRITIOUS, AND AFFORDABLE MEALS. Copyright © 2014 by Kathryn E. Payne. All rights reserved. No part of this book may be used or reproduced in any manner whatsoever without written permission except in the case of brief quotations embodied in critical articles and reviews. For information address Harper Design, 195 Broadway, New York, NY 10007.

HarperCollins books may be purchased for educational, business, or sales promotional use. For information please e-mail the Special Markets Department at SPsales@ harpercollins.com.

First published in 2014 by:
Harper Design
*An Imprint of* HarperCollins*Publishers*
195 Broadway
New York, NY 10007
Tel (212) 207-7000
harperdesign@harpercollins.com
www.harpercollins.com

Distributed throughout the world by:

HarperCollins*Publishers*
195 Broadway
New York, NY 10007

ISBN: 978-0-06-225540-2

Library of Congress Control Number: 2014934592
Book design by Suet Yee Chong
Illustrations by Meredith Dawson
Calligraphy by Alison Hanks

Printed in the United States of America, 2014

First printing, 2014

For my grandmother "Bertha Burnham"
and everyone who encountered
those unfortunate rolls.
Who cares about dinner rolls anyway?

# contents

## PART I

# Stocking Up:
# Setting the Stage for Success

## PART II

# Feeding Yourself:
# Life's Pesky Eating Requirements

## PART III
# Feeding Others: Entertaining and Sharing Food with Friends

# foreword

I met Kate Payne in 2009, shortly after I'd published a book on canning. At the time, she was working on her first *Hip Girl's* book, a millennial-generation approach to the chores and joys of maintaining a home. That first book was a swirl of tips and solutions and ideas for pulling a first household together; it took the panty hose off Héléoise. But in this book she settles down and focuses on matters of the kitchen. It makes sense: there is no space more essential to the definition of home.

Kate recognizes that the kitchen paradigm has changed. The use of fresh regional produce and proteins has become a choice rather than an imperative, and that choice is dictated by a bevy of considerations: flavor, health, economics, environment, and politics. Deciding how to eat today is laden with self-identifiers: Am I gluten free? Vegan? Paleo? What percentage of my time and dollars should be devoted to disengaging from the grid? Should I boycott General Mills, Nestle, and

Tyson Foods? Today's food choices are not just about what's for dinner. They promulgate personal truths and values.

Prewar families used local foods, put up preserves, made dishes from scratch, and utilized the waste stream of foods, even their bones and stems, out of necessity. During the Cold War era, those kinds of kitchen ecosystems were increasingly replaced with cheap, premade, high-calorie foods with an enhanced shelf life supported by chemicals. Kate is a part of, and has had her values shaped by, today's post–Cold War era, when the values of corporate America in general and industrial agriculture and its cohort, the biotech industry, in particular have become suspect.

The artisanal movement, once the arena of hereditary family operations, has risen (in part) in reaction to our fast-food culture. Every year we learn of new cheese makers, picklers, chocolatiers, preservers, and specialty farmers of all sorts who offer tempting alternatives to heavily processed, transported, or treated foods. Supporting these endeavors is a food enthusiast's passion. It's also a hobby for the rich, for while artisanal producers address key issues of health, environment, and flavor, their products are often expensive, a reflection of the David and Goliath–like challenges of competing with the industrial food system.

Community-supported foodways have evolved as a response to both the tyranny of the industrialized food complex and their allies in Congress, and the fiscal realities of artisanal products. Shared bulk purchases, co-ops, canning swaps, repurposing, reusing, recycling . . . all this is creating food communities that reinforce values and politics beyond the question of what's for dinner. When Kate describes herself as a hip girl, she is *really* talking about embracing these.

Her book shows readers how to be more food savvy; how to get hip to what their options and, actually, their obligations are. This is not a cookbook, but rather a primer for those setting up or beginning a life lived in the kitchen today, facing today's limitations and opportunities. Her recipe palette is not ethnic, it's multicultural; and her recommendations acknowledge the dietary trends of the current generation and their slender pocketbooks, too. Kate is trying to reach a large and unruly audience, but her solution is the right one: the key to successful cooking is to get in touch with what you like to eat and be realistic about what you have the time and money to prepare. If you are honest about your food preferences and priorities, and you let your conscience determine your choices, then your cooking will be easier and more satisfying.

Frugality and functionality are the pillars upon which flavor rests here, and Kate describes these virtues. Humble tools assure that the cook is preparing foods by hand, and when a food is prepared by hand, it is controlled: pestos aren't too smooth, doughs are not overkneaded—because at the end of the day, it is *skill* that determines good cooking technique, not gizmos. That is what is so untranslatable about your grandmother's recipes. Likewise, when the home cook uses regional foods that are, by nature, only marginally processed and transported, dishes prepared with those foods simply taste better. That's what makes Italian food so good; it's not about the recipes. It is about getting out of the way of fresh ingredients.

So here's the takeaway: Cooking well is synonymous with cooking with integrity. Recipes that are uncomplicated and unpretentious, that are prepared by hand using good seasonal stuff, make a kind of honest meal, and it is that honesty that is tastiest.

This is the real but often elusive truth of good cooking: values matter.

—Eugenia Bone

# introduction

I've come a long way in the kitchen, believe me. My twenties were paved with good intentions and a shameful lot of wasted groceries. Besides the fact that I was missing all that money that was literally composting at the bottom of the refrigerator, I was also missing that amazing feeling that comes when you realize you are able to feed yourself—to walk into the kitchen and use what you have on hand to make something edible, and maybe even delicious.

My version of kitchen confidence is as simple as knowing how to feed yourself from basic ingredients in as much or less time than it takes to go buy something premade from a grocery store, restaurant, or deli. And that confidence can change your day, your week, and your life.

Our society seems to like the idea of cooking much more than the actual cooking, as evidenced by our obsession with buying cookbooks, food magazines, and fancy kitchen gear; watching chefs make stuff on TV; downloading apps; and trying to technologize ourselves out of and around the matter at hand: cutting up food and cooking it. All these great resources and tools are at our disposal, and yet we often feel too busy to prepare meals at home. The disconnect between our cutting boards and the dinner plate is paramount.

## why cook, why you?

Let me rephrase that question: Why do it yourself when it's so easy to eat out or buy the packaged item? My answer to that question is quality, nutrition, and economics.

### quality

Food you buy from restaurants—unless money is no issue and you plan to dine only at local, sustainability-focused, farm-to-table restaurants—is likely composed of the cheapest ingredients the owner could find. My dad is in the wholesale food business and our family has owned restaurants in the past; he knows both sides of the industry really well. Pesticides, hormones, and GMOs are on my list of things to avoid when possible, and the cheapest ingredients often include many of these on their bottom-line price tags.

### nutrition

Food processing (the act of turning whole ingredients on a large scale into packaged and/or ready-to-eat items) strips many foods of valuable nutrients, primarily to preserve them and keep them from spoiling before they land in our shopping carts. Unfortunately, these processes also make it harder for our bodies to digest or process the foods in many cases. It's unreasonable to swear off all packaged food in busy, modern life, but it's important to understand that the less we buy in a package and the more we cook from whole ingredients the better. There are many cheap (and cheaply made) convenience items out there packed full of stuff our bodies weren't designed to consume, at least on a regular basis.

## economics

Making choices about and changes to what you and possibly your family consume is a big deal. There are long-held beliefs and habits to consider and then issues of monthly budgets to factor into the equation. My wife and I had to bid farewell to the majority of the packaged, premade goods we liked buying (oh, the convenient gluten-free cookies!) in order to make room in our budget for more expensive dairy and meats from cows and other animals raised mostly locally and without antibiotics and hormones.

I understand not everyone is able to make these kinds of choices (as those cookies or convenience items might not be in the budget to begin with). The wider problems of food access and hunger are issues I care deeply about, and I hope to see viable alternatives for those living with these realities. This book is intended not as an approach to solving these issues but rather as a tool to bring those of us with income that covers our basic needs (and this still includes tight budgets) to a place where feeding ourselves with better-quality things for approximately the same amount of money is a reality.

Learning how to make all this work on a budget is what I've tried to do for the past six years of my freelance writing career and eating life. We simply don't have the money to purchase whatever we want, so we prioritize.

## reality in small bites

My wife told someone at a party recently that the key to being successful in the kitchen is planning one meal ahead. She taught me that planning for at least one meal in the future will in large part prevent the hunger meltdowns, unplanned takeout, and impulse purchases during mealtime grocery store visits. Staying ahead of the curve is where you want to be. It's no surprise that you're going to need to eat three times tomorrow. Starting the thought process on at least one of those meals now is going to bolster success in remaining thrifty with your meal budget.

My wife cooks—in fact, she's the one who taught me how stress-free it can be. When we were living on less than $200–$250 per month for all our food costs in Brooklyn (with little to no expendable income for restaurants), she showed me how to regularly practice cooking. Approaching cooking as a continuous cycle really helps turn sporadic bursts of grocery purchases (and subsequent rot, in the downtimes) into cycles of meals you can and want to eat as the days tumble forward, whether you feel like cooking or not.

## i don't like to cook

Throughout my successes in building community around reclaiming our homes and certain empowering domestic arts, an unsettling reality remained. I don't inherently like everyday cooking; I don't find it relaxing. Rather, I find it to be a stressful thing that comes up more often than I feel prepared to handle. (When it's time to make ice cream, bread, or pickles, however, I'm your woman, your special projects task force who cheerfully steps up.)

In my earlier years, I abstained from daily cooking, thinking it took too much time (that is, when there was more than $12 in my bank account for the next two weeks), and then rushed off to that local Slow Food event or book club meeting where we chatted about eloquent food prose or changing the food system (where I felt like a hypocrite and embarked on a mini-shame spiral, thinking I *should* have it all under control and like cooking). That kind of thinking—an absent but obligatory affection for actual cooking—wasn't doing me any favors, nor was it inspiring me to get into the kitchen.

I am solidly a part of the group I think will find this book useful. I took over the task of sustenance cooking in our household while writing this book because it was important to me to practice what I preach, to be knee-deep in the endless cycle of getting food on the table.

Thanks to writing this book, I managed to reframe the act of cooking into something less ominous, and I hope to help you find a way to do that too. Not all of us have significant others or roommates who carry the responsibility for household sustenance on their backs with ease or even joy. I now try to view cooking as a challenge and opportunity to come up with creative meals from things we already have, a minor shift that keeps my wheels moving and keeps me just out of the former drudgery and stress zone. If my attitude (and aptitude) can change, I'm betting there's hope for you, too.

During the many evenings I spent writing this book—since, in true *procrastiKate* style, I left my writing for the end of the day—it was not unusual that I had to make a choice between making dinner and writing. I surely noted the irony in the fact that we were eating/ordering out because I needed every minute available to write my book on how to kick ass in the kitchen (and the other cook in our house was working late and didn't want to eat any of the prefrozen leftovers meals I had on hand for just this sort of occasion).

Life happens, and eating out is not the enemy. It's not my place to judge you for opting for store-bought meals or takeout when workweeks are crazy, confidence levels drop, or whatever. Nor should you feel bad about yourself when you need to take the easier road. Your best effort is good enough; do better in small steps.

## this book isn't going to cook dinner for you

Now that you know where I'm coming from, it's time to get in gear. I will show you how to fold budget-friendly everyday cooking and a few from-scratch projects into the context of your busy life, but it does involve you making an effort to change your habits.

This is an at-your-own-pace guide, and continuing in *Hip Girl's* style, I'll offer Hip Tricks and Words to the Wise and tools to stock. Resources at the end of each chapter will offer further reading and additional sources for honing your skills with specific projects in various aspects of the kitchen. Chapters discussing food projects will also include recipes at the end. I'd probably read first and then go for the recipes, but you can use the book however suits you best.

Part I offers the essentials for setting up your kitchen, from equipping your ship to stocking the shelves. In Chapter 1, we'll start with tools, cookware, equipment, and appliances—what you really need and where to keep it. I'll cover pantry essentials in Chapter 2, a.k.a. what you should have on hand to avoid shopping every time a meal needs to happen. Then, in Chapter 3, after you have the basics on hand, I'll help you stock up weekly on perishables and other fresh ingredients, so you don't end up pitching them (and your paycheck) in the trash the following week.

Part II is intended for a hit-the-ground-running approach, seeing as you need to eat three times daily whether you've mastered your kitchen or not. This part (Chapters 4, 5, and 6) offers real-life advice and tips to move you from clumsy to confident in the kitchen. No perfect-life pastoral, bird-in-the-windowsill kind of stuff you might see in a motivational guide; rather, I'll clue you in on some from-scratch projects that even *you* can handle—projects that are geared toward people who think it's too hard or takes too long to make food from scratch. You can be the judge of what foods you want to dish out dollars to artisan bakers and food vendors for, and what you can make sufficiently (and, God forbid, even enjoy making!) yourself.

Part III, which includes Chapters 7, 8, and 9, helps you put it all together, with entertaining recipes, preserving projects, and party ideas. After all, one thing I've come to learn about finagling food: making it can be fun, but sharing it with others is the real thrill. Plus, your newly acquired kitchen skills mean possibly adding edible gifts (ones that recipients will actually want to eat) to your gifting regime, and thus saving money while you're at it.

## another cookbook?

I used to hoard cookbooks prior to actually developing a working relationship with my kitchen. I saw them as an investment in what is possible. Unfortunately that translated to books that sat on the shelf unused while I ate out or bought prepared foods.

So, while *The Hip Girl's Guide to the Kitchen* has recipes, this isn't really a cookbook. Think of it more like a kitchen friend, someone sitting with you helping to bust your fears in the kitchen. As I researched to write this book, I discovered how many ways there are to make less-than-three-ingredient things (like mayonnaise or beans or bread) and how confusing it can get really fast. As your kitchen friend I feel compelled to tell you that there are no less than three and sometimes up to twelve different ways to do almost everything in the kitchen, and honestly, I don't think it's all that important which one you choose, as long as it works for you. You should find the way that suits you best and try to learn it by heart.

I'm sharing my favorite recipes, mostly gleaned from my five years of experience making the kitchen work for me, and some contributed by the invaluable community of authors and friends who occupy my kitchen bookshelf and blogroll. Finding your community is a large part of this book; I invite you to explore.

I'll never tell you something is too hard for you; you're smart and you can figure it out, even if it takes a few attempts. I *will* tell you when something is finicky and a pain in the ass (at first, or always) and let you be the judge. You may not find fun and easy what I find fun and easy. Maybe the art of combining components for nutritious meals on the fly won't be your thing because you like meal planning and being more deliberate about your meals. I grant you permission to find out what kind of kitchen operator you are and to tailor your experience to reality. After all, you are the only person who can make more cooking happen.

I hope you will pick a few things to add to your kitchen toolbox; more specifically, I hope to deliver you to a confident state of stocking staples and cooking simple and delicious things for yourself.

As with *The Hip Girl's Guide to Homemaking*, I claim myself as the Hip Girl (with the intentional use of an apostrophe), thus you may read on without pressure to be hip or a girl. I wrote this for anyone who has a kitchen and needs to eat from it more frequently, a swath of the population that includes both men and women, single and partnered.

So there you have it, a plan for walking up and introducing (or reintroducing) yourself to your kitchen.

Part 1

# stocking up
### setting the stage
### for success

chapter 1

# equip your ship

## setting up your kitchen
## without winning the lottery

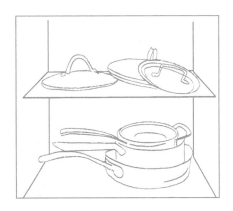

Establishing a habit of cooking starts with a kitchen that's set up to encourage daily interactions with food. I think back to my first kitchen—I copied my parents' kitchens—and how I never quite got the hang of or into the habit of cooking because I had too much stuff and not enough knowledge about what to do with it all. I shoved it all into drawers and cabinets and proceeded to eat out most of the time because my kitchen eluded me.

Most kitchens start out with a box of pots, pans, and dishes, and a random assortment of utensils that either your family or someone else doesn't want any longer. It's okay for your kitchen, like your kitchen relationship, to be a work in progress. You can accomplish basic cooking goals by compiling a few core items.

If you decide to purchase new equipment, keep in mind that there are endless ways to spend money, buying things you might (or might not) use. You can go wild purchasing kitchen equipment in a *what-if* sort of mind-set (e.g., *What if I start a mini-soufflé business? What if I decide to start making my own pasta? What if I want to poach more than four eggs at a time?*).

It's hard to know exactly what you will need when you're just getting used to the idea that eating in takes quite a bit more energy beyond the good intentions of bringing groceries home. I recommend only acquiring things you know how to use or are only one step away from knowing how to use. Feeling good about where you're at is the main goal. As your kitchen skills improve, so will your cookware.

In this chapter I will help you set up your kitchen so you can get started cooking right away. As you'll see, it's usually not a specific tool that you need to eat a good meal and have fun in the kitchen—it's a stash of ingredients and a bit of ingenuity.

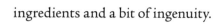

4

## cookware

While it's entirely possible (and in many cases necessary) to cook in cheap pots and pans, it can be joyless, needlessly difficult, and not representative of what cooking might be like with better equipment. Decent pots and pans will increase your chances of success, and to get them, you don't have to spend a gazillion dollars. I recommend acquiring things piecemeal and doing your research on best prices when you're in the market for an improvement. Following are the pots and pans I consider essential.

- 1- or 2-quart stainless steel saucepan with lid (clear lid is a plus).
- Cast-iron skillet: a 9-inch is standard, but get a 12-inch if you want to cook meat (or anything) for more than two people at the same time or if you plan to make pancakes. We cook at least one component (if not the entirety) of every meal in our 12-inch skillet.
- 5- or 7-quart enameled cast-iron French oven with lid (spend the extra dollars to get a metal knob so the whole lid can go in the oven).
- 8-quart stainless steel or enameled steel stockpot with lid (you can use it for the obvious—stocks and stews—or for sealing jars in small-batch canning recipes).
- Set of glass storage containers. We started with a seven-piece Pyrex set and then added a set of five containers from Bed Bath & Beyond, which is just the right amount for containing components of the week's cooking and toting a couple workday lunches.

### Hip Trick

Glass food storage containers aren't much more expensive than a set of BPA-free plastic ones, plus you can use them safely for any reheating application without worry, including sticking them directly in the toaster oven to reheat leftovers.

# dutch ovens vs. french ovens

These old-school camping pots with lids are heavy-duty tools for cooking soups, stocks, braises, roasts, and more. They are fabulous conductors of heat and make for great vehicles to fry chips or doughnuts or even bake a loaf of crusty bread. Often used interchangeably, Dutch ovens are actually unfinished cast iron that can sit atop the campfire, whereas French ovens are just as solid, but enameled both inside and out for ease (you don't have to season them) and increased utility (you can cook acidic things without fear of leaching). See page 8 for more info on cast iron.

Name brand isn't essential here, but be sure that what you're getting is

→ 1 half-sheet cookie pan from a restaurant supply store. Resist the urge to buy the more expensive, nonstick-coated versions. All you'll ever need from a cookie sheet exists in this commercial, utilitarian version. Grab two if you've got a penchant for baking.
→ 5-quart metal mixing bowl.

Get the above items secondhand if you can find them, but definitely don't buy these essentials new:

→ Glassware: 9″ x 13″ glass roasting dish, a couple medium-sized mixing bowls, liquid measuring cups (both 2-cup and 1-quart volumes), and a 9-inch pie plate.
→ Colander—metal if you can find one; otherwise, adopt a plastic one from the thrift store until the right secondhand metal one finds you.

Once you've covered the basics, here are more tools to consider. A few of these have become essential to us, but move at your own pace and adopt what makes itself clear as useful to you:

→ 2- or 3-quart heavy-bottomed saucepan with lid. I have a basic Wolfgang Puck 18/10 stainless steel one that I inherited from a friend who upgraded to a fancier set. This saucepan is my favorite pan for making custards for ice cream.

(The numbers refer to the content of chromium and nickel, respectively; 18/10 is a solid combo that resists corrosion.)

- A few 8-ounce ceramic ramekins. We use these to melt butter in the toaster oven, bake excess muffin or bread batter, or just serve soups and desserts.
- Cast-iron griddle (sits over two burners and is great for stovetop grilling; the flat flip side is great for a brunch party's worth of pancake making).
- 6-quart pot. Ours is used primarily in preserving projects like blanching greens and boiling larger batches of things like potatoes or eggs.

*unstuck on nonstick*

We are a nonstick-free household. "Nonstick" sounds like a good thing, but it's actually a chemical coating that when exposed to very high heats (which a stove range is capable of producing) releases chemicals that can kill birds outright. I'm not advising against nonstick solely for the canary in your kitchen, but for the meaning and principle behind it. These chemicals are powerful things, and the less I'm exposing myself to them the better. Nonstick surfaces also must be paired with plastic or other nonmetal utensils; otherwise, you'll risk scratching the coating and finding flecks of it in your food down the line.

Why not ditch your plastic tools and toxic pans

well made—this is equipment you could have for the rest of your life. The lower priced options ($50–$80) on enameled cast iron are great, and upgrading to more expensive versions is only desirable because certain brands—Staub and Le Creuset—offer lifetime limited warranties. We use both our lower-cost 5-quart and top-of-the-line Le Creuset 7.25-quart round French ovens often, but if I had to choose one, I would go for the 7.25-quart solely for maximum versatility. (It's also my jam and preserving pot, so I'm partial to the larger one for that reason.)

and invest in ones that embrace solid metal and the other non-leaching utensils I recommend later in the chapter? We scramble eggs, cook hamburgers, and make grilled cheese all without nonstick cookware. A cast-iron skillet is the versatile, nontoxic workhorse you might be looking for to fill the nonstick void.

## cast iron

So what's the big deal with cast iron? A cast-iron pan is one of the best kitchen tools because the iron distributes heat more evenly than other pan types. We started with a 9-inch skillet, courtesy of my local thrift store, and quickly learned that cast iron is the only way to go for panfrying and browning meats like we might find in restaurants.

Lodge makes decent, preseasoned pans that fit into any beginner's kitchen budget: $16–$25 depending on the size. Seasoning is the kitchen way of saying moisturized; Lodge's website describes seasoning as "vegetable oil baked onto the iron at a high temperature: not a chemical nonstick coating." We need to season our pans so the iron doesn't rust, which can happen when iron is not coated with the baked-on oils and thus exposed to moisture. Secondhand cast iron is also fine to use. Remove rust by scouring it off with a fine-grade sandpaper or steel wool cloth, and then reseason according to the directions below.

## caring for and cleaning a cast-iron pan

Soap is cast iron's worst enemy. But just because you can't lather it up or throw it in the dishwasher doesn't mean you can't get it clean. Well-seasoned pans are shiny and slick, forming a natural nonstick surface. Boiling water leaves the seasoning intact (thanks to the fact oil and water do not mingle), loosens stuck-on food (which a dedicated brush or a metal spatula can then dislodge), and is hot enough to kill any remaining surface microbes you don't want lingering in your pan.

I start with a deglaze—which means essentially a precleaning with broth or cooking wine (see page 152)—so as not to miss out on delicious cooking remnants (to save or incorporate into whatever I just cooked); then I pour a kettle's worth of just-boiled water into the pan. You can let it sit until the water cools a bit if you'd like, but don't leave it and forget about it or your pan will rust. Never pour cold water into a hot pan; it can cause thermal shock and possibly warp or crack the metal or layer of seasoning.

We have a dedicated cast-iron brush on our dish rack that we use to scrub and scrape food debris from our pans during their boiled

# five great places to hunt for bargains on decent cookware

1. Craigslist. Search for individual items or look up moving sales.

2. Estate sales. Go on the last day and hit up the discounts that are usually offered.

3. Outlet stores. Your favorite kitchen brands have outlet stores, so don't forget to check there first for any large purchases.

4. Overstock and discount retailers. Marshalls, Ross Dress for Less, T.J.Maxx, HomeGoods. You'll need to hunt, and there may be minor imperfections, but there are treasures to be found.

5. The houses of friends who recently got married. We inherited some of our favorite still-in-use pans from friends who upgraded to fancier versions via their wedding registry.

water baths. Find a sturdy scrubbing brush or a stiff nylon brush. If stuck-on food remains after the boiling water bath and scrub, then add fresh hot water and bring it to a boil in your pan to further loosen the residue or use a steel wool scrubber. Dry the pan with a towel (one you don't mind getting blackened) immediately and apply a light coating of vegetable oil while the pan is still warm (we use sunflower oil). Store cast-iron pans uncovered in a dry place to prevent rust.

### reseasoning cast iron

Following the postuse instructions above should keep your cast iron in good shape, but at some point you may need to reseason. If food constantly sticks to the surface, or it starts to look dull and gray, you'll know it's time for some restorative seasoning. These instructions come at Lodge's recommendation on its website:

1. Wash pan with hot, soapy water and a stiff brush. (It is okay to use soap this time because you are about to reseason it.) Rinse and dry completely.
2. Apply a thin, even coating of melted shortening or vegetable cooking oil to the inside and outside of the pan.
3. Place aluminum foil on the bottom rack of the oven to catch any drips and set oven temperature to 350°F to 400°F.
4. Place pan upside down on the top rack of the oven and bake for at least 1 hour. After the hour has elapsed, turn the oven off and let the pan cool in the oven.

Lodge also recommends you deep fry in Dutch ovens at least six times prior to cooking (notoriously acidic) beans of any kind. The acid can cause trace amounts of iron to leach into the cooked food, and for this reason some people avoid cooking acidic things entirely; I say *Oh darn, time to cook up some bacon and then make six batches of doughnuts!* It's a good idea to reseason after cooking other acidic foods, such as vinegary sauces, chili, or tomatoes.

## appliances

My list of essential appliances is short, since daily life shouldn't require a ton of mechanical gadgets. These are the bare bones of making food in your kitchen. It's best to spend a little time working through some basics, improvising, and getting your groove before you fill it up with appliances.

I've grouped my essentials into two sets, reheating/toasting technology and blending/pureeing technology. I'm listing the upgrades for various projects—baking, preserving, dessert making, and so on—in their respective chapters. As you build a relationship with your kitchen, you'll see what shakes out as enjoyable or difficult to use, and what leaves you in need of appliance backup.

### *reheating/toasting (choose one)*

- **Convection or standard toaster oven.** This is my favorite and most used appliance since it covers all my reheating, toasting, and baking needs, and it doesn't heat the whole kitchen up. We use ours to heat

## yes, you can ditch the microwave

My antimicrowave manifesto remains, though the verdict appears to be still out on the safety or harm surrounding electromagnetic radiation. There isn't any long-term research (by American universities or the U.S. government) on these relatively new devices. Microwaves were introduced to the consumer market in 1955, the year my mom was born, and a scant sixty years on the market coupled with an industry that refuses to consider their potential danger doesn't make me feel confident about cooking and nourishing my body through their use.

Obviously I'm not promoting microwave use, but I, like most people, face microwave-only reheat options on occasion out in the world. I say do your best and realize that we live in a complex world, full of hormone and other disruptors; I vote to minimalize exposure to questionable risks, at least under my own roof.

up leftovers, melt butter for baking, bake muffins, pies, or pizzas on hot summer days, and, of course, make toast. Take note, though, that the removable bottom liner, affectionately called the "crumb tray," should really be treated as if it's a cutting board or anything else you'd wash (or at least brush off) after each use (or at the start of the next use). You'll spare yourself that moment when you rush over at the smell of charred food, only to realize it's all the stuff on the bottom, not the food you just placed on the rack.

Convection is an additional and optional feature on some toaster ovens that utilizes a fan to circulate the hot air and thus bakes/cooks things faster and more evenly than when baking normally.

- **Microwave *and* toaster.** You can see where I stand on microwaves, but I have nothing against toasters. The benefit of having just one appliance that does everything in the heating/reheating/toasting category (versus two) is clear to me with my limited countertop space and small kitchen.

### *blending/pureeing (choose one, to start)*

- **Food processor.** I've never been a blender person (I always found ways to cut myself when cleaning the blasted thing), so I started out with a food processor I found at a yard sale. Then I upgraded to a Craigslist Cuisinart that I bought from a lady in Brooklyn who was moving away from NYC and had to part with her beloved appliances. I now grind my own gluten-free oat flour, puree soups, and make breadcrumbs, salsas, and pestos—all with a food processor.

- **Blender.** Blenders work for all sorts of pureeing tasks and are critical for smoothie and milkshake making. Consistent use of an inexpensive blender (making smoothies with a lot of frozen matter more than three times per week) might bring you face-to-face with blender death, and then the blender death dilemma: get another cheap blender or save up for a $400 blender with a lifetime warranty?

  While Vitamix (definitely a gift list, registry, or other major-life-event gift) was a total game changer on our home front, it was only introduced in the last couple years. A powerful blender is nonessential in that you can likely survive without pureeing everything you encounter (unless you get on a refrigerator soup kick; see page 155). My no-frills, frugal mother joined team Vitamix after the death of her $100 blender, the second such blender she owned. Many of my readers and friends love their Ninja blenders, which retail for about a fourth of the cost of a Vitamix (and, for what it's worth, is not one of the brands my mother and her smoothies killed).

- **Immersion blender.** Consider this tool if you're at an infrastructure hold (dang, Vitamix is too expensive and you don't want to buy another crappy blender) and need to puree stuff.

  Also called a stick blender, this tool can be dipped right into soup, potato, and jam pots, allowing you to fully puree or just smooth the texture a bit. Mine came with a whisk attachment and a mini-food-processor attachment, which I can't say I'd buy outright, but I end up using it rather often because it's small and easier to clean than my large one.

*Hip Trick*

In addition to brand-new machines, Vitamix sells factory-refurbished machines with a lifetime warranty for a lot less than the retail price of a new one. We own one and haven't had any issues in the two years we've had it.

13

➥ **Coffee grinder.** If you drink coffee at home (or plan to start anytime soon), get a grinder. I grant you permission to even get a cheap one (I can see my coffee friend Jonah cringing now), but whatever you do, stop buying ground coffee (even getting beans ground at the roaster). The tender aromatics and freshness—that is, the reason you go to the coffee shop instead of making coffee at home—leaches out pretty quickly after the beans are ground. Neither freezer storage nor an airtight bin can atone for that. You can free up space and stop storing beans in the freezer, too. Airtight and opaque containers are all you need to store beans prior to grinding them before your morning cup.

# cool tools: top picks for multiuse kitchen machines

- **Dehydrator:** intended purpose (dried fruits, leathers, veggies, and herbs) + making yogurt + sprouting and redrying nuts and seeds

- **Stand mixer:** intended purpose (baking/mixing) + ice cream maker (attachment) + meat grinder + sausage maker (attachment)

- **Slow cooker:** intended purpose (cooking dishes while you're at work) + fruit butters + stocks + yogurt incubator

- **Slow cooker.** If you work long hours and/or live with someone who doesn't want you to leave a simmering burner going on the stove, this is the tool for you. You can make stocks, beans, soups, casseroles, roasts, hell, even fruit butters in these. There are cookbooks dedicated to them, but usually it goes something like: brown meat (or soak beans), add stock, water, and vegetables, put lid on, eat eight to ten hours later.

*noteworthy reader faves*

- Milk frother
- Magic Bullet, which is a single-serving-sized blender
- Espresso machine
- Rice cooker

## knives

Both my parents cooked as I was growing up, and things seemed to get cut up just fine during my formative years. It wasn't until a few years back when I was an adult helping to cook Thanksgiving dinner in their kitchens that I realized decent knives were not a part of their awareness.

Cutting an onion with a dull-ass serrated chef's knife (why do these even exist?) and a sharp 7-inch Santoku knife are opposite experiences. No wonder that in my midwestern upbringing we tended to anchor meals with onion powder rather than putting knife to board over a whole onion. I'm in awe that people manage to cook every day without a sharp knife.

Whether you face a week of onions, a whole chicken, or a cantaloupe, one decent multipurpose knife is essential.

↦ **8-inch chef's knife or 7-inch Santoku.** The first serious kitchen tool I ever got was an 8-inch Wüsthof chef's knife. It was on sale for $47, down from $89. At the time, I didn't fully understand why spending that much (even the sale price) on a knife was important, but instinctively I felt it was a fine time to invest in kitchen improvement. Hell, I still had a salary, what was there to lose!

I still don't understand all the marketing surrounding knives (there are currently eight different Wüsthof chef's knives on its website), but I do know that once you've used a solid and suitably sharp knife, you're ruined forever for crappy excuses for cutlery. You can find a decent, white-handled, sharpenable chef's knife at a kitchen supply store for around $15–$20. Start here with the restaurant industry knife and move upward. When purchasing a knife you intend to treasure, you must hold it in a store. Buy it online if necessary, but only after you've held it.

↦ **Serrated bread knife.**
A good bread knife is the difference between crumbling, squished slices and normal-looking slices that could very well flank a restaurant sandwich's guts.

*acquire when possible*

↦ **Paring knife.** I lived a long time without one until a friend gifted me a set. My life changed thanks to this

16

pack of simple, low-cost paring knives, and so can yours (for probably less than $5). Steak knives work in a pinch.

- ➤ **Cheese knife.** This is a novel, well-perforated knife that won't scrunch up your cheese slices.

A few years after my first fancy knife entered my life, I moved to Brooklyn, lost the salary, and had to get serious about eating at home. At the time, the knife was sort of a dangerous object; I was still adjusting to using it and did so infrequently and improperly. (During dinner prep I still opted to pull out a steak knife. Yes, I'm ashamed to admit it, but it's true.)

To remedy my fear of my nice knife, I began paying attention to how my friends worked in their kitchens. My friend Zora taught me how to dice an onion properly, which blew my mind (and thoroughly adjusted my relationship with dinner prep).

Although no one is going to judge your knife wielding (unless you're using my Wüsthof improperly and dulling it), the best case for learning to use a sharp knife properly is that safety improves drastically in doing so. You don't need to saw away and use much pressure when working with properly sharp knives. I now head to my parents' houses and am reminded with every attempt to chop vegetables, or even slice a lemon with their knives, how far I've come with my trusty Wüsthof. Preferring that your tools do their jobs adequately is not snobbery; it's efficiency and working smarter, not harder.

### sharpening your knives

As mentioned above, during the first few years of my relationship with my knife, it didn't get enough action to warrant a sharpening. But thanks to my first attempt at making marmalade, on a

# 4 dos and don'ts in knifeland

DO
- Ditch the knife block. Look for a magnetic knife strip for a prettier and more effective conserver of countertop real estate.
- Hold any prospective knife purchase before you buy.
- Invest in a sharpening tool and actually learn how to use it properly.
- Make a $10 investment once or twice a year and have your most-used knife professionally sharpened.

DON'T
- Keep knives in a drawer where they will get pushed around and dull each other.
- Buy the set. Acquire your own set on a knife-by-knife basis. Good ones will last your whole kitchen life, so you better really like them as individuals. And really, do you need eight steak knives? Probably not. (You're serving risotto at

snowy Brooklyn night, I became acquainted with a sharpening rod. There's nothing quite so dulling to a knife as mincing citrus peels—except maybe trying to chop up a box of leather strips and rocks. My local knife sharpener, John of Assured Sharp, helped me to understand the nuances involved in sharpening and honing knives.

sharpening rod/honing steel

Most of these tools are round or oval shaped and are used exclusively for honing (if they are metal), though some are ceramic or diamond and are used for sharpening as well as honing. I suggest buying a metal one that's at least 1 inch longer than your longest knife and leaving the sharpening to the pros.

➼ **Sharpening.** This process actually establishes a new edge on the blade. Place the blade edge perpendicular to the rod, and on each side of the blade move it along the ribbed side of the steel with the smooth edge of the knife at an 18- to 20-degree angle to the rod for most thick, heavy blades (or a 15- to 18-degree angle for thin Asian-style blades). If it makes you nervous to pull out your protractor from fifth grade, just try to imagine the angle at which you'd slide the blade across the steel in order to shave off chips and divots

18

that have formed in the blade, avoiding any position that likens to cutting (which can hurt your blade). Regardless of who does your sharpening, practice regular honing between sharpenings.

↦ **Honing.** This process involves realigning the cutting edge on the knife to the blade, which gets out of whack from banging against your food and boards. Hone each side of the blade by starting at the top of the steel and moving the blade along the smooth side at a 15-degree angle; finish by pulling the knife so the tip clears the steel. Do this in slow, even swipes along the entire length of the cutting edge. Remem-

your dinner party, not rib-eyes.)

· Slide chopped food out of the way with the blade of the knife; you'll be scraping its sharp side right off. Flip it over and use the top, smooth side of the knife to slide food to the side of your cutting board or into a pan.

· Leave good knives sitting in the sink with dirty dishes. Clean and dry knives immediately to keep piles of dishes and various crusted-on foods from dulling or rusting them.

## how to hone a knife

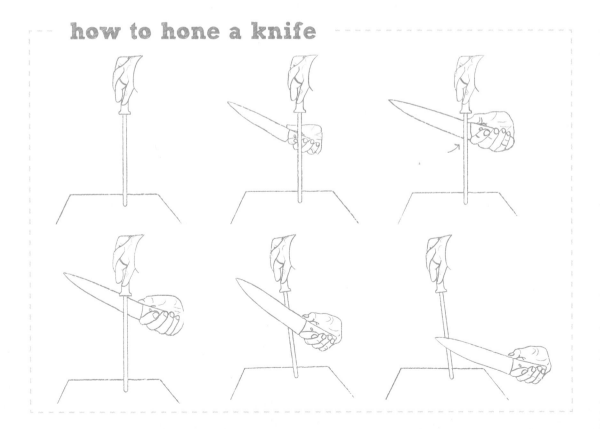

bering to hone three times—before, during, and after food preparation—will help your knives stay sharp longer and require fewer trips to the professional.

For both honing and sharpening, your speed is irrelevant. Take your time so you don't scratch or, worse, ruin the blade. As you get more comfortable with it, you can sharpen and hone with reckless abandon.

### professional sharpening

You should take your treasured knife to a professional sharpener (they're often mobile, just google "knife sharpening" in your area) at least once a year. There, they actually (should) ask you what the knives to be sharpened are used for and will tailor the sharpening to your needs, cutting off the layer of wear and tear you've accrued over the year and building you a new blade edge. Professionals then typically use a leather strop to remove burrs caused from sharpening. I take ours two or three times a year if it's been a heavy preserving season. Sharpening professionals will vary on rates, but on average it costs about $1 per inch of knife length. You can get your scissors and pocketknives sharpened, too!

### low-tech equipment and small tools

These are the last of the considerations in a well-stocked kitchen, I've listed a few of my essentials when it comes to getting the job done and which ones you can feel good about finding at the thrift store, a fabulous place to accrue low-tech tools and equipment.

20

## things to buy new

Try to get as many of the following as possible at the kitchen supply store.

- Cutting boards. Get small, medium, and large ones (or small and large if you have to be choosy).
- Microplane grater. Ideally one with both rough- and fine-grade edges.
- Vegetable peeler. A sharp peeler you like to hold will bring your relationship with mirepoix (see Glossary, page 320) to a whole new level. Steer clear of peelers with a serrated edge.
- High-heat spatula.
- Kitchen shears.
- Flat-edged wooden spatula for deglazing.
- Simple meat thermometer.
- Oven and fridge thermometers to keep tabs on your appliances. The fridge thermometer will help you assess and adjust the temperature in old or persnickety appliances, and oven thermometers are essential in old ovens so you can adjust accordingly to achieve desired temps for baked goods or dinners.
- Vacuum pump/reusable cork setup for unfinished wine.
- Muddler.

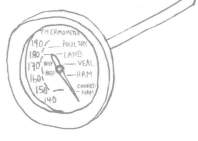

*Hip Trick*

Recalibrate your meat thermometer periodically by submerging it past the little dimple in the stem in ice water and seeing if it reads 32. If it doesn't, use a pair of pliers or a small wrench to adjust the hex that controls the dial hand to the appropriate freezing temperature.

## things to buy secondhand or vintage

- Griddle spatula, all metal (kudos on finding the treasured small, egg-flipping metal spatula).
- Measuring spoons and dry-measure cups. Be sure they're not too dinged up if they're metal.

21

- Citrus juicer or handheld press.
- Wooden spoons that are in good condition, a variety of lengths and shapes.
- Metal kitchen tongs (can also be found at kitchen supply stores; both new and old should be very inexpensive).
- Large metal slotted spoon.
- Potato masher.
- Whisks.
- Fish spatula.
- Corkscrew.

*fancy, fun additions*

- Cutting board mat. Although a damp towel does the trick, if a dedicated mat makes you happy and excited about cutting stuff up, I say go for it.
- Mortar and pestle. Go for ceramic or marble and don't get one smaller than a 10-ounce capacity.

# cool tools: top picks for multiuse kitchen tools

- **Muddler**: intended purpose (cocktails) + can serve as a mortar and pestle + packing krauts or kimchi

- **Stainless steel straws**: intended purpose (drinks) + sealing bags for freezer (see the Hip Trick on page 88)

## spatulas

This tool deserves its own section. These essential, yet majorly confusing, utensils come in a wide array of divergent shapes and materials and are used for various functions, and yet they are all still called the same thing. Never can you say with precision, "Hey, hand me the spatula"—no, instead you must describe its form or function each time.

Good spatulas are worth your investment and rarely cost more than $10 or $12. I can't count the number of times I've found myself cooking somewhere out in the world and wishing I'd brought my own spatulas. I'm attached to my Rubbermaid high-heat spatulas (found at restaurant supply stores or online), but any single scraper spatula (that doesn't detach from its base) is a great and versatile investment.

## cutting boards

Cutting boards and sanitation—someone could fill an entire book or dissertation on this topic. I'll tell you my two cents' worth, and then you'll have to make the choice that jibes with your household sanitation belief system. One thing I'd like to clear up is that you can use wooden cutting boards for meat.[*] Wood is an inhospitable host for bacteria that could get caught in a crevice or cut mark, whereas plastic is actually a fine host, which is why plastic/composite boards discolor over time.

---

[*] http://lifehacker.com/5847591/10-stubborn-food-myths-that-just-wont-die.
http://faculty.vetmed.ucdavis.edu/faculty/docliver/Research/cuttingboard.htm.
http://www.fsis.usda.gov/Pdf/cutting_boards_and_food_safety.pdf.

*Word to the Wise*
Do not stick your high-heat or silicone spatulas into the blender or food processor (when the blade is still in). You'll chip off pieces of the rubber/silicone.

With any cutting board, the best sanitation practice is to scrub it after each use with hot soapy water.

### number and size of cutting boards

You need two cutting boards, one big and one small(er).

→ **Big (21" x 15").** Yes, I mean it. You're doing yourself a huge favor by owning a board big enough to house a meal's worth of chopped veggies, seeing as it's highly unlikely that your mise en place will rely on a bunch of little glass bowls. With a big board, you can just

| MEDIUM | PROS | CONS |
| --- | --- | --- |
| Wood | Deters the growth of microorganisms. | It needs a periodic conditioning with mineral oil. |
| Bamboo | Light and easy to handle. | Thin bamboo boards can crack along the direction of the grain over time with lots of use. |
| Plastic/Composite | Can go in the dishwasher. | Cut marks are more likely to harbor bacteria, and these boards don't remain clean looking. |
| Glass | Sanitation guaranteed. | Every slice you make will shave a little off your sanity; it's such a weird noise. Your knife will hate you, too (glass is harder than your knife and thus messes with your knife's sharpness). |

chop and move them aside (with the flat side of your knife) to clear the way for the next veggie.

- ➻ **Small (11" x 17" or 8" x 10").** Our everyday-use boards came as a set (KitchenAid brand) and include both of the aforementioned sizes. We found them, gently used, in our Brooklyn neighbors' moving giveaway pile. They've lasted us three years (of heavy use) and are just now starting to develop the dingy hue surrounding darkened, too-many-cut-mark areas. Time to pull out the peroxide!

*Hip Trick*

Dampen a dishcloth or rag, wring it out, and lay it flat on the counter where you plan to set your cutting board. The damp towel will help grip the board and prevent it from moving.

For a deal on sturdy plastic/composite boards, buy them from a restaurant supply store. Be aware, though, that commercial boards won't have any gripping action built into the design, and you'll need to anchor them to the counter with a mat or a wet towel.

Cutting boards that have a little well around the perimeter of the board are my favorite, since they capture and allow you to salvage any juicy runoff.

### conditioning wooden utensils and cutting boards

If you encounter a bottle of mineral oil at some point, grab it. We received a beautiful, unconditioned wood salad bowl as a gift and it sat for nearly a year while we half-assed searched for mineral oil. Most wood you buy is already conditioned, but to keep it from cracking and to keep it looking sharp, you'll want to give it a good conditioning coat of oil every three to six months. We don't condition our spoons and wooden tools because we don't particularly care what they look like (and they get more exposure to oil than dish soap on a regular basis), but I'd oil my wooden cutting board once a week if I had one.

25

## assembly required

Now let's get you on the path of setting up the kitchen as a place to accomplish actual cooking and easy cleaning; if either of those is hard in your space, then you won't do it. Choices made surrounding kitchen setup remind me of people who set up their living rooms around the television and wonder why couch po-tatoing (not family discussions or non-TV-centric stuff) is the only thing that happens in that room. If you set up your kitchen as a facilitation station for takeout, then that's what you'll eat. Your goals are easy access to high-use items and making smart cabinet and storage decisions that help you both locate items and return them to their places.

### countertop

Your kitchen countertop is where your most easily accessible items reside, and thus it is the base of your kitchen organization. When looking at candidates for prime countertop real estate, ask your-self a few things:

*Do I use it daily (or hope to use it daily)?*
*Does it require an outlet?*
*Do I like/mind looking at it?*
*Do I use it often enough to avoid having to dust it?*

If the answer to one or more of these questions is no, you might have a prime candidate for a cabinet. Don't forget the fridge top and baker's racks as places for appliances that are bumped out of or deemed too bulky for the countertop proper. Rotating your equipment until you find the right setup is normal. When I ousted the mixer (used once every two weeks) from countertop living, my kitchen opened up to all sorts of new possibilities (and now the mixer doesn't need a full-on dusting and degunking every time I go to use it (which might seem small, but eliminating any barrier to use is important).

## stove area

Keep everything but a spoon at least a foot away (if possible) from your stove zone so it will avoid the fate of our unlucky pepper mill. He's a blue Alessi pepper mill whose formerly thumbs-up hand is now a melted and downward-dripping dagger that threatens bodily injury to anyone who attempts to crack pepper without an operation lesson. Keep hot pads or oven mitts not too far out of arm's reach from the stove.

## cabinet space

When establishing a kitchen as my own, I personally like to wash out cabinets and drawers with my all-purpose kitchen spray (see Appendix 2, page 315) and line them with contact paper. It makes me feel like I'm the first and only person to store my stuff in those cabinets. I like to use the puffy grid type of drawer and cabinet liner in areas where I'll keep cups (upside down), in drawers where utensils will just float around freely, and underneath my vertical cutting board storage area (see the next section). A dishtowel works fine as a base for these things, too, but it slides around in drawers.

You can take the puffy liner out periodically and wash it if it gets gunky, and you can take it with you to new places.

Three things to keep in mind when deciding which cabinets will house which items:

1. Proximity to where the task will usually be performed
2. Exposure to heat (above stove and its flanking cabinets)
3. What lives above or beside (to keep things clean or fresh)

It seems like a logical thing to keep spices and other heavy-use pantry goods just to the side of the stove, within arm's length of where you'll be using them, but really it's the opposite case here (see Chapter 2 for why). Instead, you want to keep things that aren't affected by constant exposure to heat in the zone surrounding your stove and oven. This means glassware, plates, bowls, baking pans, small appliances, and so on.

## organizing for frequency of use

Arrange your things in the cabinets based on how often you use them. Things you use (or want to use) more often should be easily accessible. Don't bury your appliances. If you make it a pain in the ass to dig out your food processor, I guarantee you that you won't be using it enough to warrant buying it.

Whether or not your cabinet space is officially set up this way (some homes have a cabinet with an assortment of segregated vertical slats), you should arrange one of your deeper cabinets so that you store your large flat things—cookie sheets, cooling racks, baking trays, cutting boards—standing up on their sides. Not only will you prevent them from catching unwanted dust and debris, but you'll also maximize space. Interspersing cutting boards with different kinds of flat things and sticking a square of that puffy drawer liner underneath should keep them from sliding down, but if necessary, use a not-everyday-use pot or soufflé-type (tall, but heavy) dish shoved toward the back of the cabinet to anchor them like a bookend. Use the space in front of that pot for more frequently used tools or items.

Deep cabinets are definitely not a plus for pantry goods. You need shallow storage space for foods so you don't lose track of what's in there. Use deeper cabinets for cookware, appliances that don't stay on the counter, and non-everyday-use dishware/serving utensils. If you must keep pantry goods in tall or deep cabinets, then add step-up shelving and clear stackable drawers or invest in a couple of those spinning racks so you can easily see goods that are, in the words of old-time country singer Roger Miller, "waaaay in the back."

I built a pegboard just above our stovetop since the landlord's remodel didn't include much in the way of cabinetry for pots and pans beyond the Ikea stove housing unit that has two side compartments. I moved the shelves in each up a notch in order to keep saucepans on the bottom and lids on the top. (Learn how to hang a kitchen pegboard via project photographs and detailed instructions on my blog, hipgirlshome.com.)

*drawer space*

We have a total of eight drawers in the kitchen, so we prioritized for function. Here are our drawer designations:

- Silverware
- Spices
- Small everyday-use kitchen tools
- Baking tools
- Koozies (when in Texas . . . )
- Rolls of parchment, foil, plastic wrap, and various kinds of storage bags (both parchment and freezer bags, which we stock in one-quart and one-gallon designations)

29

- Teas (individual bags and loose-leaf) and tea paraphernalia (tea balls, paper filters, etc.)
- Dishtowels and dishcloths

Notice how nowhere in the list above does "junk drawer" (a place to throw things that don't seem to belong anywhere else) take up residence. Our koozie drawer sometimes threatens to diversify into the junk realm, but then we restore order and cull any auxiliary items that are not matchbooks, rubber bands, or clothespins.

We store all our small tools in the drawer right next to the stovetop for easy access. Having just one or two drawers to store all your small tools will help keep the tools you don't really need at bay. If you operate this drawer with the one-in-one-out philosophy, you should avoid setting off in the direction of too-many-tools-not-enough-cooking.

We have another tool-devoted drawer because I'm a baker and I use these tools consistently enough to warrant segregation and functional facilitation. Read up on my baking drawer contents in Chapter 6.

When possible, place the items you'd like to keep the cleanest at the top of stacked sets of drawers; the law of gravity and the constant effect of interacting with your drawers plus the inner workings of your cabinetry can filter fragments of dust, wood, and, heaven forbid, bugs in old houses, to the lower drawers.

### sink area

If I can't easily identify how to wash and dry my hands in your kitchen, then something has gone awry with design versus function (and P.S., I don't want to wash my hands with dish soap). We also might have an issue if I can't figure out how to wash dishes by hand, since not everything goes in the dishwasher. You need some sort of dish drying rack, and if you want to hide it from public view, just don't hide it so well that you never use it.

Stock the following in your sink area:

- Two-sided sponge with nonscratch scrubber side *or* a dishcloth and a nonscratch scrubber pad
- Sturdy brush for cast iron
- Bottle-neck brush or two for cleaning out glass bottles for reuse or for cleaning tall, skinny vases
- Dish and hand soap

Make the following structural investments as possible:

- Suction-cupped stainless steel sponge rack ($5–$10) to stick somewhere on the inner portion of the sink to allow your dishcloth and/or scrubber pad/sponge to dry out completely between uses.
- A tension rod that will fit the length of your under-sink cabinet to hang any spray bottles you use often to free up valuable cabinet floor space.
- Container with a lid for starting your kitchen compost. (If you don't keep it under the sink for compost drop-off availability reasons, then you can keep your bin or a bag in the freezer.) We use a Cambro 6-quart kitchen storage container with a lid that sort of fits. You should be able to carry your full container easily to the compost pile (which eliminates the pretty—and heavy—ceramic ones for our household).
- Gloves if your hands don't appreciate all the meals you're cooking and dishes you're making.

Don't keep cookware underneath the kitchen sink. It's a great place for your kitchen compost container, your rag bin, and your cleaning supplies (nontoxic, of course), things that won't touch food you're going to eat.

## sprucing up

You're on the way to tackling prioritization so your kitchen doesn't look like the appliance section of a department store. Let's stay the course of allocating your budget to sporadic investments of better tools, not froufrou kitchen decor.

If you're making structural improvements and painting is in your future, be sure to steer clear of flat paint in the kitchen. You don't need a full-on glossy finish, just something you can wipe with a wet cloth in the event your tomato sauce bubbles with enthusiasm at the prospect of an impending dinner. Ask at the hardware store before you buy and color a base.

Beyond paint, there are tons of ways to spruce up the kitchen without a remodel. Be on the lookout for linens or other signature pieces (as mentioned below) to establish a color theme for your kitchen that fits in with your tools.

Functional ways to decorate the kitchen include:

- **Decorative dishes/pans/appliances.** As your kitchen collection shapes up, show it off. That pretty painted metal or vintage colander, a French oven, that waffle iron you found at a garage sale—all are lovely things to display from hooks or on shelves.
- **Curtains.** Tension rods and a fold-over hem can turn vintage fabric into café curtains.
- **Flour sack towels.** We have a rotating stash of various-colored flour sack hand towels, and a dish-drying

towel, which is white. I know, quite a system, but I like knowing that I'm drying clean dishes with an exclusive and clean towel. Also, you can never have too many towels in the kitchen. Both our oven and kitchen cupboard get flanked with cute and use-encouraged towels for a quick dry in the middle of a task or project.

- **Hot pads or oven mitts.** We prefer the pads to the mitts and love our silicone hot pads for setting hot pots directly on the counter or table.
- **Serving tray.** Having one pretty serving tray on hand has become an essential item around here. I'd never even considered owning a tray until entertaining became less about making a big to-do and more about facilitating time to connect with friends without rushing around being hospitable.
- **Ceramic replicas of farmers' market fruit and veggie baskets.** These make the act of storing fruit or veggie prizes a deluxe experience.
- **Mortar and pestle.** Buying a pretty mortar and pestle is a dual action device: first, it's a perfect aesthetic for the kitchen decor, and second, it's the best way to ensure the freshest spices possible (see more on that in the next chapter).
- **Vintage flour/sugar/coffee jars or containers.** These items are a great place for

## hip trick: DIY spice jar decor

Paint the exterior of small glass bottles with tight-fitting lids (or existing clear glass spice jars) with a few layers of your fave color paint and then add a circle of chalkboard paint for IDing the contents (since you won't be able to see through them any longer). Read up on why spices don't like light in the next chapter.

33

# great things to hang in the kitchen

- A fruit and veggie basket
- Hot pads, pan lids, colanders, whisks, or anything else that might affix well to wire baker's racks with S-shaped or other hooks
- An apron collection from a curtain rod mounted to the wall
- A plant designated for your kitchen's natural light scenario
- Small shelves on the walls, which make sweet nooks to stash cream and sugar service items, or opaque spice jars

keeping tools, sealed tea bags, kitchen odds and ends, basically everything besides what they're meant for (see page 42 for good vessels for keeping dry goods fresh).

## resources

*books*

➻ *Alton Brown's Gear for your Kitchen* by Alton Brown
➻ *Ruhlman's Twenty: 20 Techniques, 100 Recipes, A Cook's Manifesto* by Michael Ruhlman
➻ *Slow Death by Rubber Duck: The Secret Danger of Everyday Things* by Rick Smith and Bruce Lourie

*web*

➻ Get a trial membership—they offer fourteen days for free—to *Cook's Illustrated* online (www.cooksillustrated.com) and browse its database full of appliance, tool, and equipment reviews.
➻ Look for decor inspiration by cruising kitchen tours (mine included!) at www.thekitchn.com.

chapter 2

# pantry staples

how to skip shopping
every time you eat
a meal at home

A spare pantry, not a packed-to-the-brim one, is actually ideal. I think of all the years I filled the pantry up with all sorts of canned and packaged things, meal instigators (I thought), when in reality, this random assortment of things soon got shoved back and piled up, only to be pitched the next time I moved. Where I went wrong, and where so many pantry stockers go awry, is that unrelated, odd components of meals rarely shape themselves into the meals you hope for, especially in a pantry that's three-deep with boxes, cans, and bags.

Pantry staples are things you always have around the house, not, contrary to the popular approach, things you hoard just in case the grocery store closes indefinitely. Optimally, pantry staples reflect a constant rotation, as they're the backbone of every meal you make in a well-run ship. You build meals around your staple goods, which are replaced periodically when the stash runs low.

Sure, you can organize your way out of this conundrum, but if you have too much crap in your pantry, you'll inevitably let your meticulous coding and rearranging plan fall to the wayside. A busy couple weeks plus the next round of grocery shopping and you're right back to where you started.

Whenever I find myself in this state of affairs with my little kitchen closet, I undertake a personal, eat-down-the-pantry challenge. It's like I'm on *Chopped*, figuring out how to incorporate a few half bags of pasta, mirin I bought because it was on sale, a jar of Nutella, and the dates I'd intended to use in another recipe (which never happened; not looking like it will, either). The reality I come to after such a challenge is one that sticks; I don't need to buy a bunch of crap at the grocery store because it appeared useful. (Because, really, there's only so much eat-down-the-pantry spirit you can muster before it's just tiring and you learn your lesson.)

## when bulk buying is good

Pantry staples are the one place where buying in bulk is A-OK, but only if you have the capacity to store them properly. I discuss why buying bulk perishables or other nonessentials is actually a drain on your wallet rather than a boon in the next chapter.

Here are four examples of options to get the best deals in buying and stocking staples; I buy each of the following in bulk and store accordingly.

1. **Butter and yeast.** You not only eat the best specialty items around when you acquaint yourself with a local artisan baker, but you might also be able to sidle up to their wholesale orders. I asked a baker friend of mine to tack on an extra box of the European butter blocks

## is it worth it?

Consider these three things before buying that impulse pantry item:

1. *Do you know of more than one way to use it?* Things with a single or odd application are less likely to be useful. Having two or three ideas of how to use it (before you buy) is sufficient.

2. *Is it something you could make yourself?* Seemingly fancy, novel things are often just as easy to make at home. We'll get into ideas for that in Chapter 7, the preserving chapter.

3. *Do you already have it?* If you don't know what's in your pantry already, then leave it on the shelf until you assess your inventory.

and the bread yeast she orders for her business and she agreed. I paid about $2.50 per pound for a great butter (that retails for $4–$5) and under $5 for a year's supply of yeast.

Don't make it a pain in the ass for them to help you out, though, or they'll be less inclined to do so in the future. Be prompt in paying and picking up your goods, and don't ask them to split up a box or quantity of something. It's your responsibility to tackle splits among friend groups if a forty-pound box of butter isn't going to fit in your chest freezer (because you don't have one). Also, try to keep your "orders" to once or twice a year so it doesn't wear on a helpful friend's patience.

Granted, these items require some proper storage. The yeast is sealed in a freezer bag for freshness and lives in the back of the refrigerator. I packed five butter blocks each into freezer bags and lined my chest freezer, a stash that lasted for about a year and a half and gave me a major break from needing to buy butter and chance possibly running out in the middle of a pancake or baking ordeal. If you don't have the storage space to house such volumes yourself, then consider my tactic for stocking our gluten-free oats.

2. **Gluten-free oats.**\* When I passed on oats in our buying club's annual Bob's Red Mill company order (read more on buying clubs on page 69), I was still sufficiently stocked with oats. A busy holiday season and a lot of batches of granola later, and I ended up running out of

---

\* If you're not gluten-free, picking up regular oats from the bulk bin is not usually much different in price than buying in bulk as here, but you can extend this tactic to any other large purchase that gets divvied up among friends.

oats midyear. I called our local grocery co-op and the larger grocery store chain and priced out a 25-pound bag of gluten-free oats. I went with the better price and received a bulk discount—a 10–15 percent case or bulk discount is pretty standard—at the store. Even if you're not trying to price it out among a few stores, it's important to confirm the price ahead of time and do the math on what your bulk item costs per pound. I posted to Facebook and e-mailed a handful of my local gluten-free friends to see if they'd be interested in taking five-pound (or more) portions off my hands.

When your order arrives, you'll need to weigh out everyone's share and invest in something to pack them in (freezer bags work well for two- to three-pound portions of oats). If you anticipate buying in bulk and sharing, this is a great reason to have a kitchen scale. If packaging is expensive for you, either tack that onto the initial cost per pound or ask people to bring something to put their oats in upon pickup. We save a lot of money this way, so the extra steps are worth it; plus you get a little visit with friends that you might not normally plan—score for community building!

I didn't trust the packaging-taped-up bag's ability to fend off intruders, so I purchased a five-gallon food-safe bucket with a locking lid from the local hardware shop— which cost about $10—to store my stash of oats until next year's order.

3. **Flax meal.** Compared to the oats, this option was a breeze. I just participated in a split with a few other buying club members. Hosting a few bulk splits means you're probably more likely to be on the reciprocal end of others' orders when they host. Since flax meal is an

oily seed meal, I had to store it in the freezer to keep my eight pounds' worth from going rancid. We refill from our freezer stash when the quart-sized mason jar that lives in the fridge runs out.

4. **Vinegar, baking soda, organic sugar, and brown sugar.** I grab these items at a large wholesale store that requires membership. My friend, with said membership, takes me when the supplies run low and I pay her cash directly. You're technically not supposed to share memberships, but there are no rules that you can't bring a friend shopping with you. It's a nice opportunity to hang out with someone when you'd otherwise just be zombied out in a fluorescent store.

As for storage, the organic sugar and baking soda come in resealable ten- and five-pound bags, respectively, so I store those in their bags. The brown sugar comes in a large, multilayered paper bag, so in order to store it for the long haul and keep our pantry brown sugar jar stocked, I grabbed another three-gallon food-safe container with a locking lid.

## determining your own staples

Stocking up for things you make regularly doesn't need to involve my level of bulk acquisitions, but it does require you to sort out a rhythm in your kitchen and start looking at what you make and eat regularly. Eventually you'll fine-tune this so that you're buying less and your ingredients are doing more and more work, like various preserving projects that turn your perishables into staples; for example, peppers you bought at the farmers' market become the homemade hot sauce or rooster sauce you use frequently (and now don't buy anymore).

I don't expect you to sort your rhythm out within a week, or even in a month, but you'll know you're hitting a groove when grocery shopping becomes less stressful and more focused (you actually have a list and no real reason to veer from it).

Here are the projects and approximate frequency that determine staples for our two-person household.

| WEEKLY | BIWEEKLY OR EVERY THREE WEEKS | MONTHLY |
| --- | --- | --- |
| Roasted chicken with veggies or some sort of stew with beans and veggies, or sometimes just a big pot of beans (depends on market meat availability and wallet constraints) | Granola | Chicken or other bone stock |
| Cultured buttermilk | Muffins | Dessert (pie, cookies, cake) |
| Yogurt | Weekend pancakes | Ice cream |
| Bread | Coffee cake or snack cake | Seasonal pickles |

Since staples are things you always have and ones that help your kitchen run smoothly, it's fairly obvious that some are stored in the pantry while others are kept in the fridge or freezer. I count perishable goods in the staples category if you acquire them weekly (or on a cycle) and if your house doesn't run without them. (For us, these include milk, butter, eggs, flax meal, yogurt, whey, bone broths, frozen fruit, etc.)

# good vessels for pantry items

- Mason jars of all sizes with two-piece lids (single-piece lids may not keep out persistent pests)
- Swing-top jars with a good rubber gasket
- Specially designed airtight bins (can be pricey though)
- New freezer bags, or ones you're sure don't have any holes (though only good for shorter-term storage; they won't keep pests out for the long haul, which I found out the hard way when I discovered that moth larvae had burrowed their way into the plastic, ewww!)

## storing dry goods

It's clear you're going to need some containers. I think a case or two of quart-sized mason jars is your best bet for cost and efficiency.

I always felt like my pantry closet storage skills were fairly solid (thanks, Mom!)—that is, until moving into an old house rife with Indian meal moths (pantry moths). I tried everything to get rid of them and came to learn that, short of a total pantry remodel (in our rental house), I'd have to get even stricter about pantry storage. Hence, in the name of keeping pests out of our dry goods, my pantry now looks really cool, full of mason and swing-top jars.

Bins that look good but don't keep food fresh include most vintage flour/sugar containers. (I still keep sugar in one of our vintage bins because, thankfully, I haven't had any trouble with insurgents in the sugar. I don't store the container in the contested pantry, though; it's too pretty!)

The first rule of getting good-quality dry goods at a decent price is to shop around. At any store you visit you'll find some things will be offered at great prices and others will be higher. You don't have to go to five stores in one day, but do keep track of how much something costs at one store versus another. Next time you need to buy that item, formulate your list so you can visit the store that has the best price. If you don't have time to shop around like that, then at least try to notice prices next time you find yourself at another store that sells items you buy.

## beans and grains

We decorate with dried beans and grains primarily because we don't have the space to store them anywhere else. I saved the jars from our fave kosher dill pickles (back when we bought pickles, before I learned how to make them myself!) and repurposed them as our easy-access grain storage contain-

### Hip Trick

Sticky pheromone traps work best for combating Indian meal moths. I owe that tip to a friend who was massively relieved to find someone else who's reasonably on top of her kitchen game dealing with these little buggers. Pantry moths are one of the least-talked-about, though most-self-esteem-dropping aspects of running your kitchen. We renters (or homeowners not in a position to rip out the pantry) need a support group!

ers. We have a single two-quart jar filled with short grain brown rice, since we go through it faster than the others, and ten quart-sized jars with the following contents in constant rotation:

*Quinoa*

*Millet*

*Arborio rice (risotto)*

*White basmati rice*

*Amaranth*

*Cornmeal*

*Corn for popping*

*Lentils*

*White beans or another variety that catches my eye in the bulk bean bin\**

*Buckwheat groats*

---

\* Buying a cup of dried beans means you will have four to six servings' worth. Experiment with new beans, but don't buy more than a couple cups at a time so you're not eating the same exact bean for weeks.

*nuts, flours, and sugars*

Sure, if you're not facing any sort of pantry pest issues, you can keep flours and sugar in their bags, clipped tightly (we use clothespins, of course). For flours you use often, consider storing them in a swing-top jar that will allow you to dip a measuring cup in there. Clear containers label themselves and serve as a visual reminder to use what's in there.

We keep an array of nuts and dried fruits stocked for snacks on the go, to mix with granola, or to use for baking. Raw nuts are always more versatile (you can roast them yourself and without any undesirable oils or additives).

Our favorites:

| | |
|---|---|
| *Pumpkin seeds, also called pepitas* | *Cashews* |
| | *Pecans (periodically)* |
| *Sunflower seeds* | *Raisins* |
| *Almonds* | *Apricots* |
| *Walnut pieces* | *Mangoes (periodically)* |

Store high-protein oily flours and meals in the refrigerator, since they tend to go rancid in warmer pantry environments. Ones that definitely need to be in the fridge include:

| | |
|---|---|
| *Flaxseed meal* | *Coconut flour* |
| *Almond flour* | |

I also keep my tapioca, arrowroot, and potato starches in the refrigerator to keep them fresh.

## packaged stuff

Yes, I know our goal is cooking from fresh ingredients, using real foods as components and so on, but life doesn't always work out how we hope. A little packaged convenience shouldn't be the norm, but it's certainly not the enemy. Here's a list of things to have on hand:

- A couple cans of whole beans (black, red, or white), for days when your cooking schedule hasn't left time for bean soaking.
- A box of vegetable or chicken broth, in case you can't thaw yours in time.
- A box of an alternative milk, almond or hemp perhaps.
- At least one *full* bag/box of pasta; a few varieties are also a good idea, like rice or buckwheat noodles. If you only use half a box/bag during a cooking endeavor, you should still add another full one to your grocery list.
- A can or two of fish. We always have a can of sardines (an acquired taste, yes, but so incredibly good for you) and tuna on hand for a last-minute salad.
- A can of organic coconut milk, which has the power to turn any leftovers into a delicious curry.
- A bag of dried mushrooms, which spruce up soups, sauces, and dishes that might need some extra umami flavoring (see Glossary, page 322).
- Cereal, for the mornings you're already late. Most stores carry the economy bags (sans box). You get three or four times the cereal for two times the price of a regular box, plus you earn paper-saving credit. Generally speaking, I agree we need to veer from relying on what Sally Fallon, a journalist, chef, and nutrition researcher, calls "new

45

fangled foods"—which include flaked, puffed, and any kind of boxed cereals, among other things—but eating something for breakfast is a whole lot better than skipping out without anything in your system but coffee.

The kinds of packaged stuff you should definitely pass on are flavored rice pilaf boxes, mac and (squeezy or powdery pouch) cheese, canned soups, and flavored chips (ones that aren't usually a vehicle for other foods), all of which can shave off chunks of $3–$5 and form a landslide of savings (which could then be put to better use in the organic and/or local meat, dairy, and produce aisles).

We don't pack our pantry shelves beyond a layer of things we can see, and a shelf full of boxes means we can't see anything else.

## five things to skip in the packaged version and buy from the bulk section

1. Rice—even the most meager bulk section will have rice.

2. Nut butters—when purchased from the bulk bin section, there's an added bonus of no additives (sugar, non-nut oils, etc.). Store them in the refrigerator so the oils don't go rancid.

3. Oats.

4. Decent honey or maple syrup—not every bulk section will offer these, but if yours does, go for it.

5. Dried fruits or nuts.

# fridge essentials and storage

You were privy to the bulk of our running list of indispensable perishables a few pages back, but we also tend to keep other less flashy but often-used items on hand.

Like an overfull pantry, a too-full fridge is a hindrance to your success unless you're constantly on top of a dig-and-rotate system. Otherwise, out of sight, out of mind: your food is doomed. We combat this issue by lining the back walls of the top and middle shelves in our fridge with pickled and fermented vegetables that require refrigeration (in central Texas we don't have basements and can't keep ferments cool enough).

Fridge door storage should be confined to things that don't base their claims to staying fresh on whether they maintain a constant forty degrees (the top range of your fridge temperature) or cooler temperature.

The following items require a **constant temperature zone** (as far back as possible without getting hidden):

| | |
|---|---|
| *Dairy/nondairy milk* | *Yogurt* |
| *Butter* | *Leftovers* |
| *Eggs* | *Stocks and broths* |
| *Cheese* | |

These items are **door safe**:

| | |
|---|---|
| *Ground nut or seed meals (flax, almond, etc.)* | *Tamari or soy sauce* |
| *Starches and flours (buckwheat, arrowroot, potato starch)* | *Mustard and other condiments* |
| | *Beverages (kombucha, teas, club soda)* |

Read more about the dreaded crisper drawer and storing fruits and vegetables successfully on pages 82–83.

## counter and daily cooking essentials

Corral your everyday-use items in a vintage tray or caddy. You'll ensure portability, a little style, and a contained (easily washable) area for any salt/pepper spills or oil drips. It's so tempting to keep your olive oil bottle on or right next to the stovetop. The heat doesn't do it any favors, though. Try to keep your cooking essentials tray at least a foot or two away from the stovetop.

*vintage plate*

### *salt and pepper*

Buy a pepper mill, for the love of God, and, if at all possible, spend a few extra bucks and physically go into the store to manhandle all the options. You and your mill will come into contact at least a few times a day; you should like how it feels, looks, and works.

While you're at it, identify from your existing bowls and jars a handy vessel for kosher or cooking salt. Skip the grinder here; salt doesn't contain fragile aromatics like pepper does, so the novelty of fresh cracked salt isn't really necessary. Plus, you want to be able to grab pinches of it while cooking. We have a salt pig; I broke the ceramic spoon within a month of owning it and mended it with Super Glue. A salt pig with a metal spoon (i.e., any smallish measuring spoon on the planet) is ideal.

### *olive oil*

We buy ours in the bulk section from a local grocery and it costs $6.99 a pound; each nearly full bottle refill costs us approximately $8. We reused a green wine bottle that snugly fits an oil decanter spout (with a little topper that hangs on a chain). We are the kind of people who want to spend more on olive oil, but alas find our

48

spare grocery dollars (those not being spent on packaged things or eating out) going to sustainably (mostly locally) raised meats. (When I'm rich and famous one day, I envision the olive oil specialty shop as one of the first places I'll hit.)

Other things you might keep on a small tray near the stove (if you use them frequently):

- Cider vinegar
- Bragg Liquid Aminos (better for you than soy sauce; same liquid, salty effect)
- Fish sauce
- Neutral oil for seasoning cast iron (sunflower or canola)
- Bottle of blackstrap molasses, so you remember to spoon it straight up or add a tablespoon of it to food every day for its scores of unrefined vitamins and minerals

*other oils*

Since oils are so prominent in transforming a pile of ingredients into daily sustenance, I think it's important to discuss the nature of the fats and what happens to them when they're heated; hence, I defer to Sally Fallon on these suggestions. I've distilled into a short list her pages of text and scientific research surrounding how heat oxidizes polyunsaturated oils—primarily canola, soybean, corn, and safflower—and also causes an overabundance of omega-6 fatty acids, leaving us starved for the coun-

# choosing olive oil

Look for expeller-pressed organic extra-virgin olive oil. It should be cloudy (unfiltered) and golden yellow in color. EVOO is produced by crushing olives between stone or steel rollers versus higher heat methods that denature the antioxidants in the oil.

terbalancing omega-3s. Oil choice is something to think about and just do your best with.

*Good cooking oils*
Olive oil
Coconut oil,* also good for baking

*Okay to heat, but use sparingly*
Peanut oil

*Steer clear, or use but don't heat*
Canola oil (good luck finding anything out in the world that's not fried or cooked in canola oil; the least we can do is avoid using it all the time at home, too)
Safflower oil
Sunflower oil

## vinegars

Beyond cider vinegar, which you can make from your fall apple scraps (see page 244), stock red wine vinegar, white wine vinegar, and maybe some balsamic as additional flavor essentials. Start making your own fruit vinegars (see page 232) to expand your pantry selection. Vinegars of all sorts are best kept at room temperature, sealed tightly.

## vegetable rack staples

I love our three-tiered hanging baskets. Level one, the big base area, is nearly always in possession of members of the allium

---

\* Check prices online for this and definitely buy larger containers to keep costs low.

family (onions, garlic, shallots); bananas are on level two; and only stuff we want to forget about makes it up to level three. It's actually the place where things used to go to die in our kitchen (out of sight, out of mind), until I decided to use the top rack to decorate rather than hoard things we should have pitched or given away long ago. Hello, air plants!

## the spice drawer

It's time to take charge of your spices. Many of us spend time preparing foods and generally try to use the best ingredients, but then tend to skimp when it comes to spices. Buying spices in bulk and in their whole (not ground) state when possible is the most optimal way to stock your spice rack. The bottles full of ground spices in the spice aisle are clear glass (no good for keeping in freshness), usually more expensive, and often give you way more spice than you'll realistically be able to use.

Once a spice is ground, you enter a race against time and exposure to heat and light, thanks to the volatile and fragile oils that make up flavor. This is why it's important to buy only small quantities of ground spices and refresh them as needed.

## spice jars and storage

Creating dedicated jars for spices changed my approach to using and stocking them. I discovered I had to be choosy with what spices got their own jar, and I soon realized that many of the leftover baggies were old

### Hip Trick

Know any friends who visit an herbalist or acupuncturist? Many of their prescribed supplements come in small amber glass jars with tight-fitting lids, and many clients end up recycling the influx of jars. Scrape off the labels with a flat razor and use a dab of citrus oil solvent to remove any residual gunk. For another spice storage idea, check out page 33 for a cute *and* freshness-ensuring method of decorating with your spices.

# four spice rack dos and don'ts

**DO**

- Buy in bulk and in small quantities and get in the habit of marking the date on the jar when you refresh a spice.
- Repurpose glass vitamin or empty spice jars for spices you stock from the bulk station.
- Clean out old spices periodically. If you can't remember when you bought it, pitch it and start over.
- Repurpose a small clementine crate to corral your jars of whole spices.

**DON'T**

- Buy the prepackaged jars of spice (unless you really can't avoid it).
- Buy dried herbs like basil, oregano, or rosemary. Buy fresh (or grow) and dry them yourself (see page 223). Rosemary grows everywhere; if you can't find it somewhere

and rarely used. I suggest searching for the two- or four-ounce round, amber spice jars with lids that are sold in cases of twelve through cooperative grocery stores across the country, specifically co-ops that feature Frontier brand products. Label the contents and date of purchase by writing directly on the jar in a metallic Sharpie (erase with rubbing alcohol). When deciding on sizes, keep in mind that even the four-ounce size is a lot of a spice for things like cloves or marjoram, ones you use by the quarter teaspoon every few months.

Beyond sealing in freshness by containing them properly, you're more likely to actually use the spices if you can locate them not congealed in a uni-spice wad of fragrant plastic. Curry/paprika/cinnamon muffins, anyone? If you can't fit your spice jars into a drawer, I suggest creating depth in your pantry and storing spices in a pull-out box underneath a step-up shelf. Spices demand frequent interaction, and shoving them in an inconvenient location where you can't see all of them at

once will ensure you don't want to eat that carda-mom when you finally discover you have it.

As you start to see what spices actually get used in your house (and how frequently), dedicate your containers to those. Keep small quantities of other spices you buy (for single recipes) corralled in some sort of jar if possible. Date the baggies and toss what-ever you don't use within six months of purchase. Not including it (or substituting it for another spice) in a late-night recipe is way better than keeping your stale-ass, ancient spice indefinitely and then adding it to something you hope will be delicious.

*herbs and spices to stock*

I took a poll and discovered the following assess-ment of essential ground and whole spices and herbs from hip homies:

in your neighborhood for free, then buy a few sprigs fresh and dry it yourself.
- Buy spiced salts. They're inferior-quality salt with a not-that-fresh spice (and are sometimes full of weird preservatives). Make them yourself and taste a world of difference (see page 224).
- Buy a preassembled pickling spice mix; it's more useful to have each separately for more flavor possibility and for other projects.

| GROUND (ESSENTIAL) | GROUND (HELPFUL) | WHOLE (GRIND AS NEEDED OR USE FOR PICKLING) |
| --- | --- | --- |
| Cinnamon | Allspice | Black peppercorns |
| Chili powder/cayenne | Cloves | Nutmeg |
| Cumin | Coriander | Dried peppers (make your own flakes) |
| Ginger | Curry powder | Mustard, yellow or brown |
| Garlic | Turmeric | Fennel |
| Thyme | Paprika, smoked or sweet | Allspice |

**53**

| GROUND (ESSENTIAL) | GROUND (HELPFUL) | WHOLE (GRIND AS NEEDED OR USE FOR PICKLING) |
| --- | --- | --- |
| Oregano | Harissa | Cloves |
| | Garam masala | Cardamom |
| | | Coriander |
| | | Celery seeds |

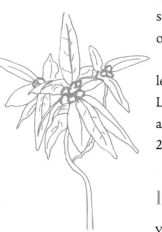

Note: onion and garlic powder appeared in many of my readers' comments about their top five faves, but I tend to flavor with sauces gleaned from scraping pan drippings from fresh versions of those.

The most important dried herb to have on hand is really a tree leaf: bay leaves unlock the flavor potential of many a soup or roast. Look for bay trees in your area and if you find one, snip a branch and hang it to dry out for free future seasoning! Check out page 223 for ways to dry and store extra fresh herbs.

## liquor cabinet

You don't need a full bar to rock general cooking, preserving projects, and impromptu entertaining. These are the basics to keep on hand:

- **Tequila,** duh (all you need to make margaritas is some sort of citrus, sweetness, and tequila).
- **Vodka,** some middle-of-the-road variety, so you can use it for drinking and preserving if necessary.
- **Everclear,** also called grain alcohol—and it's illegal in

some states—but the best thing to have on hand for bitters, liqueurs, and infusions. (Something to note: it's quite flammable, as is all alcohol, but its alcohol content is much higher than the standard forty-proof liquor you'll normally keep, so be extra careful where you stash it.) High-proof vodka will do in the event you live in one of the contraband states (but you definitely don't want to drink the high-proof vodka straight up).

- ➡ **Bitters** take the sugary edge off a drink made from homemade liqueurs or sweeter drinks. Bitters are easy to make; check out my recipe on page 286.

Liquor cabinet upgrades include the following:

- ➡ **Brandy** or **sherry** is always listed in some recipe and I rarely have it.
- ➡ **Kirsch** is in ice cream recipes, and I end up substituting vodka because I don't have it.

Move beyond the basics and learn how to upgrade your bar and beverage skills in Chapter 8.

## take inventory

Knowing what's in your pantry is the first step toward making changes. If you only look at what's behind box number three every time you move, you're missing out on whatever freshness there was to be had (learn more about date labels on page 63) and a lot of money-saving opportunities in making creative pantry meals rather than going out (because you don't think you have anything to eat).

By knowing what you have and keeping tabs on it, you also set yourself up for success in accomplishing weekly projects (e.g., bread, granola, etc.) without needing to shop. It's an incredibly satisfying feeling to look at a recipe and realize you have all the things you need already on hand.

Keeping a kitchen chalkboard or whiteboard (or painting a chalkboard wall or one side of your refrigerator with chalkboard paint) will help you keep tabs on what's getting low or completely gone. I photograph the chalkboard before going to the store. It's the easiest way to make a grocery list.

I also like to use the app Evernote for specialty grocery/kitchen and home acquisition lists, because then no matter where I am (looking at something online or in a store with just my phone), I can update the list and the changes appear everywhere.

## byob (bin)

Master the bulk section and stop acquiring plastic bags by bringing your own container and filling it at the grocery store. Be sure to write down the tare weight (what the container and lid weighs empty), and when you check out, they'll be able to subtract that weight from your purchase. It doesn't matter if it's not completely empty; the tare weight will ensure that you don't pay for more than you are buying. Don't let them give you a hard time; you're saving them money by not using their packaging. Some stores calculate weight differently, which seems impossible, but I learned that the best way to ensure a nongrumpy register attendant is to bring your container to the register first and let them mark it in their special code.

At least bring your own bag if it's not practical for you to bring the container you use to store whatever you're buying. We actually have a packaging-free grocery store in Austin called In.gredients. It's the first zero-waste grocery store in the country. And, no, you don't have to scoop almond butter into your purse if you forget your bin; you just have to buy a new reuse container.

## resources

### books

- *The Flavor Bible: The Essential Guide to Culinary Creativity, Based on the Wisdom of America's Most Imaginative Chefs* by Karen Page and Andrew Dornenburg
- *Keys to Good Cooking: A Guide to Making the Best of Foods and Recipes* by Harold McGee
- *Nourishing Traditions: The Cookbook That Challenges Politically Correct Nutrition and the Diet Dictocrats* by Sally Fallon and Mary G. Enig
- *Ratio: The Simple Codes Behind the Craft of Everyday Cooking* by Michael Ruhlman

### web

- Learn about buying clubs, or start your own: www.food club.org.
- Look into hosting your buying club through Big Tent at www.bigtent.com.
- Look for great bulk deals and ways to contain them with Frontier Natural Products Co-op: www.frontier coop.com.

# getting fresh

### an easy-on-the-wallet approach to completing the job of meals at home

Your kitchen can more or less remain in stasis with the prospect of odd little meals from your accomplishments in Chapters 1 and 2. (We all know that I-really-need-to-go-grocery-shopping dinner, which was probably one of the instigators of the put-an-egg-on-it movement.)

If you don't want to eat only beans, rice, and tamarind paste (or other dry goods you scrounge for in the back of the pantry), you need to up your game and bring on the perishables. Yes, I know it might feel like turning over an hourglass in your least favorite board game, time ticking away and your food's freshness and your sanity level slipping along with it, but I hope to change that.

## food waste

I'm not judging, especially since I've thrown out my fair share of food over the years, but we have to look at where we stand right now. At the start of any yoga practice, you're supposed to check in at your baseline, to be able to identify subtle shifts and chart improvements. I encourage you to do the same with your perishable food intake and waste volume.

The National Resource Defense Council (NRDC) has been working on reducing waste in all the different areas where food goes uneaten—left on the fields unharvested, culled postharvest because of aesthetics, overtrimmed during processing, unsold and wasted at the grocery store, or pitched after developing new life-forms in the back of our refrigerators. Here are a few shocking stats about the state of food waste right now:

➥ Our food habits waste 25 percent of America's freshwater and 4 percent of our oil. **On average,**

**a family of four spends \$1,350–\$2,275 annually on food and drinks that are never consumed.**

→ Uneaten food ends up rotting in landfills as the single-largest component of U.S. municipal solid waste, where it accounts for a large portion of U.S. methane emissions. (Why more cities don't institute mandatory composting and compost pickup baffles me.)

→ Fresh products make up the majority of household food waste; about two-thirds of the waste is due to spoilage, and the other third is the result of making/serving too much and pitching the excess.

→ The U.S. Department of Agriculture reports citrus fruits and cherries are the most commonly wasted fruits, and sweet potatoes, onions, and greens are the most commonly wasted vegetables.

Let's change this, one household at a time. Every little bit you acknowledge and attempt to change makes a difference. Here are a few ways to change these stats.

## don't overbuy

What's worse, the prospect of popping back into a grocery store or midweek farmers' market for a few additional (and not wilty) veggies, or stocking yourself up for the week and pitching half of it in the compost bin? I know the answer already, so you can just think about it.

## clean out the fridge

Rearrange things, placing the need-to-be-used-pronto items at the forefront of your refrigerator so you see those and not the things you just bought. Do this each time you buy produce or other food with a short lifespan, and do it once a week or, at the very least, once a month for other perishables.

## make a plan

I'm not asking you to plan your entire week's worth of nutrition (if you're not ready to go there yet), but it's a good idea to know roughly what you are going to eat for dinner for the next two days; that is, some sort of protein, some sort of veggie, and some sort of grain. Acquire the things you will need to make that happen and know that you may return to the grocery store if necessary. That Americans throw out $170 of food on average per month is reason enough to dismiss claims on efficient time management (i.e., not going to the store all the time). A few extra trips to the grocery store to cut out that $170 waste makes more sense to me.

## bulk down, not up

The desire to save money usually brings us to buying in bulk at dedicated bulk stores or from grocery or box stores. When presented with two options—buy a little and pay "X" or buy a lot and pay "20 percent less!"—it seems like a no-brainer, right? We're trained to get the best deal. The problem with bulk deals on perishable foods is that often a good chunk of the food goes unused and we throw it out. Think about how much money you saved initially versus what you just threw out and you'll see that maybe your best bulk option is the bulk bin section of the regular grocery store. Buy only what you need, save packaging costs, and stop throwing out all those "values."

## portion down

Portion sizes are on the up and up; so is the incidence of metabolic disorder (as discussed in Chapter 4). Cornell University did a study and discovered that *The Joy of Cooking* recipe portion sizes have increased by more than 30 percent since 1996. Recipes that used to feed ten people now feed only seven. Scaling down by a third is a good measure of how to bring portion sizes down to where they should be. See portion suggestions on page 264, for help on estimating how much of a recipe you should make.

## understand labels on food (good luck)

"Use by" and "best by" dates, which are found on both perishable and nonperishable products, are suggestions from manufacturers for peak quality; that is, they think you'll enjoy their product more if you don't let it sit in your fridge indefinitely. Contrary to common belief, these date indicators are not regulated through the USDA and do not serve as an indicator of food safety. Because "there is no uniform or universally accepted system used for food dating in the United States" (excerpted from a USDA online fact sheet), it can be mighty tricky navigating these labels. Per the USDA's website, here are the types of dates you will see on foods:

- A **"Sell by"** date tells the store how long to display the product for sale. You should buy the product before the date expires.
- A **"Best if used by" (or before)** date is recommended for best flavor or quality. It is not a purchase or safety date.

**63**

- A **"Use by"** date is the last date recommended for the use of the product while at peak quality. The date has been determined by the manufacturer of the product.
- **"Closed or coded"** dates are packing numbers for use by the manufacturer.

Don't let your roommate or spouse pitch everything with a spent date on it, especially if your nose and taste buds indicate nothing's wrong with it. You're in luck because the most common bacteria, yeasts, and molds that cause spoilage are visible or tend to make themselves known in other obvious ways. (Read more on the differences between spoilage and pathogenic bacteria on page 84.)

## shift your shopping paradigm

Visiting the farmers' market or grocery store and buying perishables is a supplemental factor to swing your staples into action every week. With a solid core of staples to work with, you'll have a higher rate of cooking success than if you purchase things that don't relate to each other or what you have in the house.

## utilize your scraps

Industry is making good use of the scraps from things you buy—for example, bones from processed meats, whey from cheesemaking—and then turning around and charging you more for things that they've created from them—like stocks, bouillon cubes, pasta, baked goods, and so on. Why not retain more of your goods' goodness and use up the entirety of what you buy? Learn simple, innovative ways to use up extras in Chapter 7.

## making meat or vegetable stock

Ever wonder why food in restaurants tastes so flavorful and rich (besides the added sodium and fat—not inherently villains, but not for everyday consumption on those levels)? Their sauces and flavor bases are built upon house-made stocks, rich with flavors you just won't get from a box of stock on the grocery shelf for $1.49. Making your own stock is the single most useful and immediately beneficial task you can undertake in the kitchen.

So what's the difference between stock and broth, which are often used interchangeably?

Stock is primarily an unclarified version of broth. Broth is a clear, pristine liquid that you won't need for anything I tell you to do in your kitchen. You can call stock broth in my book or go right ahead and follow Jacques Pépin's or any number of other chefs' advice out there for clarifying stock if a consommé found its way to your dinner menu.

When it comes to making stock, go all the way, people. There is no such thing as a quick (bone) stock, so why even try to fudge it? If it takes less than six hours, it's not worth making (you're not likely to get all the nutrients from the bones anyway). Veggie stock only takes an hour, so you can be speedy with that, but when in a pinch for meat stock, grab that box of stock you stashed in the event of an emergency and then resolve to finally start making your own to have on reserve for next time.

### Hip Trick

Keep skimmed fat from stock in a jar or container and store it in the freezer. Use it to sauté veggies or meats, or to add to simmering grains.

### scrap stock

Although it may simmer for a long time (until you're ready to deal with it), there's really only about twenty

# three ways to use homemade stock

1. Pour some in the bottom of a pan and add leftovers to reheat in your toaster oven.

2. Freeze two cups' worth in ice cube trays for handy preportioned deglazing cubes.

3. Boil grains in stock as a means of adding richness and depth to meals.

minutes of active labor involved in making a great stock. All you have to do to get started is collect trash.

We keep two gallon-sized bags in the freezer for collecting scraps, one for chicken bones, which fills up every few weeks, the other for beef/pork/other bones, which fills up every few months. We stuff veggie scraps in each bag periodically, depending on which is closer to filling. Stocks are flexible and recipeless (though I've included one for chicken on page 160 to ease you into it) and are pretty much "anything goes." Steer clear of the few things mentioned below (just say no to stinky stock) and start upping the flavor factor on homemade foods.

*scraps and things that make great stock*

- Onion ends, trimmings, and cores, or anything from the onion family (leeks, scallions, shallots, garlic)
- Celery hearts, leaves, and tough outer stalks (a.k.a. celery trash)
- Carrot peels, ends, and tops
- A bay leaf
- Mushroom scraps
- A spoonful of tomato paste
- A few crushed black peppercorns

*scraps and veggies to avoid in stock (mainly all the brassicas)*

- Lots of dark, leafy greens (kale, broccoli leaves)
- Artichokes

- Broccoli
- Brussels sprouts
- Cabbage
- Cauliflower
- Turnips
- Rutabaga

**Hip Trick**

Use the water you soaked dried mushrooms in (to reconstitute them) as impromptu veggie stock.

Take chef Deborah Madison's advice from *Vegetarian Cooking for Everyone* and leave out "anything you wouldn't eat: no funky or spoiled vegetables."

## vegetable stock

The basis of a veggie stock is mirepoix: onion, carrot, celery, and a bay leaf. You can throw anything in there, though, and the great news for vegetarians is that you don't have to cook it for nearly as long as you would a meat stock. Veggie stocks are finished after one hour, tops. I like Deborah Madison's rundown on veggie stocks, methodology, and flavors in *Vegetarian Cooking for Everyone*.

## storing stocks

See specific instructions on pages 86–88, but generally you can re-frigerate, freeze, or pressure can your stocks to store them. Stocks stored in the refrigerator for more than seven days should be re-boiled for ten minutes or longer and re-stored.

## eat food

Michael Pollan says in his book *In Defense of Food*, "Not everyone can afford to eat high-quality food in America, and that is shame-ful; however, those of us who can, should."

A year on food stamps in New York City taught us that we can eat well (non-GMO, mostly organics, and a lot of locally produced or farmers' market items) for no more than $250 a month. That certainly doesn't make me the expert on poverty and the complexity of how to make a well-grown carrot as affordable (and accessible) as a 7-Eleven Big Gulp. In the context of his book, Michael Pollan is not trying to shame anyone (nor is he speaking to an elite class); rather, he's referring to people like me and you, those who have some money but need to spend it wisely.

That we fed ourselves with high-quality foods for roughly $8.33 *per day* for *two* adults means that it is in fact possible to live well on a budget. Yes, we omitted a lot of convenience items and just plain did without some stuff (both in and out of the kitchen) to make that work, but if we could do it, I bet you can, too. We're no longer on food stamps, but we still spend less than $300 per month on three meals a day from home. Beyond issues of access (areas where good-quality food is simply not available, much less affordable), I don't especially want to hear preachy sermons about how expensive good-quality food is, especially from people who don't actively budget.

## budgeting

If you've never kept track, it's a wholly enlightening experience to record what you spend in a month on food, if only to see where you stand and make moves toward improving your model. It's helpful to segregate between the funds you spend on groceries and actual ingredients and the funds you spend on convenience items (premade or deli items, takeout, or restaurant expenses).

We keep grocery costs low by diversifying our shopping and utilizing the following tactics.

1. **Buying clubs.** I participate in a large buying club in Austin that has a ton of different sub co-op groups for different needs—baking goods, general grocery, maple syrup, clothing, kids' shoes, reusable containers, gluten-free flours, and so on. If no such thing exists where you are, start one! Round up a small group of friends or households to go in together on large orders—whole animal meat orders, bulk quantities of local vegetables, basic groceries, or hard-to-find ingredients or supplies. Organizing and coordinating the logistics of large orders will involve a learning curve at first, but you'll appreciate it when your household and five or six others start saving a bunch of money. You'll also learn a lot about local and regional farms, companies you want to support, and how to get the best deals.

2. **Rebranded products.** Places like Trader Joe's, ALDI, Whole Foods Market, and oftentimes your local grocer rebrand products purchased from other producers and companies. They offer lower prices on those rebranded products because of their ability to make large cash purchases (huge incentive for producers) or by exercising buying power on overstock items that companies inevitably end up producing.

   The only downside to all this money saving is that you don't really know what company made whatever it is you're buying and you (being hip to all this) know that it's good to know as much about the things you're buying and consuming as possible. You can find out an individual store's ethics (which should be transparent and written down somewhere), and from there you can glean what types of companies/distributors it purchases from, so if you're shopping this way, be sure you understand what your store supports.

69

I prefer shopping at Whole Foods for fruit juices, organic frozen fruit, and other 365 Everyday Value brand items. I understand their company policies and ethics—no high fructose corn syrups and mandatory labeling of products containing GMOs, among others); plus, they occasionally have overstock (thus good prices on) better-than-regular-grocery-store meats.

3. **Food co-ops.** Most large cities have a food cooperative in addition to regular grocery stores, and these co-ops all work a little differently in terms of benefits and requirements for membership. These stores often involve an initial membership fee or, if you're lucky, the option to work a regular volunteer shift for reduced prices. Retail grocery prices are double, sometimes triple what stores pay at cost. If you can join a cooperative that cuts out some of those costs, do it!

4. **CSAs—Community Supported Agriculture.** CSAs are available in all sorts of forms, but most commonly through local farms. How it works: you pay a farmer up front for the season and you get a box full of locally produced fruit and veggies grown on a farm each week during growing season. We loved receiving a CSA box, but it's a lot of produce to manage. Full shares cost on average $25–$30 per week, which, depending on your location, gets you an array of seasonal fruits and vegetables. Sometimes farms will offer discounted CSA prices for people who commit to doing farm work hours.

5. **Shop around.** As you learned in the last chapter, frugal shoppers know not only

*Hip Trick*

CSAs can be an unreasonable commitment for someone not accustomed to cooking at home at least four meals a week. (Even a half share will be a drastic influx of fresh produce, a ticking bomb of composting grocery anxiety.) If this describes you, try to find a neighbor, roommate, or friend who will split the cost and the bounty with you.

where to buy the things they need, but also average price ranges for those items. Sure, this method requires trips to a few different places and actually paying attention to what you buy, but savings add up faster than you'd expect, especially when you're pinching pennies in the first place.

## how to shop farmers' markets (and not go broke)

We shop at nearly every grocery establishment available to us plus a handful of farmers' markets in town to find deals that work for our tight budget. Don't omit the farmers' market as an option because you think it's too expensive.

Aside from the fact that small, local farmers make most of their income from direct sales at the market, market prices are usually comparable to what you'll see at a Whole Foods or the bins at your local supermarket devoted to produce you'd actually want to eat.

### seconds

My grandma grew up scrounging behind supermarkets in Michigan for seconds during the Depression years. Today, farmers often bring their imperfect produce, called seconds, to the market (and keep them stashed away); ask the vendors if they have seconds for a lower price. Snag a case of tomato seconds at hard-to-beat (for even conventionally grown, shipped produce) prices and try your hand at canning, or just freeze them for future salsas and sauces. Read more about freezing foods at the end of the chapter.

### cut out the middleman

Buying meat directly from the farmer will be the most cost-effective way to eat local meats (barring joining a buying club

71

and undertaking whole-animal kinds of purchases with friends). When we saw local meat in the frozen section of our local independent grocery store, we assumed it would cost a fortune; but it turns out that when you cut out the middleman, the prices are often comparable to any grocery store's organic meat offerings.

As the seasons for certain foods wrap up, farmers like to unload as much of their harvests as possible. Start to tune into what's in season—by going to the market every week—and you'll notice when clearance prices appear. Even if you don't buy a lot from the market on a regular basis, it's a great way to start discovering what's in season in your area.

## what's in season?

Planting zones will vary depending on your region, but here's a general listing of when most of America is enjoying foods in season.

*spring*

| | |
|---|---|
| *Asparagus* | *Broccoli* |
| *Kale* | *Cabbage* |
| *Chard* | *Strawberries* |
| *Spinach* | *Rhubarb* |

*summer*

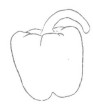

| | |
|---|---|
| *Berries (blueberries, blackberries, raspberries)* | *Corn* |
| | *Beans* |
| *Cherries* | *Melons (cantaloupes, watermelons)* |
| *Peaches* | |
| *Figs* | *Cucumber* |
| *Tomatoes* | *Summer squash and zucchini* |
| *Okra* | *Potatoes* |
| *Peppers* | |

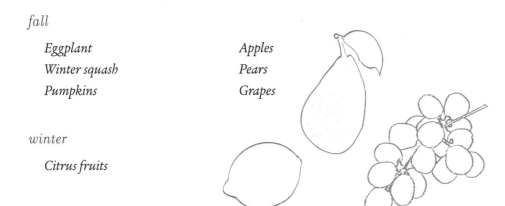

*fall*

Eggplant        Apples

Winter squash   Pears

Pumpkins        Grapes

*winter*

Citrus fruits

## buying with your brains

You should understand three basic things when at the grocery store or wherever you find yourself buying food: local, organic, and GMO. I'm not coming from the position or ideology of luxury here; we take our food (and what it ate, absorbed, or lost before we eat it) very seriously.

### local

Shifting to a more locally sourced fruit and vegetable diet will likely change your food paradigm as it did mine. I experienced what foods are really supposed to taste like and not just what I'd grown up eating: their soulless, watery, year-round (and often engineered) likenesses. I love California and all, but eating their big ol' strawberries in the fall is nothing like eating the different variety of small, tender berries that appear at our farmers' markets for a brief few weeks in spring.

Beyond taste, buying locally grown foods is important in reestablishing regional food systems, which strengthen local economies, cut down on travel/pollution costs, and provide communities with the most nutrient-dense, fresh foods. A local Austin organization, the Sustainable Food Center, advocates for our

**73**

food, and among their many great initiatives, they've introduced a double-dollar program for people on public food assistance to get half off fruits and vegetables at their markets.

## organic

As scientists continue to debate various analyses of data surrounding organic foods, it's becoming clear that there are science-based claims for both sides of the debate. This makes it increasingly difficult for us as consumers to determine what to do since even the scientists can't agree.

Eating organic food isn't a matter of marked differences in the nutritional values between conventionally grown and organics per se (though organics do contain more vitamin C and cancer-fighting compounds* according to researchers in the United Kingdom) but rather in what's not included in your food: synthetic pesticides, genetically modified organisms, antibiotics, and growth hormones. Pesticides are endocrine disruptors that change gene expression patterns and cause unforeseen harm to our health as a result.

The environmental case for eating organically grown/raised foods includes the health of farm workers and larger-scale environmental issues (e.g., pesticide runoff and fertilizers in water systems). Farm workers who are routinely exposed to pesticides develop memory problems and cancer at much higher rates than people not exposed to pesticides on that same level, noted a recent study conducted by the American Academy of Pediatrics (AAP).[†] There are many environmental concerns, but most, alarmingly, relate to water; how our water flows around the world is one of the

---

* http://dx.doi.org/10.1080/07352689.2011.554417.
† http://online.wsj.com/article/SB1000142405297020363060457807 2643615348434.html.

best reasons to support organic agriculture. The *Associated Press*[*] reported in 2007:

> *The nation's corn crop is fertilized with millions of pounds of nitrogen-based fertilizer. And when that nitrogen runs off fields in Corn Belt states, it makes its way to the Mississippi River and eventually pours into the Gulf [of Mexico], where it contributes to a growing "dead zone"—a 7,900-square-mile patch so depleted of oxygen that fish, crabs, and shrimp suffocate.*

## why organic produce?

A recent recommendation by the AAP (2012)[†] noted that prenatal and early childhood exposure to pesticides is associated with pediatric cancers, decreased cognitive function (lowered IQ, autism), and behavioral problems (like attention-deficit hyperactivity disorder).

While analyzing a series of findings, the AAP noted a study where children who normally ate conventionally grown produce switched to organic produce for just five days, and researchers found the change dramatically reduced the levels of pesticide residue in their urine.

The "organic" label, like all large-scale regula-

---

[*] http://www.nbcnews.com/id/22301669/ns/us_news -environment/t/corn-boom-could-expand-dead-zone -gulf/#.UUhxGVugnl1.

[†] http://www.healthychildren.org/English/news/pages/ AAP-Makes-Recommendations-to-Reduce-Childrens- Exposure-to-Pesticides.aspx.

# your produce sticker says a lot

- Four digits starting with 3 or 4 means conventionally grown produce.
- Five digits starting with a 9 means organically grown.
- Five digits starting with an 8 means GMO.

75

tory things, is imperfect at times. Knowing about the company touting an organic label (or about the regional farms that can't swing organic designation because of either financial or practical obstacles) is your best bet. Marketing is slick, so cut through the fat by talking with friends and grocery store staff, and researching online.

The Environmental Working Group annually assesses pesticide residues in common produce sampled by the U.S. Department of Agriculture and the federal Food and Drug Administration. I suggest downloading the free guide by visiting its website, ewg.org, and looking for its current *Shopper's Guide to Pesticides in Produce* for the most up-to-date information.

| HIGHEST PESTICIDE RESIDUES (BUY ORGANIC) | LOWEST PESTICIDE RESIDUES |
|---|---|
| Apples | Cantaloupe (U.S.-grown) |
| Blueberries (U.S.-grown) | Grapefruit |
| Grapes | Watermelon |
| Strawberries | Asparagus |
| Peaches | Avocado |
| Celery | Broccoli |
| Cucumbers | Cabbage |
| Green beans | Eggplant |
| Kale/spinach/lettuce | Mushrooms |
| Potatoes | Onions |
| Sweet bell peppers | Sweet potatoes |

You'll notice a lot of gaps in the preceding list, no mention of things you might buy regularly. So when faced with higher prices for organics, do what you can when you can. Voting with your dollars as much as possible is a part of the greater picture of fixing our agricultural system.

## why organic meats?

Eating organic meats eliminates our risk of exposure to antibiotics from eating conventionally raised animals. The AAP study also stated that organic meat options can reduce the risk of developing breast cancers and diseases related to antibiotic-resistant bacteria. Beyond keeping your body out of the test group for the unknown long-term health effects of low-level estrogen exposure from food, by choosing organic you also eliminate chance encounters with toxins like arsenic* (which the FDA found in industrial, antibiotic-treated chicken) and other drugs with which animals are treated to combat the challenges of raising them under the duress posed by industrial agriculture.

## why organic dairy?

Although the verdict is still out on the long-term human impacts of drinking milk from cows treated with rBGH (recombinant bovine growth hormone), which increases an insulinlike level in cows to keep them in high milk production mode, I'd rather not serve as a human subject for that test. Conventionally raised cows eat silage, a fodder composed largely of regional GMO crops

---

\* http://www.fda.gov/AnimalVeterinary/SafetyHealth/ ProductSafetyInformation/ucm258313.htm.

that contain pesticide residues at varying levels and environmental toxins, which tend to aggregate in fat cells.

Organic milk producers are required to allow pasture grazing for a portion of the cow's diet. As a result of the cow eating what it's actually supposed to eat, its milk has higher levels of omega-3s, which are essential fatty acids that our standard American diet is particularly deprived of—thanks to the lipid hypothesis and the campaign to switch to vegetable oils (see page 103).

## the difference between homogenized, pasteurized, and raw milk

Cow milk can be a combination of different designations.

### homogenized

When milk is homogenized, its fat particles undergo high-pressure straining and as a result shrink in size and remain in suspension rather than separating and allowing the cream to rise to the top. The fat and cholesterol are then more prone to oxidation and rancidity.

### pasteurized*

Milk that is pasteurized is heated to 161°F, the temperature that no longer supports microbial life, and thus the antimicrobial properties—lactic acid bacteria and enzymes that were keeping in check potentially harmful microbes that got into the milk—and immune-boosting enzymes, vitamins, and good bacteria are also eliminated. And pasteurization denatures the milk proteins, mak-

---

\* http://www.fda.gov/downloads/Food/FoodSafety/Product-Specific Information/MilkSafety/NationalConferenceonInterstateMilk ShipmentsNCIMSModelDocuments/UCM209789.pdf.

78

ing it more difficult to digest. *Ultrapasteurization* involves heating to 280°F. *Low-temperature pasteurization,* which is a great option if raw milk isn't available or desirable, involves heating the milk to 145°F and doesn't denature the proteins as much, though it can damage the probiotics and digestive enzymes, so making your own yogurt with this milk would be a great way to restrengthen the probiotic content of low-temp pasteurized milk.

*raw*

Sally Fallon, cofounder of the Weston A. Price Foundation, started A Campaign for Real Milk (realmilk.com) around the same time the WAP Foundation organized in 1999. The campaign promotes raising healthy cows on pasture and drinking their milk raw (i.e., *not* allowing people to drink milk from cows in current industrial processes). There is vehement, science-based opposition to raw milk, which I can understand when looking at it in the context of how our industrial dairy system operates today; no one would *ever* want to drink milk raw from industrial, conventionally raised cows, which often have udder infections (mastitis) from the increased hormone levels and other illnesses being treated with antibiotics. I support raw milk as promoted by Fallon and WAP Foundation advocates, and it's important to note that much of the opposition they face is likely because of industry and scale and not public safety; that is, it just doesn't benefit the big-ag dairy industry to revert to smaller-scale, regionally produced nonhomogenized milk.

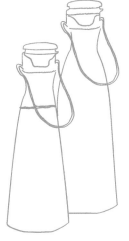

I consume both low-temp pasteurized and raw milk and I've been to the farm where we buy both; I've seen the cows and how they live and how the milk is bottled. I'm not telling you how to approach the matter, which is fraught with so much conflicting information. I just urge you to research both sides and understand what's ultimately behind FDA claims of extreme danger in this case (big industry dollars).

# these ingredients are soy based

- Hydrolyzed soy protein (HSP)
- Mono- and diglycerides
- Monosodium glutamate (MSG)
- Textured vegetable protein (TVP)

## *avoiding GMOs*

What's the big deal with GMOs? The science (which even when available might need some perspective based on who's funding it) is still inconclusive about GMOs' effect on our health and well-being. That being said, it's probably not a good idea to pump our bodies full of them. Whole Foods Market took a big step in 2013 as the first retailer in the United States to require all food sold in its stores to display GMO labeling where applicable. Trader Joe's does not allow GMO ingredients from suppliers of their private label brands (Trader Joe's, Trader José's, Trader Ming's, etc.), but there are other brands in the shop whose ingredients are not accounted for.[*]

Here are the top five commonly GMO[†] foods you should buy organically, locally if possible (and ask farmers what kind of seeds they're using) or from trusted companies who support non-GMO labeling initiatives:

1. Tomatoes
2. Corn
3. Canola (in practically all packaged food and bags of chips)
4. Rice
5. Soy

---

[*] http://www.traderjoes.com/about/customer-updates-responses.asp?i=4; http://youtube/6OMClLWQGSI.

[†] http://ecowatch.org/2012/the-top-10-gmo-foods-to-avoid/ and http://foodallergies.about.com/od/soyallergies/a/List-of-Soy-Ingredients-to-Avoid-When-Following-a-Soy-Free-Diet.htm.

Realize that most GMO consumption in our diets is not in the raw/cooked version of the ingredients above, but received as an added bonus when squeezing a ketchup packet, munching a bag of snack chips, or just eating a packaged, flavored yogurt; so you're also getting GMO corn (and maybe a few other GMO ingredients) with your meal. That GMOs are so pervasive in our highly processed diets is yet another reason to start cooking for yourself. We are currently serving as guinea pigs for the long-term research that's absent. Read more about health and nutrition in Chapter 4.

To boot, genetically engineered crops, which were designed in part to reduce the dependence on pesticides, have actually ramped up pesticide usage over the last decade. Mark Bittman shared in one of his op-ed pieces for the *New York Times* that, in general, fields grown with GMO seed crops use 24 percent more chemicals than those grown with conventional seeds.[*]

## store it

Miraculously you managed to buy produce and navigate the grocery store and/or farmers' market (and learned more than you ever wanted to know about food waste, the state of organic food, environmental concerns, and toxicity). Mastering

---

[*] http://opinionator.blogs.nytimes.com/2012/12/11/ pesticides-now-more-than-ever
http://www.motherjones.com/tom-philpott/2012/10 /how-gmos-ramped-us-pesticide-use

## these ingredients are often soy based

- Hydrolyzed vegetable protein (HVP)
- Gum arabic
- Guar gum (Bob's Red Mill brand makes non-GMO guar gum)
- Lecithin
- Vegetable gum, starch, shortening, or oil
- Vitamin E

81

the techniques for properly storing it all, so you actually want to consume it in the days to come, is the second part of the battle.

*crisper drawer,*
*a.k.a. the ticking time bomb*

No matter how technologically advanced your refrigerator is, the crisper drawer likely will not keep your vegetables as described by its misleading moniker. My best advice for a successful, extended postharvest life for your produce is to store its pieces in separate plastic bags.

I'm not crazy about plastic's pervasiveness (see page 90), but it sure does combat the drying refrigerator air well. We reuse our grocery store plastic vegetable bags by hanging them up inside out to dry between uses and then continue using them until they die. Friends of mine use nylon mesh bags and they are a good alternative to plastic for containing things, but they are not a great way to keep the contents of the bags from wilting from exposure to the drying air of your refrigerator. We store small amounts of ingredients (half a lemon or avocado, an assortment of parmesan cheese ends, etc.) in airtight glass containers, but we have to be choosy about what goes in there so we don't end up with all our leftover containers out of commission.

Hoarding fresh veggies isn't doing the nutrient content and general freshness any favors; and for a number of reasons you'd be better off cooking them in their prime and storing them as ready-to-eat veggies (in glass containers). I really like Tamar Adler's method, discussed in her book, *An Everlasting Meal,* for cooking up the entire farmers' market bounty on the day she brings it home. She roasts and boils it up and eats from the cooked stash during the week, using the veggies as ingredients in dishes she makes. This is an interesting way to manage storing food and using it while it's in its prime; plus, cooked vegetables are a lot more likely to be consumed (I'm noting the lonely raw beets lurking in the bottom of our crisper drawer at this very moment).

*produce it's okay to store at room temperature*

| VEGGIES | FRUITS |
| --- | --- |
| Onions | Apples you intend to eat within the week |
| Squash | Citrus fruits |
| Garlic | Bananas |
| Tomatoes | Tropical fruits (mangoes, papayas, pineapple) |
| Potatoes, all types (including sweet potatoes) | Pomegranates |
| Eggplant | Persimmons |
| Ginger | Watermelons |
| Herbs** (in a glass of water) | Cucumbers* (yes, I know they're technically a fruit) |

\* Once refrigerated, keep refrigerated.

\** I've had luck storing herbs for up to two weeks in water, cinched in a plastic produce bag.

If you cut into any of these veggies/fruits and don't use the whole thing, you should store it in the fridge, either in a produce bag or in a glass storage container with a tight-sealing lid.

## oh, hey, food safety

Here's a quick refresher on not giving yourself food poisoning. There are two kinds of spoilers in food:

1. **Spoilage bacteria** are the microbes that facilitate the natural method of food decomposition, what causes food not full of preservatives and artificial stuff to go bad. Food looks and smells funny (or gross), which makes the food unappealing—not usually deadly—and helps cue you in to not eat it. Molds and yeasts also contribute to spoilage, and they're both fungi naturally occurring in foods and are destroyed at temperatures between 140°F and 190°F.

2. **Pathogenic bacteria** are the ones that make you sick. There are environmental, animal, and human transmitters for bacteria that you can't see, smell, or taste. It's unlikely that you will encounter heavy hitters like *E. coli*, *Salmonella*, or *Listeria*, but proper food handling and heating will further ensure your safety against them.

### keep it clean

It's not necessary to be OCD clean in the kitchen, but starting out your cooking adventures with basic handwashing (for the amount of time it takes to sing "Happy Birthday" to your cat) and utensils that have been cleaned with warm soapy water are a good baseline of clean.

*don't double dip*

Even if you're the only person in the house who drinks the milk or eats the pickles, you shouldn't drink directly from or double dip your fork into the container because (a) that's what cups and plates are for and (b) double dipping contaminates the food with your mouth bacteria and might decrease shelf life.

*pack and date it*

Mold requires air, food, and moisture to thrive. Cut out the air as a factor and you'll decrease your chances of growing a science fair project on your leftovers. For longer-term freezing, cut out freezer burn by avoiding the standard—not freezer-quality—plastic bags or standard plastic food storage or reuse containers (those without added protections). Lightweight (cheap) aluminum foil is generally inadequate for home freezing; look for products labeled specifically for freezing.

Keep a roll of masking tape and a Sharpie somewhere near your fridge so you can label things. Go by your senses in order to determine the freshness of fridge-stored ingredients, leftovers, and long storage staples. Leftovers last on average three to five days, if they were prepared and stored without the unhelpful input of your or someone else's drool. Quality is the issue with frozen foods, so on average try to eat them within six months, tops.

# quick reference storage tips

Fridge it: 3–5 days

Freeze it: 3–6 months

Pitch it: things you can't identify or date

85

## cool it right

Allow large batches of soups, casseroles, and meat roasts to cool at room temperature (for no more than two hours) and then refrigerate; this helps prevent raising the temperature in your refrigerator. For a quicker cooling method, place large (metal) pots of food in a sink full of cold, icy water, stir the food to help the temperature to drop evenly, and then refrigerate. Alternatively, you can divide up large portions of food into smaller, shallow containers in which you'll freeze them. Allow these small containers to cool at room temperature for up to two hours and then completely cool them overnight in the refrigerator before placing them in the freezer, which will keep ice crystals small when you eventually do put them in the freezer.

## defrost it right

Thawing frozen foods should ideally be done in the refrigerator—with the item set in a bowl or container to catch defrosted drips—but the reality of defrosting means you usually forgot to do this in advance and now you're in a hurry. If that's the case, place the item in a large bowl or gallon-sized jar and allow it to sit under a small stream of cold water (capture the runoff in a roasting dish or tub below it for watering your plants). Some folks recommend defrosting in the microwave, but it partially cooks the food and provides a hospitable environment for bacterial growth if not cooked right away. So be sure to cook all of a defrosted item at the time of defrosting.

## go forth and reheat

The basic rule regarding hot/cold food is to keep hot food hot and cold food cold; that is, keep both out of the danger zone between 40°F and 140°F. When that's not possible, you get a two-hour window (one hour if food is sitting outside at temps above 90°F) to eat foods before spoilers can bloom. Reheating food so it's steaming and hot to the touch all the way through (don't burn yourself) or just to a simmer (if suspended in liquid) will kill any potential spoilers. A rolling boil for ten minutes will kill anything that might have grown in your more-than-a-week-stored stocks in the fridge.

## storing food in the freezer

The current state of your freezer may be one of two scenarios: a lonely half-eaten carton of freezer-burned ice cream, a few TV dinners, and a box of batteries and bottle of vodka in the door. Or it might be jam-packed with open boxes of waffles, bags of frozen fruits and vegetables, and mysterious freezer bags full of undisclosed, foil-wrapped things, the contents of which you thought you'd remember. Neither scenario is particularly helpful to you.

The freezer can be a really useful tool for stashing leftovers and components of meals like ready-to-cook/eat fruits, vegetables, and meats. When it comes to successful freezing, excess moisture and access to air are the top two culprits in freezing failures. Here are a few vessels and materials to help you succeed in ousting moisture and air from the mix:

- A layer of plastic wrap or waxed paper placed on top of the food in a container before adding the lid can help minimize the food's contact with freezer air.

87

➥ Any straight-sided canning jar can be used for freezing. Wide-mouth quart, pint, and straight-sided half-pint jars work best since contents can expand evenly upward during crystallization. (The regular-mouth jar that has a smaller rim than body can break when contents expand inside, unless you leave two to three inches between the food and the top of the jar.) Leave at least an inch when filling wide-mouth jars with food and leave the lid loose for the first few hours in the freezer.

➥ Reusing freezer bags in other areas of the house is fine, but try to stick with only new bags when freezing food directly in them since normal wear and tear creates small holes in bags and increases the chances of freezer burn.

Freezing halts spoilage by removing water (what bacteria needs to thrive) from the cells of food and replacing it with ice crystals. The question is quality not safety when considering what to freeze. Successful freezing minimizes opportunities for large ice crystals to form, which deteriorate the quality of your food.

### great ways to freeze common perishable foods

*fruit*

To freeze fruit quickly, space sliced fruit (toss apple or pear slices in a bit of lemon juice first to avoid browning) or whole berries (blueberries, blackberries, raspberries, etc.) on a cookie sheet (pieces shouldn't touch), place in the freezer, and throw into freezer bags once frozen (ten minutes). Keep no longer than six to eight months for best quality.

## vegetables

Blanch the vegetables and then dry them completely. Freeze in small portions. Keep no longer than six months for best quality.

## meat

Divide large packages of fresh meat into dinner-sized portions and double-wrap them with the laminated butcher paper they came in plus a layer of heavy-duty foil, or put inside a freezer bag (or with any two of these). Keep no longer than four to nine months to maintain quality. Thawed meat will lose liquid fast when cooked quickly, so longer cooking times at lower temperatures are better for retaining moisture.

# leftovers and ingredients that don't freeze well

- Mayonnaise or sour-cream-based things

- Milk sauces and gravies thickened with cornstarch or flour

- Cooked egg whites

- Meringues

- Pasta

- Rice

- Veggies found commonly in salads, such as lettuce, radishes, cucumbers, and cabbage

*Hip Trick*

If simply recycling that empty water bottle isn't enough for your eco-minded self, consider reusing #1 and #2 bottles as ice packs in coolers.

*bread*

Wrap a completely cooled loaf in foil and place it in a freezer bag. We slice our bread and stick squares of cut-up parchment paper between the slices before freezing so it's easy to grab a few slices at a time for breakfast toast or sandwiches.

## guide to plastics

When buying prepackaged foods and storing or toting leftovers, it's good to understand what those little numbers inside the recycle symbol on plastic containers mean.

Imprint this little jingle on your brain or write it in your phone notepad so you can chant to yourself at the grocery store, "One, five, four, two, all the rest are bad for you."* Stick to these numbers for storing things that come into contact with food:

- **1 PETE or PET**—polyethylene terephthalate (don't reuse for food/drink-related purposes, though, because it's designed for single use; this plastic is not sturdy enough for continued use and leaches easily with reuse)
- **2 HDPE**—High-density polyethylene
- **4 LDPE**—Low-density polyethylene
- **5 PP**—Polypropylene

BPA (bisphenol-A) is a plasticizer in polycarbonate containers and epoxy linings of most metal cans that leaches into packaged food and beverages (more reason to learn your safe plastic numbers and start making your own convenience items). France became the first country to ban BPA in all food packaging in 2013

---

* *Slow Death by Rubber Duck* by Rick Smith and Bruce Lourie.

because it is a synthetic estrogen that, even in small amounts, disrupts the endocrine system.[*] Constant exposure to this toxin is linked to a number of health issues, including infertility, breast and reproductive system cancer, obesity, diabetes, early puberty, and children's behavioral issues.

## go hyperlocal

One of the best ways to navigate the confusing web of perishable acquisitions is to grow your own. No matter what your living arrangement is, there are ways to incorporate homegrown goodness into your life. These are a few different setups you might try:

- Windowsill potted garden
- Stoop container garden
- Back deck galvanized tub garden
- Small raised-bed garden

I've included my favorite container and small-space gardening books in the chapter resources to get you going on growing. Start small and spend time observing and identifying your sunniest location—the one factor you'll need to grow food well. Use top-quality organic potting soil, since you want to eat top-quality organic food. (Definitely pass on the claims of soils with plant food

---

[*] http://www.niehs.nih.gov/health/topics/agents/endocrine/.

# decoding fertilizers

I recently learned at a seminar hosted by our county's Master Gardeners Association that a good way to remember what type of N-P-K (nitrogen-phosphorous-potassium) fertilizer ratio is best for the plants you're growing is to memorize these:

- N—leaves
- P—roots
- K—fruits or fruit quality

Get a ratio that favors whatever you're hoping to grow based on the categories above.

**91**

in them. Go with a simple soil and make or buy separate plant food based on the actual needs of your plants.) The only commitment you'll need to make is to develop a relationship with your sprouts, poking around and watching things grow and, of course, watering them regularly.

Here are a few things I've had luck growing in containers over the years:

| | |
|---|---|
| Lettuce | Nasturtiums—lovely and |
| Arugula | edible flowers |
| Spinach | Raspberries |
| Beans and peas | |

I've also been successful growing these herbs:

| | |
|---|---|
| Mint—one of the easiest | Thyme |
| things to grow | Oregano |
| Basil | Chives |

### fun things to do with homegrown foods

- Incorporate herbs into a salad dressing, herby butter, or infused vinegar.
- Make mojitos with your stoop-grown mint.
- Eat salads all summer long with your own back deck lettuce.
- Start up conversations with passersby over peas or raspberry flowers.
- Dry herbs for winter stews and soups.

## resources

### books

- *American Wasteland: How America Throws Away Nearly Half Its Food (and What We Can Do About It)* by Jonathan Bloom
- *Apartment Gardening: Plants, Projects, and Recipes for Growing Food in Your Urban Home* by Amy Pennington
- *Easy Growing: Organic Herbs and Edible Flowers from Small Spaces; Grow Great Grub: Organic Food from Small Spaces;* and *You Grow Girl: The Groundbreaking Guide to Gardening,* all by Gayla Trail
- *An Everlasting Meal: Cooking with Economy and Grace* by Tamar Adler
- *The Omnivore's Dilemma: A Natural History of Four Meals* and *In Defense of Food: An Eater's Manifesto,* both by Michael Pollan
- *Slow Death by Rubber Duck: The Secret Danger of Everyday Things* by Rick Smith and Bruce Lourie

### web

- Find pick-your-own farms and seasonal growing charts for your state: www.pickyourown.org.
- Learn what's local, in season, and sustainably produced in your area: www.eatwellguide.org; also check out information on these issues at the Natural Resources Defense Council food initiative at www.nrdc.org/living/food/.
- The USDA website has food safety fact sheets at http://www.fsis.usda.gov/wps/portal/fsis/topics/food-safety-education/get-answers/food-safety-fact-sheets.

93

- Make sense of all the various labeling and food designations, plus some limitations with labeling: www. animalwelfareapproved.org/consumers/food-labels/.

- Learn about the planet implications of unsustainable food practices and ways we can move forward with sustainable practices by visiting www.smallplanet.org.

- The Pesticide Action Network (PAN) has a searchable database cataloguing pesticide residues on foods: www. whatsonmyfood.org.

- The Cooperative Extension resource center provides information on storing fruits and vegetables for optimum flavor and quality: www.postharvest.ucdavis.edu.

- The National Center for Home Food Preservation website, nchfp.uga.edu, has detailed guidelines on how to freeze specific ingredients and food items properly.

- The Environmental Working Group helps keep our food, environment, and bodies free of harmful chemicals: www.ewg.org.

Part II

feeding yourself

life's pesky

eating requirements

chapter 4

# *methodology*
# *and mad skills*

*learning how to cook*
*without books or your laptop*

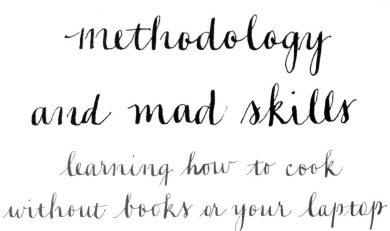

Here's what's cookin'    GRAM'S DINNER ROLLS
Recipe from the kitchen of _____

*The great thing about eating foods as compared with nutrients: you don't need to fathom a carrot's complexity in order to reap its benefits.*

—MICHAEL POLLAN

With this chapter's subtitle, I don't mean you will spontaneously erupt with intuitive chefery, but instead, you will hopefully make strides toward cooking without consulting a recipe (in a book or online) every two minutes. You'll hone your instincts and learn to shoot from there.

In this chapter, I'm giving you my lowdown on how to make heads or tails of all the nutritional information constantly thrown at us—and whose interests are at hand. Then we'll work out a solid base of methods and resources from which you'll start kicking ass in the kitchen. You don't need much inherent skill for cooking, just the aptitude to learn a few solid techniques that you'll use over and over again. The kitchen is a place to feel good at whatever level you're at and, most important, a place to keep learning; I hope you'll step on in with a bit more confidence after finishing this and the other chapters in this section.

## nutrition, funded by [insert industry here]

As you might've guessed from reading up on purchasing perishables and sorting through all the options we have before us in the refrigerated sections, my favor falls upon the real-food activists, people and groups like Michael Pollan, Slow Food, and your local farmer. Surprise, surprise, government panels and (many) academic researchers provide us with nutrition information based on the balance sheets of interested (and invested) parties. That competing industries are able to have such a heavy influence over what we're told is safe and nutritious for our bodies is pretty upsetting:

I'm considered only for the dollars I might spend on something and not at all for my health or true well-being.

The current system feels pretty broken. Obesity* and diabetes† are on the rise, with marked increases occurring in the last thirty years; oversimplified soils—with nutrient deficiencies arising from intensive mono-crop agriculture, synthetic fertilizers, and pesticides—give us fewer and fewer of the nutrients we need from food (between 10 and 40 percent loss in various produce from the 1950s to today‡); and our climate is changing rapidly. For all this brilliant industrialization and industry-centric control over what we're encouraged to eat, our health, rather than improving, is doing just the opposite. So I say, try something new, which is essentially old. You don't have to take my word for it; there are plenty of resources out there where you can read up on the matter. It's important to understand who's funding some of the research and why.

## trust and tradition

Everywhere you look there's a scientific study vilifying things found on grocery store shelves, where the majority of us go to find things to eat. Michael Pollan says it best in his book *Food Rules:* "I realized that the answer to the supposedly incredibly complicated question of what we should eat wasn't so complicated at all, and in fact could be boiled down to just seven words: 'Eat food. Not too much. Mostly plants.'" That book is a good place to start in trying to demystify dinner.

---

\* http://www.cdc.gov/chronicdisease/resources/publications/AAG/obesity.htm.

† http://www.cdc.gov/diabetes/statistics/prev/national/figpersons.htm.

‡ Michael Pollan's *In Defense of Food;* research from USDA noted in his book and http://www.scientificamerican.com/article.cfm?id=soil-depletion-and-nutrition-loss.

## sources of oxidized cholesterol

- Powdered milk (often added to reduced fat and skim milks)

- Powdered eggs

- Deep-fried foods

For a more detailed explanation of the concepts explored in *Food Rules,* you can check out *In Defense of Food*, Pollan's earlier book that inspired the grouping of those seven words, or if you're in the mood for more of a treatise, consult *Nourishing Traditions: The Cookbook That Challenges Politically Correct Nutrition and the Diet Dictocrats*, for research-based information on returning to traditional diets by preparing and eating foods that chemically resemble what our ancestors ate. No, it's not paleo, but Sally Fallon offers up rebuttals and conflicting research to all the research-based claims of the industry-funded studies on nutrition. I was particularly interested in her synthesis of exactly what it is we are passing on when we opt for cooking our own food from whole ingredients versus consuming packaged/processed food, "refined carbohydrates, oxidized cholesterol [fats damaged by heat, which alters how our body stores them], and free-radical-containing vegetable oils.*" (Cooking at certain temperatures and with certain vegetable oils releases reactive molecular fragments—free radicals—that can damage cells and lead to disease.)

### who do we trust?

I say trust yourself and develop an eating treatise of your own. If you personally want to cut down on fat, sodium, sugar, or [insert vilified ingredient here], then by all means please do, but your best bet

---

* http://www.rice.edu/~jenky/sports/antiox.html.

toward a more healthful life might just be to cut out things that come in boxes or from fast-food establishments or things that contain high fructose corn syrup or partially hydrogenated oils. Cutting out real-food items—things our bodies recognize as food, like butter or olive oil—and replacing them with low-fat concoctions misses the point of eating well (providing nourishment for your body) and, as shown in the case of certain fats (pages 103–104), might actually prevent you from absorbing and processing health-promoting nutrients properly.

Understanding how the relatively newfangled fats and sugars that compose much of what we are consuming these days are affecting our bodies in the short term and the long term can take years (if not decades) of research, which doesn't help us decide what to buy now.

Most important, though, don't hate on yourself and don't hate on food. The most fundamental interaction we have with ourselves is how we choose to feed our bodies. You're not doing yourself any favors by stressing out constantly over the food you eat. If you view every occasion where food is involved with either guilt or a sense of deprivation, you're energetically blocking part of the nourishing aspect of eating food. Why not invest that energy elsewhere, like learning to bake nutritious bread (that won't leave you puzzled over the unpronounceable ingredients label) or even yeast doughnuts* from scratch (and then eating them once every couple years—

---

* Oh look, fried food, a source of oxidized cholesterol. Honestly, your nutrition and nourishment outlook needs to be first and foremost flexible, because we are modern creatures and must participate in the modern world. To never again eat a doughnut or fried chicken is unreasonable. To not eat a doughnut and fried chicken every week is definitely doable.

the amount of time it takes to forget the involved but oh-so-worth-it undertaking they are to make).

The majority of my advice in decoding the differences between the FDA's nutritional recommendations and those of other nutritional experts comes from the Weston A. Price Foundation, founded in part to decry the current state of nutrition information being disseminated from paid experts who have industry and company profits in mind, not your actual health. While I appreciate the hard work that goes into the research done at and for the FDA and the USDA, it feels deceptive that big business interests and government corn and soy subsidies aren't discussed as part of what goes into those agencies' recommendations on what we should and shouldn't eat. What I do support in the government's generally accepted nutrition course: balanced meals and eating from different food groups (including fermented) at every meal. I extend this challenge of diversity to you in populating your plate and thus understanding how to put together a meal so you're not strapped to recipes.

## food chemistry 101

The food we eat fits into a series of complex combinations of the following four elements: water, fat, carbohydrate, and protein.

### water

Water is pretty simple—thankfully so, because the other three molecules can be quite confusing.

### fat

There are four main types of dietary fats: saturated (from foods like butter, cream, tallow, and tropical oils such as coconut or palm), monounsaturated (including olive, avocado, peanut, canola, safflower, and sesame oils, and animal sources like lard and duck fat), polyunsaturated (including flaxseed, grapeseed, soy, corn, and fish oils), and trans fats (which are produced by the partial hydrogenation of unsaturated fats). Fat is the single most vilified ingredient in our diets today and we have George McGovern and his 1977 panel primarily to thank for it. The lipid hypothesis, which remains an (unlikely) hypothesis (still without scientific backing), advised us to eat polyunsaturated fats and pass on saturated fats to avoid heart disease, obesity, and generally not fitting in at the diet counter during the '90s nonfat craze. Jennifer McLagan wrote an entire book on it (*Fat: An Appreciation of a Misunderstood Ingredient, with Recipes*), and health and integrative medicine expert Dr. Andrew Weil has even changed his position on saturated fat.* Here's a recap of why you might consider ditching the low-fat diet plan:

*Word to the Wise*

Not all butter is created equal. Buy butter made from the cream of cows who ate plenty of grass to get immune-boosting, LDL-cholesterol-lowering, and mineral-packing benefits.

↠    Everyone agrees that trans fat is bad for you, and it is, but passing up animal fats for heating food in vegetable oils derived primarily from soy, corn, safflower, and canola is actually increasing our consumption of omega-6 and decreasing our ability to absorb the balancing omega-3 fatty acids. A safe ratio is 2 to 1 (two 6's for every 3), and our mostly polyunsaturated diet (plus consuming meat and eggs from animals fed too much grain and not enough grass) puts our standard ratio of 6's to 3's at around 20 to 1. This overconsumption of 6's

---

\* http://www.drweil.com/drw/u/QAA400919/Rethinking-Saturated-Fat.html.

has been linked to cancer, heart disease, liver damage, weight gain, and immune, digestive, and reproductive system dysfunction.[*]

↠ Fat is essential to brain function (our brain is 60 percent fat; neurons are sheathed in it) and an essential component of our cell wall structure, that is, how everything moves in our bodies. Many vitamins are fat-soluble (A, D, E, and K specifically) and can't pass through our intestines and get absorbed by our bodies without fat.

↠ Cutting the fat in baked goods is actually doing you more harm than good because fats like butter, coconut oil or milk, egg yolks, cream, or whole milk actually slow the absorption of sugar in the bloodstream and have a nourishing effect on the glands that regulate blood sugar.[†]

Beyond practicing moderation with fat intake, the only other good reason I can see for reducing fats in your diet (if not purchasing organically or pasture raised) is because that's where environmental toxins tend to aggregate in large animals' bodies. Vegetarians and vegans have many great plant-based sources of fat that meat eaters can incorporate more often to make buying well-raised meats and dairy products affordable in tight grocery budgets. (See my suggestions for good cooking oils, ones that won't oxidize when heated, on page 50.)

---

[*] http://www.drweil.com/drw/u/QAA400149/balancing-omega-3-and-omega-6.html.

[†] Sally Fallon, *Nourishing Traditions*, p. 535.

*carbs*

Carbohydrates break down in our bodies as starch and sugar. Look to increase the carbs that come in whole form—those in vegetables, whole grains, and fruits—and avoid the ones that are refined; that is, those in white flour, sugar, white rice, or snack foods composed primarily of the preceding ingredients. The process of refining (to extend shelf life) strips these carbohydrates of the vitamins and enzymes that (when digested as a part of the whole) help us to process them, requiring our bodies to use our own reserves of vitamins and enzymes to do that work, which further taxes our system. Current dietary guidelines (released every five years by the USDA; latest issued in 2010) don't really talk about the type of grains that should make up the bulk of our eating, a whopping 6 to 11 servings; refined grains are the norm, and whole grains have to be sought out from confusing terminology in food packaging.

Refined sugar is the most notorious of the bad carbs, though curiously it's one of the only things the USDA doesn't assign a number for how much we should be consuming on a daily basis, just that we should reduce empty calories (by what?).

sugar

Understanding what happens in our bodies when we eat sugar is a helpful way of keeping ourselves on a moderation track. Studies (not funded by the sugar industry) have found the following major issues with sugar (among many other minor issues):

- An increased risk for heart disease, diabetes, and stroke
- An increased risk for cancer (tumors absorb sugars)
- An imbalance in the way we process calcium by de-

105

# the scoop on sodium

Salt, like fat, is on the hit list for health fanatics. As with carbs, the highly processed and refined salts are the ones that, when consumed in excess, are bad for you. Eat unrefined, mineral-laden sea salts that have the essential sodium chloride we need plus extra minerals derived and retained from natural production methods.

My take on this essential mineral is that you should not omit salt when preparing your own food; rather, you ought to skip that Ramen noodle packet or salty chips that contain your whole day's allotment (plus an added bonus of hydrogenated oils and MSG). Cutting out packaged foods in general will help you cut down on the unwanted sodium and leave more room for incorporating the potassium you need to process it.

creasing the amount of phosphorous in our blood, which then leads to bone loss and dental decay

Having some sugar in your life is not the issue; the path of overconsumption of refined sugars packed into refined carbohydrates is the problem. Most often, it's not the homemade pies or ice creams that are the majority of our "empty calories," but rather the sugar-laden things we don't think too much about, like soft drinks, sweetened beverages and teas, energy drinks, and even many fruit juices. When looking to cut down on sugar at home, try substituting unsweetened applesauce, honey, molasses, agave, and maple syrup where sugar is called for. These are still sugars, but they are not refined and come with other components that help our bodies break them down. Avoid substituting with fake, fabricated sweeteners like those made of aspartame, saccharin, and sucralose, things your body has no idea what to do with.

## *proteins*

There are eight essential amino acids that your body cannot make on its own and you must get from your diet. A complete protein contains all eight of these amino acids. All animal foods are complete proteins and so are quinoa and soybeans.

When assembling your lineup of protein candidates for a meal, consider diversity and cost as your guiding factors.

## animal proteins

Consume good-quality animal proteins—pasture-raised meats and wild-caught fish (see why small fish are the best in Chapter 5). Eggs and cheese are good lower-cost sources of complete protein, too.

If your pocketbook looks anything like mine, you'll be focusing on assembling other complete proteins to fill in the spaces between less-frequent (read: higher-cost) purchases of good meats and animal products.

## vegetable proteins

### legumes

Bean protein chains are completed by combining them with whole grains like rice, wheat, and corn. The exception in the legumes family is soybeans, which are high in lysine and form a complete protein on their own.

### nuts, seeds, and grains

Do not forget about the nut as a good source of protein. Add roasted unsalted nuts or seeds to salads, pilafs, or casseroles. Nut butters on whole-grain bread or in smoothies with yogurt can form complete proteins. Seeds like quinoa and amaranth are complete on their own. Adding cheese, egg, or nuts and seeds to grains will help complete the protein.

# good whole food sources of potassium

- Asparagus

- Avocado

- Broccoli

- Brussels sprouts

- Lima beans

- Cooked spinach

- Winter squash

- Pumpkin

- Bananas (though they have about half the amount as the green veggies)

**107**

## skills and stratagems

Bless your heart for braving the grocery store; decoding labels (or skipping things with labels in the first place and buying vegetables and whole food ingredients); getting food home via bike, train, or automobile; and then putting it away properly so you can use it for a week if not longer. Now I'm calling upon you to cook it. I promise this gets easier, or at least more replicable and routine.

### *understanding measurements*

The only thing I can tell you with confidence regarding measuring with precision is how to get better at eyeballing it and making approximations. You'll see as I get into the thick of it in Chapter 5 that I'm all about using as few dishes, cups, spoons, and so on as possible when undertaking baking and cooking ventures. You have enough to clean up and put away already; do you really need every single measuring cup and spoon you own in order to complete a single recipe?

My meals are full of imprecision (yes, even my baked goods) and they turn out more than fine most of the time. Here are some exercises in imprecision to get you started.

- **Fill half the spoon.** Take your teaspoon measure and fill it halfway from side to side, not rim to base. Do this by keeping the spoon nearly vertical as you measure your half scoop (so the granules all stay to one side).

This only works well with the spoons that are round and cuplike versus flat and wide.

◦ **Feel it out.** Use measuring spoons to give yourself a feel for what a quarter and half teaspoon measure of salt or spice feels like in your fingers or palm. Discover larger measures, too, like learning how much of something will fit in your palm; for example, a heaping palmful of beans or pasta for me is about a half cup.

◦ **Assisted eyeballing.** Use canning jars to measure stuff. They come in convenient measuring cup sizes that are somewhere in between liquid and dry measures when filled all the way to the rim, which, in my experience is a hair lower than liquid standard. (Translation: add an extra splash if measuring liquid and lowball it if measuring a dry ingredient.)

## liquid versus dry measurements

Use as few scoops and tools as you please, but don't put liquids in your dry measure cups; a cup of buttermilk in a glass measuring cup is more voluminous than a cup of buttermilk poured into a dry measuring cup. The best way to remember this is to note that most dry measures are made from opaque materials (think metal, plastic, or ceramic for measuring flours and sugar) and most liquid measures are clear glass or plastic.

# mason jar measures

· 4-ounce jelly jar = ½ cup

· 8-ounce jelly jar = 1 cup

· Pint jar = 2 cups

· Quart jar = 4 cups

## weight measurements

Some folks swear by measuring ingredients by weight. It's definitely the most exact way to measure since an ounce is an ounce is an ounce. You'll obviously need a kitchen scale for this type of cooking, but weighing your inputs as Michael Ruhlman describes in his book *Ratio: The Simple Codes Behind the Craft of Everyday Cooking* can help you learn to improvise and become a more intuitive cook.

### *prepare as you go versus mise en place*

Sometimes it's great to be überprepared and have all the things you need measured out and displayed before you in an array of little glass bowls. Other times reality strikes and you don't have a zillion little bowls, and even if you did, they wouldn't all be clean at the same time anyway.

Yes, it's culinary school practice to measure out everything in advance so you're paying the most attention to your food and how it's cooking. But that's theory and we live in a world of practice. Start by identifying fast-moving parts of a recipe or method and prepare for those (e.g., have all your meat sliced and your veggies cleaned and sliced or chopped if you're doing a stir-fry for dinner).

## recipes

We are a culture of recipes; they're free, they're on our phones—inside hundreds of apps or within hundreds of thousands of cookbooks. You will spend your life acquiring recipes. I've seen families make cookbooks for their kids with all the family or favorite recipes they've collected throughout their lives.

Here's what's cookin'   GRAM'S DINNER ROLLS
Recipe from the kitchen of _____

Recipes are sacred to me. Following someone's instructions in preparing food is an act of trust. Willingly going into a cooking experience—with all the work you've already put into getting the ingredients—and then selecting a random recipe from the Internet is a gamble.

Since cooking under someone's direction is a trust issue for me, I have a few sources I turn to for the majority of my kitchen projects. When faced with a new ingredient or a hopeful idea for a dish, I first turn to Eugenia (Bone) or Irma (Rombauer) or Alice (Waters). Consider those in your life who've been cooking for years. Maybe it's your aunt Janice or your friend from college. Who can you turn to to talk out a project? Remember that once you've mastered something, you needn't reinvent the wheel every time. How many recipes for mayonnaise do you really need? Personally, I just need the one that always works.

Obviously some blogs have great recipes (wink, wink), and just because you don't know them doesn't mean you shouldn't trust them. Generally speaking, I'm more apt to try an Internet recipe from an independent blogger than one from a massive recipe database. It's not a fail-proof strategy (some people are better at designing blogs than cooking), but things usually work out just fine. If you're looking up a recipe for a popular dish and need to choose from the hundreds of results that pop up, scope out a few from both larger sites and indie blogs and pick the one that appeals to you most.

Even when you follow trusted sources, not all recipes will work for you. Sometimes it's just the way they're written (confusing), sometimes it's a matter of equipment differential (what, you don't have a mandoline?), or the blasted thing just doesn't work out, even when you followed it meticulously. One of the main

# good places to start when looking for your bible

- *The Joy of Cooking* by Irma Rombauer, Marion Rombauer Becker, and Ethan Becker
- *CookWise: The Secrets of Cooking Revealed* by Shirley O. Corriher
- *The Fireside Cookbook: A Complete Guide to Fine Cooking for Beginner and Expert* by James Beard
- *The Way to Cook* or *Julia's Kitchen Wisdom: Essential Techniques and Recipes from a Lifetime of Cooking* by Julia Child
- *The Art of Simple Cooking: Notes, Lessons, and Recipes from a Delicious Revolution* by Alice Waters
- *The Best Recipe* by the editors of *Cook's Illustrated* magazine
- *The New York Times Cookbook: The Classic Gourmet Cookbook for the Home Kitchen* by Craig Claiborne
- *Better Homes and Gardens New Cookbook* by the magazine's editors

112

reasons I took to *The Joy of Cooking* was the discovery of a recipe I didn't suck at following. Irma's formatting—(bold print) ingredients in line with the steps of the preparation method—changed my recipe-phobic perspective almost immediately. I no longer got lost between an ingredient (which was not measured out in advance per the Boston Cooking School and Fannie Farmer's directives, tsk tsk) and the area within the method where I was supposed to use that ingredient.

My eyes ceased glazing over when reading recipes and I didn't get olive oil or flour in my laptop from having to scroll up and down constantly. You might hate *Joy*'s format, so I encourage you to find a format *and* a person you trust.

*find your bible*

You should believe wholeheartedly in whatever book you choose to be your main kitchen reference. You should also like the person who wrote the book; if there's no style that you can discern, find a different bible. Don't own more than two or three cooking essentials volumes or else you'll start to feel schizophrenic. I put holds on nearly every kitchen and cooking basics tome in the library and then hauled them home (thank goodness I had a car for this round of book research). I was surprised by how different they all are, yet all are full of the exact same information. Furthermore, when amassed on my living room floor, I found how little

I wanted to cook when surrounded with methodology. Major TMI.

We're each different in terms of how we gather and retain information; a particular book's style and your preference for one over another is something that's unique to you. One that works well for me or other hip kitchen homies might not work for you, so I urge you to get tight with your library card and see what's out there. It's well worth waiting for your hold to come through at the library before taking the plunge on a $40 or $50 book.

My bible became *The Joy of Cooking* many years ago after getting my mom's voice mail in a hot moment of dinner prep when I called to ask her what temperature my chicken ought to be. It turns out I had one of the least "Irma-tastic" editions—though one of the better recipe success editions—but I appreciated the detail and tone, and as I mentioned above, the recipe format captivated me. No matter which bible you choose, I think it's important on occasion to try guessing what they recommend when faced with a kitchen question, then look it up. Making educated guesses builds instinct and makes you feel good when you finally start getting it right.

## halving or reducing recipes

Many of you can pass right by this section. You understand algebra and ratios and use

## veggie-centric (not only for vegetarians)

- *The Modern Vegetarian Kitchen* by Peter Berley
- *Moosewood Restaurant Cooks at Home: Fast and Easy Recipes for Any Day* by the Moosewood Collective
- *Vegetarian Cooking for Everyone* by Deborah Madison

your phone calculator like a pro. You obviously don't have to make the whole thing when it comes to recipes. It's usually pretty easy to cut something in half, except for recipes that call for half an egg after reducing. (I usually use the whole thing anyway.)

But increasing or making some portion of a recipe can get complicated. The two essential factors in recipe volume editing are to figure out how much of the main ingredient you actually have and, similarly, how much of the food you'd like to end up with. Consider the following example (from the buttercream frosting recipe on page 204):

1. Set **2 sticks of unsalted butter** on the counter and allow to come to room temperature.
2. Combine butter with **3 cups sifted confectioners' sugar** and mix on low until sugar is fully incorporated. Bring mixer up to medium and add **1 teaspoon vanilla extract** and **1 tablespoon milk or cream** to achieve spreading consistency. Add additional milk/cream if frosting is still too stiff to spread.

Now let's say you only have 2 cups of confectioners' sugar on hand for the preceding. Here's where you pull out your calculator. Divide 2 (how much you actually have) by 3 (how much the recipe calls for); the answer is 0.66666666667 . . .

This is your core ratio; you (we) are making approximately 67 percent of the original recipe. You now **go through each ingredient listed and multiply by .67** (I rounded up to make things neat). How much is 1.34 sticks of butter, you might wonder? Well, it's about 1⅓, which might lead you to refresh yourself on fractions and algebra, possibly with kids in the fifth to seventh grades. Spices or small measurements get a little crazy in the reducing process, that is, when you're reducing a teaspoon or a tablespoon of something. In those cases, usually "a pinch" or the old half- or third-full eyeballing technique (see page 109) suffices.

## cook what you have

I have a crazy idea: start your meal planning based on what you have in the pantry. We should be building meals out of the components we already have, not some recipe we looked up online at work and must buy every single ingredient for, except the salt.

Pantry cooking (versus whim cooking) means starting with an ingredient or two (or more!) you have, maybe a can of stewed tomatoes or a tangle of greens you impulse-bought at the farmers' market, and building a meal around those. You can still search for recipes, but you're working with items you already have as the basis. Meal planning can get interesting once you get to the things in the pantry that you must either use or get rid of. We had great, impromptu Asian nights after I bought a bottle of mirin on sale (and we always have rice noodles from the Asian market and sriracha).

After a month or two, you'll actually be able to see the back of the shelves, you might have more room (instead of a mysterious back pantry full of food you're never going to eat), and you'll feel a sense of accomplishment every time you look in there.

## cooking methods

Now that you have a working knowledge of nutritious food and how to prepare it on your own, let's chat about how to heat it. Geek out with me for a moment, and let's take a trip back to your high school chemistry class. Who knows, understanding the basis for all cooking might earn you points on trivia night (or date night).

*the heat is on*

I discuss each of the following methods and how they pertain to your dinner in the next chapter, but for now I'll keep on with the geeky science. Heat transfer happens by one of three ways: conduction, convection, or radiation. There are chemical differences between these ways of cooking things and nutritional benefits associated with each (which I wouldn't worry about too much).

- **Boiling/steaming.** This method uses water or steam to heat foods directly. Plain old boiling is a great tactic to know. A simmer (160°F–180°F) is enough to kill many microorganisms, and a rolling boil (212°F) held for ten minutes kills all microbes that generally reproduce with oxygen present.
- **Sautéing/stir-frying.** This method, which exposes foods to the heat source directly, develops flavors with the addition of fat, most commonly through the browning situation called the Maillard reaction (which translates to delicious food and pan juices for deglazing). The average temperature of a sauté pan is about 350°F.
- **Baking/roasting/braising.** These three methods caramelize sugars and slowly develop flavors. Baking is usually done around 350°F; roasting around 400°F–450°F. Braising involves browning a meat and

# five ways to kick ass in the kitchen

- **Have a stash of master recipes.** Build a small but solid stash of dishes that work and can be modified with different bases, vegetables, sauces, and so on. Gravitate toward recipes whose leftovers, or initial ingredients, are useful as components in other things.

- **Take notes.** Keeping a kitchen journal will help you remember what went right (or, hopefully not the case, wrong) when you improvised up a storm. No need to rewrite an existing recipe; just note your source, page number, or URL and write down what you did differently. The number of times I've sworn I'd remember my modifications versus the times I had a viable, replicable recipe are sadly not the same. For complex, oddly written, or confusing recipes, you can rewrite them in your kitchen journal, expanding upon and explaining the confusing parts for the next time you make it (or you can warn yourself not to make it again).

- **Ditch your bible.** I know, I just told you to find your bible, but losing it on occasion is a good idea. Go rogue and skip looking up something that won't make or break the meal. Recall previous experiences or seeing it done somewhere and go for it. The first time you do a particular task—fileting a canned sardine, deglazing a pan, or pureeing a soup, something you can't really mess up—based on intuition, your reserve of kitchen confidence skyrockets.

- **Skip the store.** At least once a week focus on ingredients you have and decide what to make with them. Switching to an on-hand ingredient-based, not wild-idea-based version of dinner planning will help you cut down grocery bills, reduce food waste, and plan better for stocking staples in the future.

- **Plan one meal ahead.** Follow the sage advice of my wife and have a plan for your next meal. It's no surprise that you will need to eat lunch or dinner, so having a rough idea or a game plan for that time will help lessen cooking-related stress and prevent hunger-induced purchasing.

then cooking it fully on low heat in some sort of delicious liquid at anywhere between 150°F and 200°F.

- ⇢ **Induction/microwaving.** These methods use electromagnetic fields to cook food. Electrons start banging around, creating friction, and then heat when water molecules start banging into other molecules. Some sources may say that microwaving is the best way to retain the most nutrients in foods since it takes the least amount of time and not a lot of direct exposure to heat; however, other health experts say it's better to stick to reheating food than performing the initial cooking stage in the microwave because you lose certain nutrients, antioxidants, and other benefits of foods.

Honestly, anything you're cooking yourself is likely to be much more nutritious than a boxed or takeout version; so don't fret too much over the subtle differences in what retains more nutrients.

*how to thicken stuff*

| THICKENER | RATIO OF THICKENER TO LIQUID | WHEN TO ADD IT AND HOW |
|---|---|---|
| Flour* | 2 tablespoons:1 cup | Melt equal part butter and whisk with flour; add small amounts of liquid and continue whisking to completely incorporate it before adding more. |
| Cornstarch* | 1 tablespoon:1–1½ cups | Whisk cornstarch into small amount of cold liquid and add at the very end of simmering the sauce, then remove from heat. |

118

| THICKENER | RATIO OF THICKENER TO LIQUID | WHEN TO ADD IT AND HOW |
|---|---|---|
| Arrowroot | 1 tablespoon:1½–2 cups | Whisk arrowroot into small amount of cold liquid and add at the very end of simmering the sauce. |
| Tapioca | 1 tablespoon:1 cup | Add tapioca starch to liquid and bring to a simmer, remove from heat, and let it rest for 15 minutes to set. Great for sauces served cold or frozen. Never let a tapioca-thickened sauce fully boil, as it will become stringy. |
| Egg yolk | 2 yolks:¼ cup | Whisk yolks in a separate bowl with warm cream, milk, or stock. Add small portions of warmed yolk mixture back to simmering sauce to temper it. Bring the sauce to a simmer and whisk or stir until it slightly thickens. |

* Will thin out the longer it's exposed to heat.

## substitutions

Needing to find some sort of suitable substitution pretty much sums up my experience with most from-scratch projects. I never seem to have everything on the list of ingredients, and rarely do I feel like going to the store (like for cream of tartar).

If you find yourself in a position of always needing to substitute for certain ingredients (eggs, wheat, nuts, dairy, or other common allergens), then chances are there are cookbooks and blogs devoted to cooking without those things and you need to do a bit of

R&D to discover which of the camps within that camp is the one that works for you. For example, within gluten-free baking there are several camps, the xanthan crowd, the guar peeps, and the chia and flax proponents; and everyone thinks their camp is the only one doing it right. I advise you to pick your camp based on the success level and stress level involved when making the recipes, not on the vehement claims of camp leaders.

## no egg?

For every egg needed, try using one of the following:

- 1 tablespoon flaxseed meal and a pinch of baking powder soaked in 3 tablespoons warm water
- 3 tablespoons mayonnaise
- Half a banana mashed with ½ teaspoon baking powder

## no buttermilk?

- Sour cream mixed and whisked with milk
- 1 cup of milk mixed with 1 tablespoon vinegar or lemon juice

## no stock?

- Soak dried mushrooms in warm water for a half hour. Reserve the mushrooms for whatever you're cooking and use soaking water in place of stock.
- Boil veggies and use the boiling water as stock.

## no sugar?

Natural sweeteners are things that are sweet but not stripped of their nutrient compounds. Look for these as sugar substitutes in cases where cutting back on refined sugars is the intent (research diabetic-friendly substitutes when regulating blood sugar is necessary):

- ⟿ Maple syrup or raw honey. Use three-fourths the amount of sugar called for in the recipe.
- ⟿ Stevia leaf extracts (powder or liquid volumes will vary; follow the lead of the product you pick).

## other things you might need to substitute

- ⟿ Cream of tartar: For 1 teaspoon, use 2 teaspoons lemon juice or vinegar.
- ⟿ Self-rising flour: For 1 cup, use a scant cup of all-purpose flour (also called AP flour) with ½ to 1 teaspoon baking powder and ½ teaspoon salt.
- ⟿ Molasses: For every cup, use ¾ cup brown sugar with 1 teaspoon cream of tartar (or above substitutions).

## resources

### books

- ⟿ *CookWise: The Hows and Whys of Successful Cooking* by Shirley O. Corriher
- ⟿ *Food Rules: An Eater's Manual* by Michael Pollan, illustrated by Maira Kalman
- ⟿ *The Food Substitutions Bible: More Than 6,500 Substitutions for Ingredients, Equipment and Techniques* by David Joachim
- ⟿ *In Defense of Food: An Eater's Manifesto* by Michael Pollan

**121**

- *Jamie's Food Revolution: Rediscover How to Cook Simple, Delicious, Affordable Meals* by Jamie Oliver
- *The Joy of Cooking* by Irma S. Rombauer, Marion Rombauer Becker, and Ethan Becker (the 1997 edition remains my go-to source for successful recipe bases despite the Irma-infused, charming pile of earlier years' editions on my shelf)
- *Julia's Kitchen Wisdom: Essential Techniques and Recipes from a Lifetime of Cooking* by Julia Child
- *Nourishing Traditions: The Cookbook That Challenges Politically Correct Nutrition and the Diet Dictocrats* by Sally Fallon and Mary Enig
- *On Food and Cooking: The Science and Lore of the Kitchen* by Harold McGee
- *The Science of Good Food: The Ultimate Reference on How Cooking Works* by David Joachim and Andrew Schloss

*web*

- Visit the resources section of Michael Pollan's website, www.michaelpollan.com/resources, for answers to FAQs and links to people doing research and great work surrounding sustainable eating, nutrition, cooking, animal welfare, and many other topics.
- If you enjoy food geekery you might enjoy the site www.cookingforengineers.com.
- Learn more about fats and which oils are safest for cooking at http://www.wholefoodsmarket.com/recipes/food-guides/cooking-oils.
- Discover alternative scientific studies and information surrounding traditions in nutrition, farming, and healing arts at www.westonaprice.org.

122

*chapter 5*

# kitchen kick-ass

## tapping into your inner depression-era granny

*My mother didn't burn everything like I do.*

—BERTHA BURNHAM, MY GRANDMOTHER

I like how M.F.K. Fisher talks about her first experience with "day-to-day meal-after-meal cooking" in her memoir, *The Gastronomical Me*. It takes place in the 1930s, when Fisher is figuring out how to make meals happen in an odd little apartment without the luxuries we are used to today (particularly running water). "[It] was only a little less complicated than performing an appendectomy in a life-raft," she wrote.

The difficulty of cooking lies not in the assembly of this or that meal—because any meal on its own is pretty easy to work up—but rather in the connection between them; you just prepared dinner last night and it's time to start anew with your same set of resources twelve hours later. Being the kind of person who cooks means embracing the connectivity between our meals and changing our expectations of food as isolated incidents. We don't live in the bubble assumed by most recipes; we have previous meals' odds and ends, leftovers, and weird things in our pantries.

Throughout my twenties I was never very good at continuous cooking; in fact, I was a terrible food waster and frequent restaurant visitor because I was generally overwhelmed by the fact that we need to eat three times a day. I found my way out of that situation with a series of small steps:

1. Develop a two-meal plan, a loose knowledge of what you are likely going to eat at least two meals ahead of time.
2. Know one thing by heart, a versatile thing that's easily modified, like how to sauté stuff so it tastes good.
3. Eat in when there's food in your fridge, even if it's food that doesn't sound appealing. Find a way to ramp it up,

**124**

instead of throwing it out days later when you've forgotten about it.

4. Buy groceries that are related to each other, sort of like clothes that will mix and match well in your wardrobe.

Come up with your own meals with seasonality, availability, and affordability in mind. Maybe it's a beans week where you spend money on good cheese and eggs from the farmers' market because good meat didn't fit the budget. Maybe you got good meat and are now charged with figuring out how to make days two and three of leftovers interesting and how to use every last bit and bob that came with the meat.

Whatever your week looks like, being ready to handle the impending three meals a day starts with making a habit of actually cooking in your house. Start with breakfast, a meal that's relatively easy, really flexible, and offers great promise of success.

## breakfast

Don't skip breakfast. It helps buffer the highly acidic coffee you're likely to drink, regulates appetite throughout the day, and helps your brain do better work. There *are* ways to fit breakfast in, even for those "I'm way too busy in the morning to eat" people.

You can make a fine meal out of any of the following; just make sure to mix and match when possible so you get enough protein.

### breakfast checklist

➡ Yogurt, with nuts, dried or fresh fruit, and honey or maple syrup.
*Skip the individual yogurt containers. It's more cost-effective to*

**Hip Trick**

Try adding blackstrap molasses to your coffee instead of sugar for a great-for-you mineral boost. Add your preferred milk or cream and it's like an iced or hot mocha.

125

*buy the quart and divvy it out yourself. Buy plain yogurt and flavor it yourself with fresh fruit, bits of jam, honey, agave, or whatever else sounds good.*

- Eggs, any way you like them.

  *A fried egg takes all of three minutes. Plus it's a complete protein to get you off to a good start. Scramble your egg instead and pair with leftover beans tossed in a tortilla—welcome to Austin, Texas: breakfast taco! (See pages 130–134 for egg basics and more in-a-hurry egg ideas.)*

- Toastlike product with a nut butter and honey or applesauce.

  *Stash homemade bread or muffins (see Chapter 6), English muffins, bagels, or your favorite bread product in the freezer for mornings when you're on the run.*

- Fruit or 100 percent juice (not from concentrate if possible).

  *Pair with yogurt, cheese, nuts, or granola.*

- Oatmeal with raisins and cinnamon.

  *If you soaked the oats the night before, it's all of two minutes before you're eating the best consistency oatmeal ever; if you went to bed without breakfast in mind, it's only 10–15 minutes' time before you're having a creamy hot breakfast.*

- Granola, sprinkled over yogurt or with any kind of milk.
  *Toss some in a small jar with dried fruit and stick it in your bag for your ride/drive to work.*
- Something leafy and green.
  *Breakfast roughage with a drizzle of olive oil and salt and pepper is a nice complement to what can be a heavy breakfast of eggs and grains. Or skip the skillet and stick some spinach in your smoothie.*
- Smoothie.
  *Requires a little technology, but a fruit-and-veggie-stocked freezer/fridge will be your best defense against running out without eating (and a great way to pack great, raw nutrients into your diet).*
- Avocado.
  *Add this to just about any of the above and find yourself with a breakfast secret weapon. Avocado infiltrates toast, smoothies, eggs, and greens exceedingly well.*
- In case of emergency: cereal and milk.
  *Eating something is better than nothing at all.*

Following are more specifics on two protein-boosting breakfast foods.

### *making granola*

Homemade granola is the perfect project for a beginner. Granola is easily adaptable to what you actually have on hand and darned near fail-proof. Contrary to popular food blog searching, you don't have to spend your week's grocery budget on a single batch either. My recipe (see page 158) is a starter formula that you can alter based on your pantry inventory. You can buy rolled oats, nuts, and spices in bulk to keep costs low.

**127**

## making smoothies

If you have to look up a recipe for making a smoothie, then you're not doing it right. Smoothies are by nature an improvisational act, a fine way to sneak vegetables, beneficial oils, and other good-for-you stuff into your own or your favorite picky eater's mouth. This is my personal formula for success: 1 part frozen/solids:1–2 parts liquid:1 part wild card.

## frozen/solids

I prefer to use frozen fruit or veggies instead of ice, which makes the consistency more like a milkshake than a crunchy icy smoothie, but you can add ice to your frozen/solids situation for a more liquidy, drinkable smoothie. Bananas are on the essential list for our smoothies because of both the texture they impart (when frozen) and the sweetness that usually balances out the tang. Peel and freeze them in halves or slivered if you wish.

Here are some solids to include:

- Banana
- Avocado
- Fresh spinach or kale
- Frozen greens (blanched and frozen, heartier greens won't add a pulpy, possibly stringy layer to your smoothie)
- Blueberries
- Strawberries
- Cranberries
- Almond or other nut butters
- Fruit juice frozen in ice cube trays

*liquid*

Use less liquid than you think you need and add more if the smoothie is too thick. (You can't unadd it.) We use varying combinations of the following, as available in our fridge:

- Apple or other juice
- Whey
- Milk (cow, almond, or coconut)
- Yogurt
- Water kefir
- Kombucha
- Water

*wild card*

Spice things up with nutritional powerhouse foods, seeds, and spices. Here are some ideas to get you going:

- Ginger, fresh or ground
- Cayenne
- Cinnamon
- Flax meal or flax oil
- Chia seeds (will add some crunch to your smoothie since they're so tiny and don't usually grind any smaller)
- Sprouted hemp seeds
- Kelp or other sea vegetables; can be powdered, dried, or fresh
- Parsley or other fresh herbs
- Apple cider vinegar

## Hip Trick

Knock out some of the sugar in your morning sips by pouring your cup only half full with juice and filling the rest with chilled club soda or seltzer water. This makes a bubbly, no-alcohol spritzer that's fun for kids and grown-ups alike.

## weekend brunch

Of all the things to spend your money on, take brunch at a restaurant off that list. I used to love brunching, until I discovered how easy it is to make just about everything on a great brunch menu. Follow the egg action plan (see "Eggs 101" below) for eggs that rival your favorite brunch spot's offerings, less the $14 fee. Here are a couple common menu items that you can make as well, if not better.

### french toast

French toast was the first thing my dad taught me to make. I'd kneel on a bar stool on the other side of our open kitchen and watch him until I was old enough to dunk the bread in the egg mixture myself. Make scrambled egg batter, add cinnamon, nutmeg, and maybe some cardamom, and locate any sort of bread (the crustier the better), then dunk and panfry.

### pancakes

You probably already have all the ingredients you need to make pancakes from scratch. Stick any kind of fresh fruit, jam, or chocolate chips in the batter to fancy it up. See Chapter 6 for the lowdown on making pancakes.

## Word to the Wise

Farm eggs don't come with expiration dates, so how do you know when your local eggs are no longer good? Fill a cup or bowl with water and place the egg in it—if it floats, toss it in your compost bin.

### eggs 101

Stay home and make that egg you swoon over at your fave brunch restaurant. Unless you're dining at a farm-to-plate restaurant, I bet you'll use better eggs and still spend a lot less money.

In all methods of egg cookery, it is essential to add the egg to the pan or pot once it is at temperature. A not-quite-hot enough pan will leave you with an egg disaster. Starting breakfast off grumpy is not fun. Read up on how to separate eggs on page 190.

### Word to the Wise
Do not crack your egg into the pan until you've located your spatula. Many an egg has overcooked in our house while we were learning this lesson.

## scrambled

My dad taught me how to scramble eggs when I was young. His were fluffy and as far from dry as I am from the Arizona desert where I grew up. The key to a perfectly fluffy scramble is to keep the heat low and resist the urge to scrape the pan every ten seconds. By giving more time between swipes with your spatula, you allow the egg proteins to set along the bottom and form a network of larger curds. I think the larger curds hold in moisture and flavor better, but some people are keen on small, finer-curd scrambles that resemble polenta more than eggs. Prepare batter by cracking as many eggs as people you're feeding plus two. Add a splash of milk or half and half, cracked pepper, and salt and whisk to thoroughly combine.

## fried

This is by far my favorite way to eat an egg. My mother-in-law, Rose, taught me how to make the perfect fried egg. The success of this egg dish requires the perfect metal spatula, too. (See page 23 for illustration.) Use a small pan (a 6-inch cast-iron skillet is ideal) and add a dollop of butter for best flavor (or other fat) to the pan, heat until it sizzles, and crack your egg into the pan. Let it cook without

**131**

touching it until the white sets. Do a swift scrape with your metal spatula and gently flip the egg over, being careful not to break the yolk. Serve over toast or grits.

## poached

Welcome to fancy town. My mom taught me this method. Poached eggs are a fine way to dress up leftovers, make your brunch table look just like your fave brunch restaurant, or just generally impress people.

Bring a small pot of water with a pinch of salt and a hearty swig of any vinegar to a simmer. Set a large metal spoon across the top of the pot and gently crack your egg onto that (alternatively, crack it into a small bowl or ramekin). Gently slide your egg in. Don't make more eggs than your pan will accommodate in a single layer. If poaching larger volumes of eggs is in your future, you can use a skillet filled almost to the top. Stir gently to keep the eggs from sticking to the bottom, and then fish them out after about three minutes (that's if there are only a couple in there; more eggs poached at one time take more time). The water should remain at just below a simmer. Turn down the heat if it starts to boil.

## omelet

Successful omelets are essentially scrambled eggs that you don't mess with. They require the right size pan, a good spatula, more patience than you think you have, and a dose of confidence. It's all in the flip. You can fudge a good flip by placing a plate over your pan once the omelet is no longer runny in the middle and flipping that contraption over. Slide the uncooked side of the omelet (now facedown on the plate) directly into the pan and then fill with sautéed or cooked veggies, cheese, or anything that sounds good. Once the bottom has set, carefully fold half the omelet over your added filling.

## frittata

This is the easiest way of making a substantial meal (or dinner party appetizer) from whatever you have going on in the crisper drawer. Prepare scrambled eggs batter and add shredded cheese and any fresh herbs to it and set aside. Add fat to a cast-iron skillet and sauté onions, garlic, peppers, asparagus, or any vegetable (already cooked if it's not quickly sautéable). Pour the egg mixture over the veggies and cook over medium heat until the sides start to pull away; finish in a 350°F oven for about ten minutes.

## hard- and soft-boiled

I had my first soft-boiled egg in Ireland when I studied abroad and lived with a family just outside of Cork. I didn't eat meat at the time and this stumped my Irish host mother, so I enjoyed many an egg (or salmon, since I was a pescatarian). I liked watching my Irish host sister artfully crack the top off and slide my eggcup over. The best part of soft-boiled eggs is dipping strips of toast right into the eggshell.

Fill a pot wide and deep enough for the eggs to boil in a single layer with water to cover them by about double their height. Bring the water to a boil and add the eggs gently using a slotted spoon. Start timing when the water returns to a boil.

- ☛ **Soft-boiled:** four minutes for large eggs; add/subtract thirty seconds for other egg sizes. Crack the top off and serve in a special eggcup that allows you to scoop

**133**

out the contents with a small spoon, or dip pieces of toast cut into slices that fit inside the hole.

→ **Hard-boiled:** fourteen minutes for large eggs; add/subtract a minute for other egg sizes. See my friend Mary's trick for hard-boiled eggs on page 141.

## lunch and snacks

Your fear of a life of endless sandwiches need not prevent you from brown-bagging it. You will have to work within your constraints; for example, your office kitchen may only have a microwave. But maybe you have a toaster oven at your disposal, which will effectively crisp up quick-assembled bruschetta or simply heat up your leftovers (just add an extra splash of stock or broth at home to balance the dry oven air and keep your food moist). If you don't want to microwave, then consider taking delicious cold salads to work, and maybe treat yourself to a hot lunch once a week.

### *workday lunches on the go*

I asked *The Hip Girl's Guide to Homemaking* blog readers for workday lunch ideas, ones that made them excited to pop open the lunch bag. Here are a few of the great ideas they shared:

→ Sandwiches made with homemade bread

**134**

- Mason jar–portioned pasta salads
- Brie, fresh spinach, and cranberry sauce or raspberry preserves on French bread
- Homemade leftover mac 'n' cheese in a jar
- Egg salad, because it's usually something made especially for lunch and not just leftovers
- A homemade cupcake, which always brightens the afternoon
- Quinoa with cucumbers, tomatoes, red onion, olives, feta, and sunflower seeds, and a light vinaigrette of olive oil, red wine vinegar, and honey
- Last night's couscous (or quinoa) tossed with dried cranberries, walnuts, and slices of deli turkey, with a quarter of an orange squeezed over it (and eat the remainder of the orange, too)—a light, refreshing lunch that's great for summer
- Chicken salad with grapes and walnuts on either toasted bread or lettuce with crackers
- Easy caprese: any sandwich with some combination of tomato, mozzarella, and fresh basil

*mayonnaise*

Homemade mayonnaise is its own religion; you will find me front and center in the pews. I deem it supremely useful and essential in the lunchtime operations of our kitchen. Yes, it's a raw egg yolk, so babies and pregnant women and the immune-compromised elderly should steer clear, but that leaves a lot of us who are fully capable of ingesting emulsified yolks of well-raised chickens' eggs. I don't feel like I'm living on the edge, really; we buy eggs

*Hip Trick*

Go bento! Get yourself a grown-up lunchbox and pack its various compartments full of different bits from your week's cooking.

from a farmer who lives a mile away from us. We know how her chickens are raised, what they eat, and where they sleep.[*]

Eugenia Bone taught me to make mayonnaise in her book *At Mesa's Edge: Cooking and Ranching in Colorado's North Fork Valley*. The supreme usefulness of mayo is obvious when it comes to lunch. There's nothing I can think of that doesn't taste doubly better sheathed in (or dipped in) homemade mayo. See the only recipe you'll ever need (because it always works) on page 163. If, by some gush-of-oil chance, your mayo doesn't thicken, add buttermilk or yogurt and call it a salad dressing or sauce. If it congeals, then add a teaspoon of cold water to a clean bowl and slowly pour in your congealed mixture, whisking it back together. My experience is that if it doesn't thicken (and doesn't congeal either), it likely needs another egg yolk and for you to use your runny mayo instead of adding more oil to round two. If you're not committed to using another yolk, just use it as dressing or sauce.

### making a flavored mayo, a.k.a. aioli

Aioli is just a fancy name for mayo with tasty stuff in it. Traditionally speaking, aioli is a garlicky version of mayo, but I like to go wild with flavors and use whatever fresh herbs or fragrant components I have on hand.

---

[*] http://www.theatlantic.com/health/archive/2010/03/a-raw-egg-a-day-keeps-the-doctor-away/38096/.
http://www.westonaprice.org/childrens-health/feeding-the-family-when-its-too-hot-to-cook.

*salad dressing*

Never buy salad dressing again; the bottled stuff is full of stabilizers and other random stuff to keep otherwise volatile ingredients in a constantly suspended state.

My go-to method of dressing up greens is a few shakes of olive oil tossed with salt and fresh ground pepper. It's delicious and simple and lets the freshness of your salad shine.

If you buy vinaigrettes you're throwing your money away, since a simple vinaigrette can be made by a five-year-old. Put yours to work by setting them to the task of making the dressing for salads and fresh veggies:

1. Use an 8-ounce jelly jar.
2. Fill it halfway with olive oil.
3. Add 1 tablespoon vinegar, preferably raw.
4. Add 1 teaspoon Dijon or yellow mustard.
5. Place lid on jar and seal tightly, then shake it until blended and pour it over your greens!

The more complex varieties—like America's favorite "ranch" or a tasty Asian-inspired mix like cashew tamari—have a few more ingredients, but not much else beyond the method above. Making salad dressings from scratch is guaranteed to be cheaper and less packed with unpronounceable additives. All the cooking bibles have recipes for homemade salad dressings suited to your taste. I suggest trying out a few to see how they compare.

*sardines*

Learn to love the small fish, or as Michael Pollan puts it in *Food Rules*, "Don't overlook the oily little fishes." Sardines, anchovies, and mackerel are great, affordable wild-caught fish whose stocks are not taxed by overfishing and whose body composition—being so small—contains the least amount of mercury of all fish options.

They come whole in cans, in oil or water. We get the ones in oil and use the oil in the salads where their meat ends up. They require a quick peeling open at the already-cut side to allow you to pull out their bones, a simple exchange for all the balancing omega-3 fatty acids and protein they impart.

### hard-boiled eggs

Your best defense against crappy airport food or slim pickings near your office might just be the hard-boiled egg. An egg on the run makes a great snack; chop it up and add homemade mayonnaise, as well as whatever herbs and light oniony things you have to step it up, and have an egg salad dipping fest for your lunch. My friend Dawna is the queen of hard-boiled eggs, and her mother, Mary, reigns supreme over deviled eggs, a project that involves a lot of peeling but is so worth the work; her eggs always get swooped and cleared at gatherings.

## dinner:
## the belly of the beast

This is the test of your preparations, or of your creativity if you're not all that prepared. Regardless of your skill level, making simple, delicious dinners (and future lunch components) is within your reach. I ascribe to a utilitarian agenda when it comes to the dinner menu: cooking using as few pots and pans as possible. This is not because I don't have enough pots and pans, but because I'm lazy by this time of day and the prospect of cleaning up dinner-

138

# my top seven dinner recipes to master

1. **Shoulder roast.** The braised pot o' food is probably my favorite way to roll. Any meat, any cut (especially the more affordable shoulder pieces), on top of any vegetable with something acidic and flavorful poured over them and cooked until you're ready to eat. Yes. (See page 292.)

2. **Risotto or polenta or pilaf.** Once you master one of these, your dinner is 80 percent to 95 percent finished. Assimilate random vegetables and/or additional protein and anything else lurking around your fridge, and call it a night. My friend Zora mentioned how she often rolls with the basic idea of rice pilaf. Explore other grains while you're at it, like bulgur wheat, orzo, farro, barley, and so on, and cook it with anything you have on hand: dried fruit, tomatoes, mushrooms, assorted herbs and veggies, and even little bits of meat. Whatever you do, don't forget the two fancy factors: something crunchy and something cheesy in or sprinkled on top, like toasted nuts, grated parmesan, crumbled feta, whatever you like. See my recipe for risotto on page 291.

3. **Chili or minestrone.** Knowing how to make chili opens up a wide swath of multi-ingredient soups and stews. We hardly ever eat traditional chili, but I make a mean whatever's-in-the-pantry improvisation of it (or its boiled-down cousin, goulash) pretty often.

4. **Pan-sautéed anything.** This project has two rounds, the first kicked off by starting a pot of more rice than you will eat for dinner, and while that's going sautéing whatever you have on hand—any meat and some sort of veggie. Round two is fried rice: the masterful assimilation of random things held together by the common bond of rice, a tactic that makes leftovers you aren't that excited about into something you'd go pay for again.

5. **Mac and cheese, from scratch.** The cream-sauce-and-baked-pasta thing encompasses anything delicious you ever want to do with pasta. It's a good place to start when aspiring to make lasagna. You'll also never go back to the box.

6. **Frittata.** When in doubt, sauté it and pour whisked eggs over it.

7. **Cream of anything soup.** Or any richly pureed soup; you can always go lean and omit the creamy factor when you're dairy– or coconut milk– poor, but knowing how to make a luxurious, creamy soup will set you up for a lifetime of amazing refrigerator soups (see page 155).

pocalypse after enjoying that fine home-cooked meal makes my stomach turn.

## phase 1: boiling stuff, a.k.a. remembering you already know how to cook

You know how to bring something to a boil, I presume. Congratulations, you cook! Boiling is a simple and universal way to turn ingredients into dinner.

Here's a little bit of terminology to send you on your way:

➺ Simmer = little bubbles
➺ Rolling boil = an all-out ruckus. I hope you realized the potential for ruckus (and the displacement of water when adding food to the pot) when picking out your pot (I often do not).

Use water from boiled projects for other applications. Go from least starchy to most starchy; that is, boil veggies and then use that water for pasta. Flavored water imparts flavor to the grains you're cooking.

| STUFF YOU BRING TO A BOIL | LIQUID/ INGREDIENT RATIO | WHAT ELSE TO ADD AND SPECIAL NOTES | COOKING TIME |
|---|---|---|---|
| Beans | 3:1 | At end of cooking time add a generous sprinkling of salt, butter, or skimmed fat from stocks. | 6–8 hours |

| STUFF YOU BRING TO A BOIL | LIQUID/ INGREDIENT RATIO | WHAT ELSE TO ADD AND SPECIAL NOTES | COOKING TIME |
|---|---|---|---|
| Rice | 2:1 | 1 teaspoon butter or olive oil, salt. Wild rice requires a 3:1 ratio of liquid to rice. | 20 (white)– 30 (brown) min |
| Quinoa | 2:1 | | 20 min |
| Millet* | 2:1 | Take liquid ratio to 3:1 if you want a creamier (vs. dry pilaf) result. | 15–20 min |
| Amaranth | 2½:1 | | 20 min |
| Farro | 3:1 | | 25–40 min |
| Barley (pearled or hulled) | 3:1 | If using hulled barley, use the longer cooking time. | 45 min or 90 min |
| Potatoes | Enough water to cover potatoes by one inch | Add 1 teaspoon salt for every quart of water. Cooking time depends on size of potatoes or sections of cut potatoes. | 15–45 min |
| Eggs | Enough cold water to completely cover a single layer of eggs by one inch | Add 1 teaspoon salt. Cover pot, bring to a boil, then reduce heat to a simmer for 5 minutes. Remove lid and let sit for 10–15 minutes. Place hard-boiled eggs directly into an ice bath to prevent continued cooking. | 15 min |

\* Millet isn't great for leftovers because it dries out too much.

| STUFF YOU ADD TO ALREADY-BOILING SALTED WATER | WATER/INGREDIENT RATIO | SPECIAL NOTES | COOKING TIME |
|---|---|---|---|
| Pasta | 6–8 quarts/16-ounce package | Stir pasta within first minute of adding it to boiling water to avoid sticking; do not rinse pasta after cooking. Reserve ¼ cup cooking water to help thicken your sauce. | 5–15 min |
| Couscous | 1:1 | Bring water to a boil. Remove from heat and add couscous; stir well to combine. Let sit covered to fluff up. | 10 min |
| Orzo | 3 quarts: 1½ cups | Prepare like pasta; see note above. | 8–10 min |
| Most vegetables | 3:1 | Salt the water so it tastes like the ocean.** | 5–15 min |

** One of salt's chemical properties includes reinforcing cell walls. Salting the water when boiling veggies helps preserve nutrients, keeping them from leaching into the cooking water. Salt less heavily when making pastas and dry grains because they actually absorb the salt.

### gallo pinto

Costa Rica's signature breakfast is gallo pinto, made from beans and rice. Everyone needs to know how to make beans and rice, regardless of whether you plan on eating them all the time (budgetary restrictions) or whether they're your Meatless Monday conquest (like ours: to try a new bean from the bulk bin every week). When you make them correctly, you'll forgo the unfortunate nature of beans and just get cheap, delicious vegetable protein.

My former roommate, Wanalee, taught me how to make both beans and rice. Her years on a grad student budget made grocery shopping a pretty easy experience; head straight to the bulk bin section and locate simple, inexpensive ingredients that form a complete protein. Wana has her Ph.D. now, but I'm still more impressed at the scope of knowledge she imparted to me in our years living together.

*rice*

Rice is beyond easy to make, but incredibly complex to the uninitiated, namely because there are so many doggone people out there telling us different methods.

For the record, there are also all sorts of varieties of rice out there, which you're welcome to try at your leisure; our staple variety is short-grain brown rice. Rarely (read: never) do I look up the fifteen modifications for cooking all the different varieties of rice. The following method works for nearly all varieties you'll encounter (exempting wild rice, which isn't actually a rice grain at all; it comes from marsh grass, and arborio rice, the variety used for risotto, which involves a different process to make that signature creamy dish).

There is no recipe for rice, only attention to vessels. Rice requires a small saucepan with a lid (a see-through, glass lid is ideal for beginners) first and

# meatless monday

Meatless Monday is an initiative started by the Johns Hopkins Bloomberg School of Public Health, a throwback to the World War eras when Presidents Wilson, Roosevelt, and Truman organized voluntary meatless days to conserve resources. We rock out at least one day in our house without meat, not for good reasons like conserving water, halting climate change, and reducing fossil fuel dependence—all truths of large-scale meat production—but to save money and buy better-quality meat directly from farmers who are raising it more sustainably.

143

# reconstituting dried beans successfully

For whatever method you plan to follow, don't skip soaking your beans. If you forgot to soak, you can sub a quicker method for the omitted foresight.

- **Overnight:** Before bed, pour beans in a pot and submerge them in a few inches of water. Let sit until the morning, then drain and cook them using one of the methods on pages 145–146.

- **Quick soak:** Pour beans into a pot that will allow you to cover them with about five or six inches of water. Bring them to a boil and turn off the heat. Let beans sit, covered, in the hot water for one hour. Drain and rinse them and cook as desired.

foremost; then things get flexible. For every one scoop of dry rice (whether that's a 1-cup measuring cup, a juice glass, or a ceramic ramekin), follow that up with two identical scoops of filtered water or stock.

Combine your three parts (1 part rice to 2 parts water) in a saucepan that contains it all and is half or less than halfway full and add a generous pinch of salt and a pat of butter or splash of olive oil. Close lid and set over medium heat until rice begins to boil. (Pay attention so it doesn't boil like that for long or, worse, boil over the edges. The moment you walk away from it is when it boils over, just an FYI.) When boiling, reduce heat to lowest possible setting and let simmer for twenty minutes. Do not open the lid before then—really, I mean it! Do not do it. The lid will rattle and shake, but stay strong. If, after the twenty minutes has elapsed, your rice has a series of little crater holes in it, it's done. If it doesn't, it's not (and you should put the lid back on asap).

## beans

A pound of dried beans usually costs around $1.50, which affords about 2 to 3 cups' worth or 8 to 16 servings. When soaked and rinsed properly, beans become less notorious. I like how Tamar Adler put it in her book, *An Everlasting Meal: Cooking with Economy and Grace:* "What gets flushed out of the beans on their overnight wallow is what inspires musicality in eaters. Feed their soaking water to your plants, who will digest it more quietly, if you like."

Wanalee's method for dried beans is in line with

one-half of the bean-cookery divide. There are two very strong opinions resonating in bean cookery: one camp (the one I've joined) is a no-salt-till-it's-done group, and the other says what the hell, why not? For most of the things in my life, I'm in the what-the-hell camp, but I've had consistently great results with Wana, so I remain resolved.

What should cooked beans taste like? Not the canned version, which are often dry, brittle, and undercooked. A properly cooked bean requires little to no interaction with your teeth (because it melts in your mouth). Aim for that.

### stovetop beans

Vessel size makes all the difference in your experience with beans on the stovetop. If you have a big enough pot, you can make a lot of them at once and not be very involved. If you're challenged in the large pot category, you can still make a bunch o' beans, but you'll need to add boiling water periodically as the water soaks into the beans.

Wana used to fall into the latter category (that is, until I gave her a nice big French oven for teaching me so many useful things). In the event your pot is not suited for a 3:1 water:bean ratio without fear of boilover, you can do a 2:1 ratio and keep a kettle of water full and at the ready. If you're not good at remembering to check on it, then set some sort of timer to remind yourself to go check on the beans every hour and add water when the water level drops. (Wait until the water is at a boil before you pour it in,

*Hip Trick*
In a pinch you can rinse canned beans and cook them as described in the quick soak method (with a little less water) to help turn them into beans that you might enjoy eating.

You can stick dried, unsoaked beans directly in the slow cooker and allow them to cook on the longest setting (or overnight), but I find they come out better and more tender with even just the quick soak method before they are added to the slow cooker. Regardless of how you choose to cook your beans (stove or slow cooker), check out the instructions in the chart on page 140 for Wana's tips on when to add salt.

145

though, so your beans don't crack.) This iteration of bean cookery is obviously one of those things you'd do when planning to be around the house.

If your pot *is* large enough, then your involvement in a large pot of beans drops to nil after you've got it going. I'll leave it up to you to decide if leaving the burner on low is appropriate and safe if you're not home. If you deem it unsafe, then you can always turn off the burner if you need to leave, and restart the beans by bringing them to a low simmer once you return, no harm done.

### slow cooker beans

Among all the fine things one can do in a slow cooker, beans are my favorite. You pay them no mind and they pay you a bounty of protein and future snacks and meals (see page 156). I'll stop gushing about beans one day, I suppose, but I just can't get over how amazing it is to walk in after a long day and have tender beans at the ready for your week's eating endeavors.

### phase 2:
### vegetables 202

You've already got boiling them under control, so here are a few other ways you might prepare veggies. Almost any meal ideally starts with a sautéed onion. Why not learn to cut the thing up right?

#### how to dice an onion

This tutorial, courtesy of my author friend Zora (and inspired by chef forager Hank Shaw's rendition at a blogging conference), changed my life.

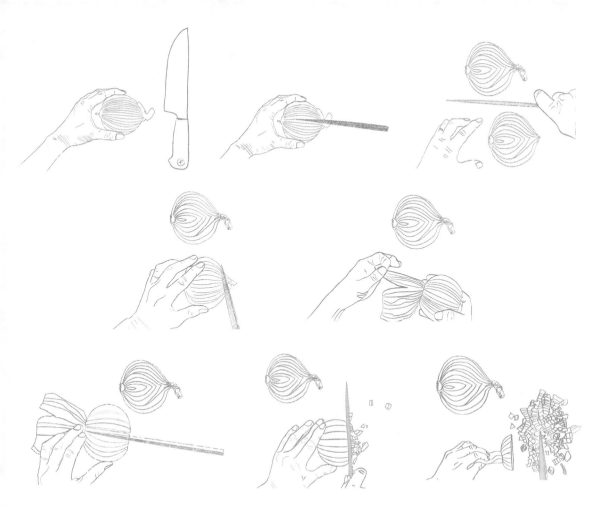

1. Slice onion from pole to pole, leaving you with two halves. Set each half so it's flat on the board and work on one half at a time.

2. Cut off top (not root end) and stick it in your freezer bag of scraps for stock (see page 66). Peel dry outer layer of skin toward the root end and use that as a handle.

3. Score the onion as shown into strips about ½ inch apart, taking care not to cut all the way into the root end. This will keep your onion strips together as you proceed with the next step. (If your goal is to end up with long strips

**147**

of onion, then your work here is done. Slice off the root end after scoring the strips and put it in your scraps bag.)

4. To produce finely diced onion pieces, continue to cut as shown. As you run out of onion to hold, grab the handle you created from the outer layer of skin.

If you are cutting more than one onion, no matter how sharp your knife or honed your technique, I suggest wearing swim goggles to avoid a tearful interaction with your alliums (onions' family name).

### how to cook vegetables

The following methods for cooking veggies all have redeeming qualities, though starting with the panfry/sauté and working your way through the rest is completely acceptable (and worked as the only thing I knew how to do for a number of years).

### panfrying/sautéing/stir-frying

Hands-down, panfrying, or sautéing, is the easiest way to cook and eat vegetables. The only things you have to pay attention to are the order of operations (charred garlic is not tasty) and making sure to cut up your ingredients with density and cook time in mind (it takes a lot longer to cook a carrot stick versus a thinly sliced carrot round).

### steaming

My fave way to soften firm veggies prior to a quick stir-fry is to place them in a wire mesh strainer that sits over a pot cooking something else. Noodles or potatoes are excellent candidates for this project.

(Obviously, you can also just boil water in a pot with a lid and put the strainer over that, but why not make your dinner earn its keep by multitasking to keep energy and resource inputs low?)

## blanching

Blanching is pretty much the same as steaming, but you actually drop the veggies into the water, instead of having them hover over it. Pull the veggies out when the water returns to a boil and in many cases you'll drop them right onto your plate, or into an ice bath to halt the cooking process.

## roasting

Roasting is another easy way to prepare large quantities of veggies, though it requires a little foresight and planning (since it takes about an hour, maybe more, depending on the veggies). To roast, preheat your oven to 400°F, cut the vegetables into pieces about 1 to 2 square inches, load them onto a cookie sheet with walls (very important), and then drizzle olive oil over the veggies and toss them around to coat evenly. Make a final pass over the tray with a judicious sprinkling of salt and freshly ground pepper, and then bake the veggies until they can easily be poked through with a fork, or until they taste good to you, whichever. Large squash and pumpkin are best hacked into halves or quarters for roasting.

## tossed in something you're braising

Slow cookers or French ovens full of stewy, simmery deliciousness are an excellent place to stick vegetables that won't disintegrate (i.e., anything you'd roast). Hell, even if they disintegrate, they'll make the *jus* (cooking liquid) taste good.

## phase 3:
## cooking meats

The good news is you've pretty much mastered methods you'll use for meats when assessing what to do with veggies, so now all you need is to get the heat right and to not forget to use your pan juices to make delicious sauces (see Deglazing, page 152).

Here are a few common meats you'll possibly encounter at the local butcher counter, bring home, and then receive way too much advice for how to cook them. See Appendix 1 (page 314) for the obligatory list of meats and their internal temperatures. Here's what we do.

### sausage

Use a cast-iron or stainless steel skillet that has a lid. (We put our wok lid or a plate over our two lidless cast-iron skillets.) Put some sort of fat (see page 50 for suggestions) in the pan and turn up the heat to medium-high; add the sausages when the pan is hot. Sear them on both sides and then add a splash of water or broth and cover the pan to allow them to cook through without drying out. (Same goes for cooking chicken pieces when you want a nice crisp skin.)

### whole chicken

Buy it whole, people; why pay for someone to cut it up for you (and remove all the parts you need for stock)? The most efficient way to roast a chicken is by placing it over any assortment of cut-up veggies in a roasting pan or Dutch oven; trussing it (a fancy way of saying tie it up so the legs stay together and the breast meat stays plumped up) if you feel like it; and then putting it in a 375°F oven for 1–2 hours.

Even if you don't plan to cook it whole, buying a whole chicken and cutting it into the pieces you'd purchase for panfrying, deep frying, or baking ends up being a better deal for the array of meat areas you get.

*steak*

Per *Cook's Illustrated*'s advice, we achieve the perfect medium-rare by starting our expensive steaks in the oven at 250°F for 30–45 minutes (until the steak reaches an internal temp of 110°F) and then finishing by searing each side for 60–90 seconds (depending on the thickness of the steak; use your judgment) in a hot skillet. If you want it done more than medium-rare, then cook it longer in the skillet. We don't really buy inexpensive steaks; at our house that's called stew or roast meat. It's imperative to let the steak rest for ten minutes after cooking and before you cut into it, so the juices are able to redistribute throughout the meat.

# testing for doneness

Use the thumb rule to identify by touch when your meat is cooked to your liking. Start by putting your index finger and thumb together and pressing the area just below your thumb with the index finger of your other hand; this is how medium-rare feels. Use your middle, ring, and pinky fingers to assess medium, medium-well, and well-done, respectively.

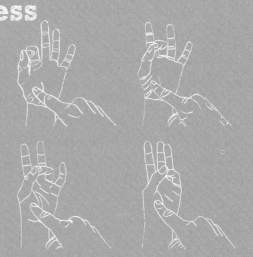

*pork shoulder (or roasts or stew meat)*

Add some sort of fat (see page 50 for suggestions) to a solid pan and turn up the heat to medium-high. Salt and pepper the roast (or other meat) well and brown both sides. If cooking the whole meal in a Dutch oven, add liquid directly to the pan; if cooking in a slow cooker, deglaze the pan (see below) and pour the sauce over the roast in the slow cooker. Add any array of veggies and other liquidy things like stock or beer to cover it all, and press go.

## phase 4:
## flavors and sauces

Think of how uninteresting a plate of rice and chicken and bland veggies is, and think of how many times you'll likely cook that for yourself before digging around in the takeout menu drawer for something with more flavor.

Creating flavors on your own is simple once you know what kinds of things work well together. Consult *The Flavor Bible: The Essential Guide to Culinary Creativity, Based on the Wisdom of America's Most Imaginative Chefs* for advice on the topic of pairing flavors on a per-ingredient basis.

*deglazing*

The only thing I think you really need to know about making home-prepared food taste great lies in the art of deglazing. This is just a fancy word for making use of pan juices and stuck-on stuff. (Hence, it also cleans up your pan quite nicely.) When you've finished cooking whatever you cooked (veggies in an animal fat* and/or meat browned over high heat), make the base of any number of sauces by pouring off any excess fat (and reserving it; see page 65), and then adding to the pan a 1:2 combination of wine to stock and bringing it to a boil. Let the sauce thicken, stirring occasionally as it boils. If you don't have or don't want to use wine, then use the acidity of a splash of vinegar to deglaze or just use all stock.

Your boiled-down creation can also be thickened either by whisking in butter and allowing it to simmer a bit at a low heat or through the addition of a starch—flour, cornstarch, or arrowroot—to form a luxurious reduction.

## white or cream sauce

Okay, I lied. One more thing will boost your homemade dinners up to at least decent restaurant quality. A cream sauce is the base of all dishes where comfort is involved, and when you don't want to use fake cheeselike products or weird boxed sauce packets, learning the homemade base will serve you well. Fannie Farmer's classic 1896 *Boston Cooking-School Cook Book* taught me the art of white sauce, which is essentially a couple tablespoons of butter melted in a saucepan, a cup of milk poured over it and brought to a simmer, and the postheat whisking in of a tablespoon of cornstarch dissolved in a little cold milk. If you're down with wheat flour, you can just add an equal measure of flour to the butter in the pan and whisk it well, let it cook for a few minutes, and then add portions of the milk, whisking thoroughly before each addi-

---

\* If sautéing only veggies, or lean meats without much fat, it's best to do it in an animal fat like butter or skimmed fat from a stock in order to develop a more flavorful sauce.

tion so your sauce doesn't clump. If you're making a cheese sauce, you can simply add shredded cheese to a white sauce. (Read about thickening sauces on pages 118–119 for details on each thickener.)

Modify this with veggie broth and coconut milk to create a delicious vegan cream sauce.

## phase 5:
## the grand salvage

As you read in Chapter 3, the average American family throws out about 25 percent of the food and beverages they buy*; those dollars add up.

When I say salvage, I'm talking leftovers and odds and ends from other cooking projects. I'm not saying you need to eat the same meal for days on end. We need to get good at making our meals taste great on days two and three by turning them into components for new meals.

My default application for dealing with a bunch of random things in the fridge: soup. Refrigerator soup, as I call it with the three-year-old I watch weekly, is the best way to keep food waste at bay and food safety at an all-time high (even with dodgy or wilty ingredients). The secret to soup's universal success is twofold: (1) it's pretty hard to make bad soup, and (2) boiling anything for ten minutes kills most bacteria, yeasts, molds, and any other surly insurgents. This is not to say you should just pour water or stock over some gross, moldy thing in the back of the fridge; don't do that. I'm just saying it's possible that, on occasion, one might lose track of the date on something, and a long-boiled soup is a great recourse for those of you who live with (or happen to be) hyper-expiration-date-sensitive partners/housemates.

---

\* http://www.nrdc.org/food/files/wasted-food-IP.pdf.

*refrigerator soup method*

1. Sauté whatever you can find, hopefully in conjunction with an onion or something oniony; doing so in a combo of butter and olive oil is a great flavor base.

2. Deglaze directly in pan by adding stock or a stock and water combo to make about as much soup as you're hoping to end up with; a good ratio is 1 part veg to 3 parts water; add bay leaf, salt, and pepper.

3. Find additional vegetables (if the sautéable ones were scant) and cut them up.

4. Steam additional veggies (if eating with noodles) over your simmering pot of stock and onion matter, or just drop them in and cook until tender (if pureeing).

5. Two options now include adding noodles and any leftover bits of protein, then cooking for another 10–15 minutes, or keeping it simple and pureeing (after you remove the bay leaf).

6. Add a dollop of cream, half-and-half, buttermilk, or coconut milk; a sprinkling of parmesan cheese; or a squeeze of lime.

You can follow this general method or consult my inspiration in this undertaking, Tamar Adler's *An Everlasting Meal*, for slightly more detailed examples of off-the-cuff soup advice.

## phase change

The following are the top three high-mileage foods I make and the next phase of meals they inspire.

*beans*

•» Portion out a serving of beans and some of the broth (add stock if you're low on bean broth) and bring to a simmer. Then toss in raw chunks of kale, collards, spinach, or other leafy greens, and a half-cup of brown rice pasta or whole-grain pasta; cover and let the bean broth and stock infiltrate the dry pasta. Eat bean soup when the pasta is cooked through and soft.

•» Puree them into a creamy, delicious soup and sprinkle with fresh herbs.

•» Bake them into a casserole.

•» Make cornbread or biscuits or something luxuriously bready and pour hot beans over it.

•» Strain liquid (save it for other cooking) and mash them into a dip. Add shredded cheese or whatever you like in or on your dip.

*turkey or whole chicken*

•» Make stock from the carcass and other saved bones. Even a single chicken carcass makes 4 cups of amazing stock.

•» Make chicken salad, especially from the drier breast meat that doesn't love a reheat.

•» Create a stock, as noted above, or pour in stashed stock and make soup from leftover meat.

*grains, noodles, and odds and ends*

•» Use up leftover rice, noodles, meats, or veggies by wrapping them into spring rolls. Add homemade sriracha and kimchi and whisk up a peanut sauce; enjoy that you're halfway around the world with your new cuisine. Reconstituting dry rice paper (the outer wrapping of spring rolls) is as easy as boiling water and turning it off and then dropping the papers in.

- Turn stale tortillas into chips.
- Pop stale tortilla chips in the oven for a crisp-up or break them into pieces and add them to weekend egg, veggie, and cheese scrambles and call it *migas*.
- Use excess rice for rice pudding and fried rice.
- Puree a roasted pumpkin into soup, pumpkin butter, pie, bread, and muffins.

## recipes

### oatmeal for one

*Yields one bowl*

1. Pour **1¼ cups water** into a small saucepan with a **pinch of salt**. Bring to a boil.
2. Add **½ cup rolled oats** to the pan, stir to incorporate, and allow the mixture to reach a boil again. Reduce heat to low and add **1 teaspoon butter** (optional).
3. Place lid on pan, leaving a crack for steam to vent. Allow pot to simmer for 5–8 minutes or until most of the water has evaporated, leaving a moist porridge consistency.
4. Stir oatmeal and add any of the following flavors:
   - **1 tablespoon brown sugar**
   - **¼ teaspoon cinnamon or ginger**
   - Pinch **cardamom**

**157**

- A sprinkling of **almonds, raisins,** or **other nuts/seeds/dried fruit**
- A splash of your **milk** of choice gives it a creamier texture

## brown sugar and honey granola

*Modified from www.foodinjars.com. Yields about 9 cups.*

1. Preheat oven to 350°F.
2. Combine in your largest mixing bowl:
   - **3½ cups rolled oats** (not instant!)
   - **1 cup raw almonds,** roughly chopped or left whole
   - **1½ cups any combination of raw pepitas** (pumpkin seeds, husked), **walnuts or pecans** (chopped), and **sunflower seeds**
   - **¼ cup flax meal**
   - **1 teaspoon ground cinnamon**
   - **½ teaspoon salt**
3. Place in a small saucepan and melt to a liquid over low heat:
   - **¾ cup light** or **dark brown sugar**
   - **½ cup honey**
4. Mix liquid sugar and honey into the oats, nuts, and seeds mixture. Use a spatula to thoroughly combine.
5. Add **¼ cup extra-virgin olive oil** to the mixture and stir to combine.
6. Line an 11" x 17" walled cookie sheet with aluminum foil and spread granola evenly. Bake for 15 minutes. Use a scraper spatula or wooden spoon and mix to ensure even browning. Bake for another 15 minutes.

7. Remove pan from oven and let cool for 15 minutes until granola hardens. Break up larger chunks and place in bags, jars, or your own gallon-sized mason jar for storage.

## *whole chicken on a vegetable roasting rack*

1. Preheat oven to 375°F.
2. Cut up **1–2 pounds of veggies**, any mixture of potatoes, onions, carrots, leeks, beets, eggplant, zucchini, tomatoes (whatever is in season and available) into 1- to 2-square-inch pieces, trying to keep them for the most part uniform. Toss cut veggies into a French oven or cast-iron skillet and drizzle olive oil or other oil of choice over them. Add salt and freshly ground black pepper and toss veggies to coat them evenly.
3. Truss (tie with kitchen twine) a **2- to 3-pound whole chicken**. Trussing allows for the juiciest results. Watch me do it on YouTube or come up with your own way to tie so that the legs stay together and the breast meat gets plumped.
4. Salt and pepper the bird on both sides. Stick a **bay leaf** or a few sprigs of **rosemary** into its cavity if you have either on hand. Place chicken on top of cut-up veggies.
5. Bake for 45 minutes to 1 hour, or until a thermometer stuck in the leg or thigh meat reads 165°F. You'll also know it's done when the juices that ooze out from the thermometer- or knife-poke in this area run clear (as opposed to red). Let chicken rest for 5–10 minutes after baking before carving.

*chicken stock*

*Method based on Sally Fallon's recipe in* Nourishing Traditions *and verbal instruction from Eugenia Bone. Yields approximately 6–10 cups.*

1. Cut a **3-pound chicken** into pieces, or use about **3 pounds of chicken parts** and add them to a large stock-pot. (Alternately, as you learned on pages 65–66, you can use bone scraps and carcasses from previous chicken dinners. Save these scraps in your freezer and make stock once you have a full gallon bag's worth.)

2. Chop roughly and add the following aromatics:
   - **3 celery stalks**
   - **2 carrots, peeled**
   - **1 large or 2 small yellow onions**

3. Add whatever you have on hand that suits you and tastes good boiled; avoid things like cabbage, broccoli, and eggplant. You can also save veggie scraps from other cooking projects in your freezer bag of bones! If you don't have any veggies, it's okay too. (Bones are the only essential here.)

4. Add **2 tablespoons vinegar** and fill pot with cold, filtered water to cover bones by two to three inches. Let sit at room temperature for 30 minutes.

5. Bring stock to a simmer and skim off the layer of foamy residue that rises to the top. Reduce heat to maintain a continuous simmer (not a rolling boil). Cover and simmer for 12–24 hours. As you're finishing the cooking process, add a **handful of fresh parsley** to the simmering pot for the last 10 minutes.

6. Remove pot from heat and allow stock to cool at room temperature for 2 hours. Strain solids from stock and, if pressure canning the stock, let sit at room temp for a few

additional hours to continue to cool, or flash-chill stock
by filling your sink with ice and cold water and setting
strained stock in the ice bath.

7.  Refrigerate stock for at least 8 hours, so fat rises to
    the top and hardens and may be easily skimmed (and
    saved!). Don't be alarmed if your cold stock is more like
    Jell-O when you pull it out; bones are a natural source
    of gelatin. A nourishing broth is wiggly when cold! Por-
    tion for freezer storage or pressure can stock for shelf
    storage.

## *stovetop popcorn*

Making popcorn at home always feels like a magical act. All you
need are dried corn kernels, a good oil (see page 50), salt, and a
frying pan with a lid. Most store-bought packets not only contain
perfluorooctanoic acid (PFOA)—linked to several forms of cancer
and infertility*—but often also include partially hydrogenated
oils† and way too much sodium in their flavoring lineup.

Our pan's lid is transparent so we can see all the action, which
is fun, but not essential. (I don't see this happening on a glass-top
stove since you need to shake the pan and it might scratch your
cooktop.)

1.  Heat **2 tablespoons oil** over medium-high heat for a few
    minutes until the oil runs easily and looks hot.
2.  Drop a few kernels of dried corn in the pan and put the
    lid on.

---

\*   http://www.care2.com/greenliving/8-of-the-worst-foods-for-your-
    body.html#ixzz2OUHvxGhy.
†   *Slow Death by Rubber Duck* by Rick Smith and Bruce Lourie, p. 4.

3. When those kernels pop, remove them and pour ½ **cup kernels** into the pan, and then replace the lid.

4. Shake the pan back and forth on the burner so the kernels are evenly coated in oil and distribute properly throughout popping. This will take about 5–10 minutes.

5. Flavor the popcorn by transferring it into a big bowl when it's finished (the pops are few and further between) and drop a pat of **butter**, a slosh of **olive oil**, or your favorite **butterlike spread** onto the still-hot pan and swirl till it melts. Pour the popcorn back into the pan and swirl it around or mix with tongs to coat the popped corn; return it to the bowl and add **salt** and other **seasonings** as desired. Our standby flavor is sea salt and nutritional yeast, but we occasionally venture into a curry or truffle-salted detour. The seasoning adheres better on the popcorn with the little butter or olive oil swirl, but you can omit it and sprinkle your seasonings anyway (just be sure to dredge spices up from the bottom as you eat the popcorn).

## baked tortilla chips

*Makes one half-gallon jar's worth*

I started using this chip-making method after my friend Suzanne introduced me to it. She eliminated corn from her diet and began making her own brown rice tortilla chips. She uses a twelve-ounce bag of Food for Life brand brown rice tortillas, but you can use wheat, corn, or any other kind of prime- or not-so-prime-quality (just not moldy) tortillas.

1. Preheat oven to 450°F (or 425°F if using a convection oven's bake setting).

2. Cut **tortillas** into evenly sized chips. Toss them with enough **olive oil** to lightly coat them, which translates to a few hearty sloshes from the bottle. Grease a baking sheet with olive oil.

3. Place coated pieces on the baking sheet to form a single layer without overlapping them and bake for 7–10 minutes, or until chips are evenly lightly browned. Pay close attention, because these can go from perfectly crunchy to nearly burned at a moment's notice. Dump finished chips into a bowl and toss them with **sea salt** (I like to use coarse sel gris, which I get in the bulk section of the specialty grocery store.)

4. Repeat the process of baking in single-layer batches until all the chips are crispy; there's no need to regrease the baking sheet each time. Allow chips to cool before placing them into a half-gallon jar or other airtight vessel for storage. If any of your chips are still chewy after they've cooled, just put them back on the baking sheet and continue to cook them.

*mayonnaise*

*Based on original recipe by Eugenia Bone in* At Mesa's Edge: Cooking and Ranching in Colorado's North Fork Valley. *Yields ¾ cup.*

1. Combine **1 egg yolk** and **scant 1 teaspoon Dijon or yellow mustard** in a small bowl. Place the bowl on a damp dishtowel to hold it in place.

2. Measure out **¾ cup neutral oil** (we use sunflower or canola) and pour it into the yolk mixture in a very thin

stream (no larger than the diameter of a piece of kitchen twine), whisking constantly. The mayonnaise should start to thicken immediately. This requires some degree of coordination, so stop pouring periodically if necessary and make sure you whisk thoroughly. Pour slowly to produce a light stream. Pouring too quickly will produce a heavy stream that will result in the mayonnaise not thickening.

3. After the oil is fully incorporated and the mayonnaise has thickened, add ½ **teaspoon fresh lemon juice**, **salt**, and a few twists of **freshly ground pepper**. Use immediately or store in the refrigerator for up to five days.

## slow cooker white rice

*Recipe courtesy of Hilah Johnson, creator of www.hilahcooking.com and author of* Learn to Cook: A Down and Dirty Guide to Cooking (for People Who Never Learned How).

Here's a pretty foolproof and hands-off way to make rice in your slow cooker. Most slow cooker rice recipes tell you to stir the rice every thirty minutes, which not only takes thought and time but also destroys the integrity of the rice. Don't do it. Following this method instead will always yield fluffy rice. You might occasionally get a little toasty-brown rice layer on the bottom, which actually has special names in Persian and Korean cuisines. This recipe can also be halved and made in a 1–2 quart slow cooker.

1. Rub the inside of a 4–6 quart slow cooker with **1 tablespoon butter**.
2. Add the following and stir gently:

- **2 cups long-grain rice** *(short-grain rice turns to mush)*
- **3 cups boiling water**
- **1 teaspoon salt**

3. Include any seasonings you want, like a minced clove of garlic, a bay leaf, or a pinch of saffron threads.

4. Cover and cook on high 2–3 hours, and resist the urge to peek (you'll let out valuable steam). The rice can be kept warm on the lowest setting for another hour.

## *vegan cream sauce*

*Makes 1 cup*

1. Whisk **1 tablespoon cornstarch** into **2 tablespoons almond or other nondairy milk** (cold), incorporating fully. Set aside.

2. Combine ½ **cup coconut milk** and ½ **cup vegetable stock** and bring to a simmer. Remove from heat and whisk in cornstarch mixture. Sauce will thicken as it cools. Add salt, pepper, and other ground spices to taste.

## resources

### *books*

- *An Everlasting Meal: Cooking with Economy and Grace* by Tamar Adler
- *The Fireside Cook Book: A Complete Guide to Fine Cooking for Beginner and Expert* by James Beard
- *The Improvisational Cook* by Sally Schneider
- *In the Green Kitchen: Techniques to Learn by Heart* and *The Art of Simple Food: Notes, Lessons, and Recipes from a Delicious Revolution,* both by Alice Waters

- *Jamie's Food Revolution: Rediscover How to Cook Simple, Delicious, Affordable Meals* by Jamie Oliver
- *The Joy of Cooking* by Irma S. Rombauer, Marion Rombauer Becker, and Ethan Becker
- *The Kitchen Ecosystem* and *At Mesa's Edge: Cooking and Ranching in Colorado's North Fork Valley,* both by Eugenia Bone
- *The Meat Lover's Meatless Cookbook: Vegetarian Recipes Carnivores Will Devour* by Kim O'Donnel
- *Pleasures of the Good Earth* by Edward Giobbi
- *Ruhlman's Twenty: 20 Techniques, 100 Recipes, A Cook's Manifesto* by Michael Ruhlman

*web*

- If you're a recipe gatherer, check out aggregate cooking and recipe sites like www.food52.com or www.thekitchn.com.
- Read about the environmental benefits of cutting meat from your diet even just once a week at www.meatlessmonday.com.
- My friend Hilah is a great source for simple, from-scratch recipes. Her videos will make you laugh; visit www.hilahcooking.com.

chapter 6

# baking
# and desserts

staples and sweets
even you can manage

Baking gets a bad rap. There are so many factors that influence success—heat, temperamental microorganisms (yeast), science, your attitude, minerals in tap water, and so on—and so many companies trying to sell you boxes of stuff you don't really need to be successful. In this chapter I'll start with staple baked goods, and things you might even be able to call healthy, and then move on to the brazen among the baked goods, desserts, and homemade sweet treats.

As you learned in Chapter 4, I'm a terrible measurer, an incorrigible improviser, and a downright crappy recipe follower. Still, I feel capable of handling almost anything in the baking realm (with the exception of level scoops). Life rarely provides us with the conditions for level scoops—the late-night baking project discovery that you're out of all-purpose flour, pouring the buttermilk and finding yourself just shy of what you need—so why place so much pressure on exactitude?

Anyone who chimes in about how precise baking must be probably isn't a baker. Rather than relying on measurements and hoping for the best in your kitchen's *environs du jour,* I think your better bet lies in making the project once with someone who knows what they're doing, so you know what the ideal batter is supposed to look and feel like and how to judge when you should add more flour or liquid or let it alone.

The key to successful baking is experiencing success more often than failure. Duh, right? Well, to do so, I recommend finding trusted, master recipes for the staples in your house and making them over and over again until you get it just right. This doesn't apply to fun, side-project baking (like making a lemon tart or persimmon pudding).

Baking what you have is the extension of cooking what you have. I start any baked good endeavor with the "what are my assets" conversation, and move forward from there. Finding projects that work with your existing ingredients and staples will trim your monthly grocery expenses and start to show you how to use every part of the foods you purchase and cycle them through many stages of utility.

*things i've learned about baking*

1. When you have a bad or stressy attitude, something is bound to go awry.
2. Improvise freely but understand what constitutes wet/dry and acidic/alkaline; this will ensure that improvisations remain edible and similar to, if not exactly, what you were hoping for.
3. Excessively opening the oven to check the progress of your baked good does more harm than good.
4. Skip the prepackaged mixes. Starting with simple flours, leaveners, and other essentials are easier on the wallet and will help you be more successful in your modifications, since you have more control over all the ingredients going into the recipe. (Plus, you're still going to use the same number of dishes; what's another measuring scoop or two?)
5. As with other kitchen projects, write it down! If you use a base recipe and modify it, note what you changed so you can replicate it in the event you just made the best muffins on the planet.

If you want to bake more, keep your baking equipment somewhere it's not a pain in the ass to access. Our baking drawer is right below my swath of counter workspace and just above the cabinet where the mixing bowls live. I don't really have to move from one area to make baking magic happen. I know that won't work for everyone, but attempting to minimize the number of areas you need to visit in order to make something like muffins (and the separate bowls for wet and dry ingredients) will set you up for mental success in baking. I keep a 4-ounce mason jar on the counter with toothpicks to test for doneness, a small measure in cutting off the frustration of always searching for toothpicks in a tense moment of baked good doneness uncertainty.

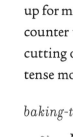

*baking-tool-drawer staples*

- Muffin batter spring scoop, for evenly proportioned baked goods
- Whisks of all size
- Icing spatula
- Dough scraper
- Pastry brush (don't get a silicone bristle one)
- Spoon spatula
- Array of high-heat spatulas

# essential bakeware you can find at the thrift store

- 8- or 9-inch metal baking pans

- Loaf pans, medium and large

- Muffin tin—or silicone muffin cups, though it's unlikely you'll find them at the thrift store. Both are a pain in the ass to wash, but you manage because muffins and cupcakes are delicious

- 9- or 10-inch pie pans

- Kitchen twine
- A second set of kitchen shears for easy access
- If the counter doesn't work for you, you may want to keep your toothpicks in here

*tool upgrades*

- A silicone baking mat (saving the parchment tree, one batch of cookies or scones at a time).
- 2 quarter-pan cookie sheets from the restaurant supply store—same reason you bought the bigger sheet from the restaurant supply store (see Chapter 1), but two smaller versatile pans are so useful for baking projects.
- A baking cooling rack. There are lots of ways to improvise this, but having a real one is pretty dang nice when you've embarked upon the quest for cupcake mastery.
- A stand mixer if you whisk, whip, or bake more than once a year. Since our kitchen churns out a steady stream of gluten-free baked goods, where it's all about emulsifying and not so much the hand knead, the stand mixer is one of my most used tools. This is another investment piece, of course, and certainly one to purchase way after you discover you love baking (or maybe around the time you decide you really love making marshmallows). Be very sure you're going to use it all the time by spending time not having it and making do. There *are* deals to be had and ways to acquire them on the cheap. I found mine on Craigslist when visiting my mom in North Carolina, where the original owner was packing for a move overseas and had to sell it. I forked over $140 plus

*Hip Trick*

Turn your toaster oven or oven rack into a cooling rack by propping it up on a few towels or oven mitts to let air pass under the rack.

$25 to ship it home, and I've been in love with it ever since. It's also pretty fun to acquire the attachments as possible, like the ice cream churning setup (my ice cream maker of choice) and the meat grinder (we made sausages!), which could arguably save space in the kitchen closet by consolidating the machinery you own. (You know, in case you need help justifying, I'm here for you.)

⇥ A bread machine if you have other things to do besides thinking about bread, but still want to make homemade bread. This likely falls into the diehard baker's redundant or nonuseful list, but not all of us make bread in the same fashion. A friend recently reported that her thrift-store-acquired machine has lasted their family for many years without incident and provided the twice-weekly loaves they consume (which would have been a lot of baking by hand). As a gluten-free baker, I've tested all different types of ovens, from our apartment oven to culinary school top-of-the-line ovens, and the bread machine loaf trumps all, rivaling a regular, gluten sandwich bread.

## yeast bread basics

You can read entire books on making breads with yeast (and every other project in this chapter, for that matter), but my guess is that going at it on your own will be better learning than engaging in a how-to-make-bread overload. Yeast is a living thing, thus temperamental and unpredictable, and your best breads will be ones where you rely on knowledge of what good dough feels like (and if you need more flour or water to achieve it). I'm partial to my bread teachers, Irma and Marion (*The Joy of Cooking*) and James Beard (*Beard on Bread*), but others gravitate toward *The Bread Bible*, *CookWise*, or anything by Peter Reinhart. You needn't pick a bible, though, until you decide you'd like to make more than just sandwich bread (see page 194). Here's what makes bread taste so dang good.

## *yeast*

Yeast gone wild (in the good way) involves activated spores eating liquids and sugars, producing another generation, called buds, and giving off alcohol and carbon dioxide gas in return. The gluten network in your bread traps these gases and stretches around them to produce light and fluffy bread.

## basic yeast bread method

1. Activate yeast and let sit for 10 minutes.

2. Combine flour with all ingredients and add to yeast water.

3. Adjust with additional flour or liquid to form a (generally) not-sticky dough.

4. Knead for 10 minutes.

5. Let rise for an hour or two, then punch down.*

6. Shape in a greased pan and let rise again, this time for 30 minutes. Bake.

---

\* Gluten-free projects only need one rise, so you should skip the first rise and let them rise in or on whatever holding instrument you're using.

High-gluten flours are best for yeast breads because they stretch and trap gas from yeast promiscuity. Various flours are used to accomplish different bread goals; a combo of whole wheat and unbleached white flours will yield a loaf most similar to the wheat sandwich bread you probably buy. Having some bread flour or wheat gluten on hand (and storing it in the refrigerator or freezer to keep it fresh) will help turn an AP flour into a better bread.

Gluten-free peeps like me can use varied combinations of flours from rice, nuts, starches, and meals, plus a binder like xanthan or guar gum and some emulsion action from the wet ingredients (hello, eggs!) to help our nongluten flours behave glutenously.

*other ingredients to note*

- **Sugar.** Increases yeast activity (when added in small quantities), slows staling, and retains moisture.
- **Salt.** Halts yeast activity; enhances flavor, texture, and color; helps control enzymes that weaken gluten structures; firms dough; and increases elasticity.
- **Fat.** Tenderizes, aerates, contributes to flakiness (depending on how it's added), carries nutrients, and adds flavor.

Making yeast breads can involve a lot of or little technology. Despite having all the "time-savers" like our stand mixer and a food processor—both great ways to mix and knead bread doughs—I still prefer to make loaves of gluten bread for friends with my hands and an oven. My gluten-free weekly loaf needs no help from my hands to become the light, flexible slice that hauls our homemade mayo or dips into fried egg yolk breakfasts; the eight-year-old bread machine I picked up from Craigslist is a trusty workhorse that gets it right every time. Figure out what works for you each week in the context of your regular life and do that.

These are the top three types of bread that are easy to make well at home:

- ➥ **No-knead:** Makes crusty artisan-like loaves. Made ideally in a Dutch oven or cast-iron skillet.
- ➥ **Sandwich:** Makes the right shape for toasters, lunch bags, or bento boxes; usually keeps well for a few days. Made in a simple loaf pan or in bread machines.
- ➥ **Rolls or breadsticks:** *Minibread*, a huge and impressive hit at dinner parties.

### quick bread basics

No time for yeast, go soda. Quick bread constitutes the genre of baked goods that include muffins, cakes, biscuits, and breads like those of corn, veggie, nut, and fruit fame. They use the alkaline power of baking soda (sodium bicarbonate) in conjunction with something acidic to create carbon dioxide gas to add lift to your baked goods. A small volcano erupts inside your muffins every time you combine wet with dry ingredients—fun!

*Baking soda* breaks into carbon dioxide and washing soda (which should linger in your laundry, not your muffins), so that's why recipes that call for extra baking soda in addition to baking powder are the ones that also utilize acidic dairy products.

*Baking powder* contains a small portion of baking soda paired with the exact amount of acid necessary to match the alkaline breakdown of the soda. Baking powder also contains cornstarch

no aluminum in here

only

baking powder

*Hip Trick*

Test your vintage canister of baking powder by putting a spoonful in a bowl and pouring hot water over it. If it doesn't bubble up, then use it to clean your bathtub and buy a new container for baking.

to keep these two reactive things separated and dry until you're ready for them. Most brands on the market are double acting, which means they pack a punch both when initially added to the wet/acidic ingredients and again when they do their poofing work while heating in the oven.

## flours

Low-gluten flours (like all-purpose or cake flours) are best for the quick bread lot. The quick combining directives are usually to avoid working with the flour too much and activating its gluten network (which will make tough muffins, cakes, and breads). Gluten-free flour combinations are excellent for quick breads; gluten-free peeps go wild!

## fat

Fats serve the same roles in quick breads as they do in yeast breads. Although I think full-fat baking is essential (especially with sugary treats; see pages 102–104 for why you don't need to freak out about fat), you can compromise by substituting a portion of the fat (butter or oil) with equal portions of unsweetened applesauce or other unsweetened fruit puree to cut down the oil or butter called for in a recipe.

## modifying quick breads

Good recipes are written with a chemical balance in mind. Whenever you modify a quick bread, be sure you allot for not only wet versus dry ingredients, but also acid versus base ingredients. The wet/dry thing will help your end product resemble its goal; the acid/base thing ensures your end product doesn't taste like washing soda (because there wasn't enough acid to counter the baking soda).

## wet and dry ingredients

If you increase the amount of a wet ingredient, decrease another wet ingredient by that same amount or increase a dry ingredient by that amount.

| WET | DRY |
| --- | --- |
| Banana | Flours |
| Other fresh fruit or jam | Nuts (butters or rough ground) |
| Fats (butter, oil), fat substitute (applesauce) | Seeds (meals and whole) |
| Dairy (milk, buttermilk, sour cream, or yogurt) | Oats |
| Shredded or pureed vegetables (squash, carrots, etc.) | Cocoa powder |
| Eggs | |
| Sweeteners (sugar,* honey, molasses) | |

* Sugar is solid and might seem like a dry ingredient, but when prepared in quick breads it actually serves as a liquid.

## acid and base ingredients

Don't make yourself crazy, but do your best to try and make substitutions with their respective acidity/alkalinity in mind. Counterbalance any substitutions to these common things with respective acid/alkaline adjustments.

| MILD ACIDS USED IN BAKING | ALKALINE-LEANING INGREDIENTS |
| --- | --- |
| Citrus juice | Milk |
| Molasses | Soda leaveners |
| Brown sugar | Salt |
| Honey | Dutch-process cocoa |
| Chocolate and natural cocoa | Hard water |
| Sour cream | Egg whites |
| Buttermilk | |

## muffins

Muffins are the most forgiving baked good you can make. Ugly muffins are almost never inedible, and in fact, most of the time a homely muffin is delicious. I include muffins as an essential tactic for shuffling an abundance of fruits or veggies (see Chapter 7) into a now or later snack. If in doubt, bake it into a muffin.

My base recipe includes buttermilk, since the end of our weekly-cultured jar of buttermilk is usually the instigator for making muffins, but you can find a solid muffin recipe surrounding ingredients you always have on hand. (My definition of solid is one that works more than twice with the same results.) Flavor muffins with squash, zucchini, bananas on the way out, any fruit or excess jam, frozen blueberries, or whatever you have.

These are my top three tips for muffin making:

1. Don't overmix the batter. It's okay if it's bumpy and there are tiny pockets of flour lurking around the bottom, but

overmixing and incorporating everything evenly will make a tough,
dense muffin.

2. If you run out of muffin tin space,
   or room in your toaster oven on a
   hot summer day, just keep muffin
   batter out and use it later.

3. Wait 5 minutes before attempt-
   ing to extract muffins from the tin and then gently
   wiggle them out. If they want to stick, run a butter knife
   around the edges of the muffins and they should pop
   out. If you try to bust them loose without the proper
   wait time, you'll rip them in half. (I relearn this once
   every four batches.)

### storing muffins

We keep muffins we'll eat within the next three days out at room
temperature in a not completely sealed container or in a parchment paper bag. Keeping baked goods in non-airtight containers

# basic muffin method

1. Whisk together dry ingredients.

2. Combine and whisk wet ingredients in a separate bowl.

3. Pour wet into dry and combine without overmixing.

4. Bake in a greased pan.

allows them to breathe. If you use an airtight container, you run the risk of moisture getting trapped in, which will cause the goods to mold faster. We freeze what we won't eat in the immediate future and pull them out on an as-desired basis.

## pancakes

Pancakes are here rather than in the breakfast section in Chapter 5 because they're a special project. I try to make them once a weekend, but sometimes life gets in the way. We end up eating pancakes once or twice a month.

Pancakes are a quick bread because their poof, while it may be small, relies on baking powder's punch; pancakes are prepared just as you would muffins. The trick is to let the combined batter sit for a few minutes before you pour out your first pancakes. It's easy to wait because you need to make sure your pan/griddle is hot. The first round of pancakes will likely not be your prettiest because you're impatient and the pan's not quite hot enough. Hide that batch on the bottom of the plate, or better yet, eat those while you're making the rest of the pancakes.

## desserts

Desserts are my favorite kitchen project. As with all aspects of the kitchen, they can be as simple or as involved as you wish. I've included my favorite projects and how to make them friendlier to everyday life and regular (vs. super-) human capacity.

By now, you're probably quite familiar with where I'm coming from on matters of food and nutrition, so it won't come as a surprise to you that I default to one of Michael Pollan's other food rules when it comes to moderation and dessert. Here's the gist: eat as many sweets as you like as long as you made them from scratch yourself. (I suppose the one exception would be barring you're not a professional pastry chef, which I'm not.) I don't usually have the time to make more than one sweet a week, and sometimes just once every two or three weeks. Lean or busy weeks include a bar of dark chocolate after meals.

I find the trusted recipe thing most essential with dessert. Not because your hopes are high for a flashy finisher (homely desserts usually taste great), but because good ingredients are expensive. A failed dessert based on five or more precious-commodity farm eggs is traumatic.

## whipped cream, a.k.a. instant dessert

Turn anything into dessert by dropping a dollop of whipped cream on it. The good fortune of ripe fruit is an excellent place to start. Trade the hissing cold metal bottle of whipped cream in for a little postmeal manual labor and the tinkling of whisk on glass. All you really need to make your own fluffy whipped cream is cream, a pinch of sugar, vanilla (or a splash of any liquor/liqueur), and a whisk.

Whatever you do, don't lose hope on your whipped cream. Older cream or boozy whipped cream might take longer to whip itself into fluffy shape, but if you wait it out without too much panic, it usually comes through. See recipe on www.hipgirlshome.com.

## cookies

Cookies are the most impulsive treat made around our house, seeing as making them is one of the only good answers to what to do with too much milk

## Hip Trick

Roll out batter for shaped cookies directly onto your baking sheet: press cookie shapes and remove excess dough all without chopping off your snowman's head, Santa's toy bag, or any limbs from a four-legged cookie creature.

(beyond a few ideas in Chapter 7). My impetuous relationship with them keeps us stocking cookies on an every-few-months basis. Only once a year are cookies a planned and thought-out ordeal, when I pull down the mixer to cream butter and sugar and eggs in solidarity with the rest of the holiday-celebrating world. During the rest of the year, I'm texting neighbors asking for the missing ingredient to my 9:00 P.M. batch of oatmeal-raisin cookies.

# basic cookies method

1. Sift sugar (which may sound finicky but it helps to produce that fine cookie texture you're hoping for) and beat with butter until creamy.

2. Add eggy, vanilla-y things and mix to incorporate.

3. Sift (whether or not I actually do this depends on my mood) in dry ingredients and mix in shifts with portions of milk/liquid and beat until well blended.

4. Add nuts, fruits, or other dried additions.

5. Shape the batter into a roll, wrap it to protect it from drying refrigerator air, and chill for 2–8 hours. This process will often make a better cookie because chilling allows the gluten to relax and keeps cookies from becoming rubbery, helps keep the dough from being too sticky when spreading roll and cutout cookies, and helps to keep the cookies from spreading everywhere when baked. Here's where you freeze dough, well sealed, for future cut-and-bake action.

6. Cut chilled dough into slices and place on greased pan; bake when dough returns to room temp.

The best way to roll with cookies is to inflate batch size and freeze an extra portion for future cut-and-bake convenience. One mess, future hot-out-of-the-oven rewards.

## cakes and yeast-leavened desserts

Cakes fall into the quick breads category because they're almost always leavened with baking powder, not yeast; but on occasion I do make a yeast-leavened cake (like coffee cake) or cakelike objects (like cinnamon rolls). I've lumped these two kinds of projects together because they're both rather particular when it comes to process and involve quite a few steps (and double that amount of dishes). These are the kinds of dessert projects you might advance to when you're feeling confident that you've mastered their predecessors—for example, yeast sandwich bread, muffins, or my in-a-jam cake.

## in-a-jam cake

My go-to, anytime/any event dessert is either a buttermilk cake inspired by my friend Julia or a modified version of banana muffins baked in a pan versus a muffin tin. This fine dinner party whip-up treat saves the day when, as usual, I've run out of time for my grand finale dessert plans; plus, both cakes pair quite well with your morning coffee if any leftovers make it till the next day. I adore the utility of these sorts of cake in that they're not overwhelmingly sweet and serve to sop up whatever topping I have on hand, whether it's fruit in season needing to be dealt with or one of the too many jars of jam I have crammed

## Hip Trick

Use those butter wrappers as greasing devices. You use up every spare bit of butter on the wrapper and possibly save a hand-wash by keeping your hands relatively grease-free during the final pour and delivery to the oven. I learned this invaluable tip from Amy McCoy, author of *Poor Girl Gourmet: Eat in Style on a Bare Bones Budget*.

on pantry shelves (hence the name). Julia's buttermilk cake recipe, which she modified from a couple great sources, is included at the end of the chapter.

## fancier cake basics

Essentially, the only difference between a fancy cake and a muffin is the flour and how you handle it. Cake flour is superlow protein (of all the kinds of wheat flour, it retains the least of what it came from, a wheat berry), and beyond the flour's protein content, the flour and sugar are usually sifted for the lightest possible crumb formation. Cakes fall into butter or sponge categories, and both benefit from having all your ingredients at room temperature. We prefer butter cake so that's what I'm focusing on.

When making a cake for a special occasion, I tend to skip right over the plain yellow cake and go for a flavor-packed base, like lemon or chocolate cake, both ideal bases for (read: vehicles for) a luxurious frosting. (Yellow cake should be yellow because of egg yolks, not artificial colors.)

# basic butter cake method

1. Cream butter and sugar to a foamy fluff.

2. Add eggs/yolks one by one and mix well.

3. Sift in dry ingredients and mix in shifts with three portions of milk/buttermilk/liquid and beat until well blended.

4. Bake in a greased pan.

# basic yeast cake method

1. Activate yeast and let sit for 10 minutes.

2. Mix batter, add yeast mixture, mix with mixer on medium-high for 7–10 minutes.

3. Let dough rise for an hour,* then roll out (cinnamon rolls) or shape in baking pan (coffee cakes) and add flavor stuff; let rise for another 30 minutes.

4. Bake in a greased pan.

* Gluten-free projects only need one rise, so you should skip the first rise, assemble, and let it rise on whatever you're baking it on/in.

### yeast cakes

The two kinds of yeast-leavened projects I make on occasion are cinnamon rolls and coffee cake. I grew up knowing these as grocery-store, special-occasion foods, which always came from a blue pop tube and white box, respectively. My first few times making these from scratch were revolutionary experiences. I instantly felt connected to my domestic goddess great-grandma Rose, the daughter of German immigrants who rocked the hell out of both of these projects.

### frosting or icing, a.k.a. the reason you make a cake or cinnamon roll in the first place

Decorating cakes is so not my thing. By the time I reach the final stage, I'm exuberant that I even have something to decorate at all and that it looks nothing like my first cake. As a teenager I made a sad squashed pancake (courtesy of using AP flour instead of self-rising flour). My mother ate her birthday cake anyway and told me it was good—and then taught me about flours.

I tend to stick with the one frosting that enhances any conglomeration of butter, sugar, and eggs: cream cheese frosting. When you discover your cream cheese stash to be moldy because you were coveting it so fiercely, make buttercream, the ingredients for which you probably already have. In the event none of these ingredients work for your dietary needs, I'd seek Erin McKenna's advice, as her BabyCakes bakeries' vegan and refined-sugar-free frostings are celebrated by anyone lucky enough to encounter her treats.

### pies

I'm not going to lie to you and say pies are easy. Pies are a bit of a process, but as with all this stuff, when you find a groove on a recipe that works for you, I hope you'll pull out your rolling pin and get down to business (at least twice a year). The most important rule of pie: you have to let it cool so the filling thickens properly.

### crust

Piecrusts—a more advanced form of biscuits—are sort of like houseplants: the less you interfere, the better off they do. If you're making one, you may as well make two and freeze the second. Having piecrust around the house is always an asset. With the bulk of the labor out of the way, you get homemade pie with half the work. Plus, there'll usually be scraps, and from the scraps you can make minipies or pie pockets.

# basic piecrust method

1. Combine dry ingredients.

2. Cut butter into dry ingredients to form pea-sized pebbles.

3. Add ice-cold liquid to form a just-cohesive dough.

4. Smash dough into one or two rounds, place in sealed bag, and refrigerate overnight (or freeze for 2 hours).

# pie-filling method

1. Prepare filling and let sit.

2. Roll out bottom crust and shape in pie pan.

3. Brush bottom crust with egg white, add filling and chunks of butter (I always forget the butter and as a result have to bust into my shell or shove it between lattice pieces).

4. Top with second crust, lattice, or streusel.

# pie-finishing method

1. Brush top with egg yolk for golden glaze (using the counterpart of your bottom crust glaze).

2. Bake on a walled cookie sheet at a high temperature initially.

3. Reduce heat and continue cooking; cover with a round of aluminum foil if pie is browning too much on top.

4. Let cool for 2–4 hours to allow the filling to set or you'll end up with a gooey, runny piece of pie (that still tastes good).

When making a lattice top for your pie (or a gluten-free pie lattice with less stretchy lattice strips), rather than weaving it on top of the pie filling, cut strips and weave it together on a piece of parchment paper. When it's time to transfer the woven lattice to your pie, use a swift, book-page turn and flip with intention onto your pie.

## 8 things to do with a homemade pie

1. Pull it out of the oven and stare at it until it cools.
2. Take its photo and post it to Facebook; then watch as the photo receives more likes than you've ever seen on your page. (A good thing to do while you're doing #1.)
3. Top it with homemade whipped cream.
4. Give it to someone special for their birthday. (Always make two crusts when you do this, in case of separation anxiety.)

My weapon of choice in preventing a soggy-bottomed piecrust (and ensuring a golden brown top) is an egg. I separate the egg and, using a pastry brush, I paint the white onto the pie shell before I add the filling. After the top is in place, I brush it with the yolk, which serves as a lovely glaze.

*fats*

The flake of your crust depends on your fats. Yes, you must use some sort of fat, and here are a few good options:

1. Butter.
2. Leaf lard (not the gross hydrogenated stuff at the grocery store; buy this from your local butcher).
3. Vegans can use shortening or a butter substitute. Steer clear of standard brand (cheap) shortening, which is made with partially hydrogenated oil (vegetable oils were not meant to be consumed in that fashion).

I made a video with my friend Hilah; you can watch us do all the stages involved in making pie and see what things are supposed to look like at each point. Go to http://hilahcooking.com/gluten-free-pumpkin-pie/.

1. **Sweet potato or pumpkin.** Great easy start to pie making because you don't have to do much beyond making the filling and sticking it in the oven (you can skip the last stage of pie methodology entirely).

2. **Everything else.** I love *The Joy of Cooking*'s formula for making any fruit pie filling: combining all of the following and letting it sit at room temp until you're ready to pour it in your piecrust.

   - **5 cups sliced fruit or berries**
   - **¾ cup sugar**
   - **3 tablespoons tapioca starch** (substitute same amount of cornstarch for a lattice top)
   - **1 tablespoon strained fresh lemon juice**
   - **2–3 tablespoons unsalted butter, cut into half-inch pieces**

   In fact, I love the entire pie-making section in *Joy*: it's a thorough, illustrated, and exhaustive resource on all versions and kinds of pies.

The following thickeners are all used in equal measure in pie fillings:

- *Tapioca* and *cornstarch* make clearer fillings that melt in the eater's mouth.
- *Flour* is used for a creamier and nutty flavor.

5. Take it to a potluck and watch it disappear.

6. Trade it for a mound of delicious things at a food swap.

7. Tell seven friends to bake different flavored pies and host a gathering where everyone trades slices. (Read more on hosting food parties on page 302.)

8. Pull out your homemade ice cream, scoop it on a rewarmed piece, and eat it. (Duh.)

## eggs 202

In Chapter 5 you learned all about rocking the hell out of breakfast and snackage with eggs. Now you can kick some dessert ass with these egg techniques.

### separating eggs

I owe this lesson to my mother, who taught me early on how to separate yolk from white without any equipment besides a butter knife. First, have two bowls ready, one for the whites and one for the yolks.

Gently tap your knife along the equator of the egg in a line so you get a break that separates the shell in two halves pretty cleanly. Let the white seep out into one bowl while delicately transferring the yolk back and forth between the two shell halves. Fresh eggs sometimes put up a fight when breaking up this perfect pair and sort of pull on the yolk, making it seem as if it's going to yank the yolk (or sever it at least) right into the whites bowl with it. The answer to this dilemma lies in a few deft transfers between shell halves to let that tense moment pass.

After you've got most of the white in the bowl, use the shell edge and a few more transfers between halves to cut the stringy

 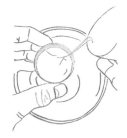  

# basic curds method

1. Whisk together citrus juice, egg yolks and eggs, sugar, and salt in a double boiler.

2. Add butter sliced into cubes and whisk frequently until butter melts.

3. Continue to whisk until mixture thickens to the consistency of sour cream, which takes about 5–9 minutes.

4. Press curd through a fine-mesh strainer to remove any imperfections.

cords (hopefully without piercing the yolk). Spoon out wayward yolk drops from the whites bowl if whipping or foaming them is on your agenda, because it might affect your success. It's okay if a little white gets mixed in the yolk bowl, though; nothing bad should happen to your yolk projects.

### custard or citrus curds

Curds incorporate butter, citrus juice, and eggs to make a creamy filling or topping for treats. I love making lemon or lime curd to spread on muffins and take them up a notch on the dessert scale. One thing's for sure, scrambled eggs for dessert is a major bummer, so making curds using a double boiler setup—a heat-safe metal bowl placed atop a simmering pot of water, not touching the water—is sometimes a helpful way for beginners to get the knack for this custardlike project. (See more on custards in the ice cream section that follows.)

Bringing the eggs past a simmer temperature of 180°F will

curdle them if they're not being constantly whisked to reduce temperature, but pressing the finished curd through a fine-mesh strainer will filter out any imperfections in your curd.

## *ice cream*

There is something terrifying and seemingly un-attainable about homemade ice cream.

Maybe it's a fear of curdling five eggs, since good ones are not cheap. Maybe it's the two-day factor.

Ice cream from scratch can be done using a few differ-ent methods. My favorite, French style, is totally worth the work. Another method, Philly style, involves simply bringing all the in-gredients to a boil and whisking in flavor components, and yet another method is similar to making a jam and then folding that into the cream. Sorbet is like Philly style but without the dairy. I got the itch to make ice cream after purchasing one of David Lebovitz's dessert books, still my go-to, trusted source for desserts done right.

## french-style ice cream

To a kitchen novice, a French-style ice cream recipe is sort of like assembling something from IKEA—fussy, laborious, and just complex enough to be annoying. In my first attempt, I puzzled over how many bowls I needed, what size and what to put in them, and how this was all going to go down. I broke down and illus-trated it after winging it and making a total mess of the kitchen (and using every single bowl we owned).

French-style ice cream is a four-step process and spans two days. Here are the four steps in detail:

1. **Make the custard.** This is the finicky part; you temper eggs in the warmed milk and sugar mixture and then stare down the mixture (possibly holding your breath—no, don't do that), stirring it until it thickens. Everyone says stir "until it coats the back of a spoon," but that's dumb because even that is open for interpretation. Keep stirring until you can clearly see a line that doesn't immediately reincorporate in the bottom of your pan after you make a swipe with a high-heat spatula.

   Don't plan on doing anything else for at least fifteen minutes, like talking on the phone or checking your e-mail or letting the dog out. You have a date with that saucepan and your high-heat spatula. If a crisis of any sort emerges during this stage, remove the saucepan from the stove and return it to the heat once the crisis is under control.

2. **Fold it into the cream.** A fine-mesh strainer will prevent any wayward curds from making the custard and keep them from chunking up your ice cream. Whatever bowl you poured your cream in, the one you're straining the custard into will be the final resting and cooling place. Choose wisely based on the instructions in the next step.

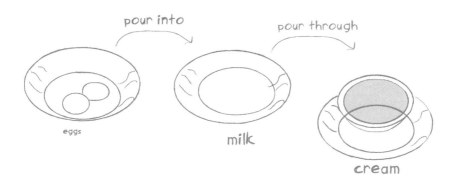

pour into

pour through

eggs

milk

cream

**193**

3. **Cool it.** Prepare an ice bath, keeping in mind you don't want water to seep into the ice cream bowl. Ideally your ice cream bowl will be tall-sided, much taller than the water level in your ice bath. Nothing is worse after all that custard work than your bowl tipping over and taking in water, which will transform what would have been smooth, velvety ice cream into a grainy and crystalline form. Once the ice cream mixture is no longer warm, cover it tightly and put it in the refrigerator overnight. Churning it without giving it sufficient time in the fridge will also make your ice cream grainy.

4. **Churn it.** Congratulations. You've made it to the end. Now stick the ice cream in the freezer and wait till tomorrow to take the scoop-in-a-pretty-bowl glamour shot; just-churned ice cream is soft, but it hardens after a night in the freezer.

If you have more time or want to learn the best methods for making desserts other than those I've covered here, check out the resources section at the end of the chapter for great baking and dessert books.

## recipes

### *american white bread*

*Recipe courtesy of DPaul Brown via Hedonia (www.hedonia.seantimber lake.com), adapted from* Time-Life Foods of the World: American Cooking

The original recipe for this American white bread calls for 4 cups of flour, but I've found that to be far too much, given the temperature of my home. You'll need to use your own sense of touch and judgment to determine when your dough has enough flour. The dough should be silky rather than sticky, and dense and springy, almost like the consistency of a marshmallow. It is imperative that you let the dough rise in a truly draft-free place, or else you risk developing a crust on top.

This recipe also makes fabulous dinner rolls.

1. Sprinkle **2 packages dry yeast (4½ teaspoons)** into **½ cup lukewarm buttermilk** (no hotter than 90°F). Add **1 teaspoon sugar** and stir until thoroughly dissolved. Place the mixture in a warm, draft-free place, such as an unlighted oven, for 5–8 minutes, or until the yeast has begun to bubble and has almost doubled in volume.

2. Pour the yeast mixture into a large mixing bowl, add another **½ cup lukewarm buttermilk**, and stir until combined.

3. With a large wooden spoon, slowly beat into the mixture **1 cup flour** and continue to beat vigorously until the mixture is smooth. While continuing to beat the dough, add the following:
   - **4 tablespoons softened butter**
   - **1 tablespoon sugar**
   - **1 tablespoon salt**
   - **1½ cups flour**

4. Transfer the dough to a lightly floured surface and knead it by folding it end to end, then pressing it down, pushing it forward, and folding it back. Knead for at least 10 minutes, sprinkling the dough every few minutes with small handfuls of flour—as much as you need

to prevent the dough from sticking to the board and your hands. When the dough is smooth and elastic, place it in a large, lightly buttered bowl. Dust it with a sprinkling of flour and cover the bowl loosely with a kitchen towel. Let the dough rise in a warm, draft-free place for 45 minutes to an hour, or until the dough has doubled its bulk and springs back slowly when gently poked with a finger.

5. Punch down the dough to reduce it to its original volume. Let it rise again for 30–40 minutes, until it has doubled in bulk.

6. Preheat the oven to 425°F. Lightly but thoroughly butter a 9" x 5" x 3" loaf pan. Shape the dough into a compact loaf, somewhat high and round in the center, and place it in the pan. (Be careful not to punch or deflate the dough.) An optional step here is to rub the top with soft butter, such as the leftovers on the wrapper, to keep the top of the dough moist. Cover with a towel and let the dough rise in the same warm place for about 25 minutes, until it reaches the top of the pan.

7. Combine **1 egg,** lightly beaten, with **1 tablespoon milk** to make a glaze. Thoroughly brush the top of the loaf with it. Bake the loaf in the lower third of the oven for 30–40 minutes, or until the loaf is golden brown and a toothpick inserted into its center comes out clean and dry. Invert the bread onto a cake rack and allow it to cool completely before you slice it.

*whole grain pizza dough*

*Recipe courtesy of Kaela Porter of localkitchenblog.com. Adapted from Basic Pizza Dough in* Pizza *by James McNair. Yields enough dough for two 12-inch pizzas, one 16-inch pizza, two 10-inch calzones, two 9-inch deep-dish pizzas, or one 10-inch double-crusted stuffed pizza.*

If you are used to making pizza dough with regular white all-purpose flour, you may want to use half whole wheat and half AP flour and slowly reduce the amount of white flour as you get used to working with the whole grain dough. Other whole grain flours (spelt, triticale, rye, etc.) can be substituted in part or in whole for the bread flour and white whole wheat flour. I generally try to use two cups bread flour, for gluten and protein content, plus one cup of any other flour, for flavor and variety. If you'd like, you can parbake the pizza crust and then freeze it for a quick and easy homemade pizza on a busy weeknight.

1. Proof **scant 1 tablespoon active dry yeast** (about 1½ packets' worth). Stir yeast into **1¼ cups warm water** (110–115°F) and **1 teaspoon honey**. Let stand for 5-10 minutes, until foam and small bubbles start to form on the surface of the yeast mixture. (If using instant yeast, omit water and honey and simply add yeast directly to the flour.)

2. In a large bowl, combine the following:
   - **3 cups whole grain flour** (I use 2 cups whole wheat bread flour and 1 cup white whole wheat)
   - **1 teaspoon sea salt**
   - **3 tablespoons olive oil**
   - **2 teaspoons honey** (optional)

3. Stir vigorously with a wooden spoon or spatula until a loose, wet dough is formed. Add water or flour here as needed to form a cohesive, but very sticky, ball of dough. Let rest in the bowl for five minutes.

4. Turn the dough out onto a lightly floured work space. Pat the dough out into a rectangle. With floured hands and a bench scraper fold the dough into thirds, like a business letter, and then fold in half so the dough is roughly the shape of a square "ball." Cover with a clean kitchen towel and allow to rest for fifteen minutes.

5. Use a **tablespoon of olive oil** to oil a bowl for the dough's rise. Set a small bowl of water nearby to wet your hands. Knead the dough, alternately flouring and wetting your hands, using the heel of your hands to push out and away from you, until the dough feels smooth and springy. It should be elastic but still somewhat sticky; this will take about 5–10 minutes. Resist adding too much flour: use a combination of water and flour on your hands to keep the dough from sticking. If the dough starts to resist you, allow it to rest for five minutes, and then resume kneading. Form it into a ball, transfer to the oiled bowl, and turn once to coat the whole ball in olive oil. Then cover tightly with plastic wrap and leave in a warm spot to rise; the heat from your gas oven's pilot light works well for this. If you have an electric oven, you can still use your oven for rising dough by heating it to 200°F and then turning it off. Wait ten minutes before placing dough in the oven to rise. Allow dough to rise until it has increased 50 percent in bulk, which takes about 45 minutes.

    If time allows, punch down the dough, form it again into a ball, replace the plastic wrap, and transfer the bowl to the stove while you preheat the oven. The second rise should take about half the time of the first, about 25 minutes. If you're pressed for time, skip ahead and use the dough after only a single rise.

6. Preheat the oven as hot as it will go (that's 550°F on my oven). If you do not have a baking stone, set an oven rack at the lowest level and place a baking sheet on it to preheat.

   Turn the dough out onto a lightly floured work surface. Cover a pizza peel with a piece of parchment, or sprinkle liberally with flour or cornmeal. Cut the dough in half to make two 12-inch pizza crusts. Pat one half into a rough circle; then, using a combination of light rolling and stretching, shape it into a 10–12-inch round. The dough will be a little soft and will tear more easily than a traditional white flour dough, so use a light touch and try to form the pizza shape with a minimum of handling. The more you manipulate the dough, the stickier it will get and the more difficult it will be to shape. If the middle tears, patch it together and continue shaping. Spread the shaped dough onto the parchment and pile on your favorite toppings. If desired, brush the edges of the dough with olive oil and sprinkle with grated cheese to form a cheese crust. Slide pizza, on parchment, directly onto a baking stone, or onto the preheated baking sheet. Bake topped pizza for approximately 7–9 minutes. If you plan to freeze the crusts, parbake the plain crusts for 2–3 minutes. Allow to cool completely and then wrap well and freeze for up to three months.

*pancakes for almost everyone:*
*gluten-full, gluten-free, and sugar-free pancakes*

*Modified from* The Joy of Cooking. *Yields about 24 three-inch pancakes.*

1. Combine the following in a large mixing bowl:
   - **1 cup brown rice flour**
   - **¼ cup buckwheat or millet flour**
   - **¼ cup arrowroot starch or tapioca starch**
   - **½ teaspoon xanthan gum**

   (If you are *not* gluten free, sub 1½ cups all-purpose flour for everything above.)
   - **¼ cup flaxseed meal**
   - **1½ teaspoons baking powder**
   - **½ teaspoon salt**

2. In a separate, medium-sized mixing bowl, whisk together the following wet ingredients:
   - **2 eggs**
   - **1½ cups any milk** (I have used with great success whole cow milk, almond milk, and 1 cup coconut milk mixed with ½ cup water)
   - **3 tablespoons unsalted butter**, melted
   - **1 tablespoon honey or agave nectar** (if not adding fruit butter or applesauce, below)
   - **splash of vanilla extract**

3. Fold wet ingredients into dry ingredients and stir to incorporate. Don't beat the batter, though. You want an even consistency; that is, you want the baking powder to activate inside the pancake on the stovetop (and produce fluffy little cakes), not spend all its puffing powers in the mixing bowl.

4. Once batter no longer contains any dry flour pockets, add ½ **pint blueberries** (or other small berries) or ½ **cup applesauce** or fruit butter to batter (optional).

5. Let batter sit for 5 minutes to thicken before dolloping 3-inch pancake portions onto the hot griddle or skillet. Cook until lightly browned on both sides.

### maple banana bread (or muffins)

*Recipe courtesy of Marisa McClellan of www.foodinjars.com.*

1. Preheat oven to 350°F. Grease a standard-size loaf pan (or muffin tin) and set aside.

2. Combine the following ingredients in a large mixing bowl:
   - ↔ **¼ cup butter, melted**
   - ↔ **¼ cup fruit butter** (or applesauce)
   - ↔ **½ cup maple syrup**
   - ↔ **1 egg**

3. Beat with a wooden spoon or a hand mixer. Stir in **2 ripe, mashed bananas** and **½ teaspoon maple extract** (vanilla extract will work fine, too). Set aside.

4. In a small bowl, combine the following with a whisk:
   - ↔ **1 cup all-purpose flour**
   - ↔ **1 cup whole wheat flour**
   - ↔ **1 teaspoon baking soda**
   - ↔ **½ teaspoon baking powder**
   - ↔ **½ teaspoon salt**

5. Add the dry ingredients to the wet ingredients in thirds, each time mixing to fully integrate before adding more. Optional: Stir **½ cup chopped toasted walnuts** into the batter. To toast the walnuts first, spread them out on a cookie sheet or wide flat pan and place

them in a 375°F oven for 5–10 minutes until they are lightly browned and start to smell toasted.

6. Pour batter into the greased loaf pan (or muffin tin) and bake for 50–55 minutes (25–30 minutes if making muffins), until a toothpick inserted in the center comes out mostly clean.

## julia's buttermilk cake

*Recipe courtesy of Julia Sforza of whatjuliaate.blogspot.com. Adapted from* Bon Appétit *and* Gourmet.

1. Combine the following dry ingredients in a large mixing bowl:
   - **1 cup flour**
   - **½ teaspoon baking soda**
   - **½ teaspoon baking powder**
   - **¼ teaspoon salt**

2. Mix the following ingredients together and then add to the bowl of dry ingredients:
   - **⅓ cup olive oil**
   - **½ cup buttermilk**
   - **½ cup sugar**
   - **½ teaspoon vanilla extract**
   - **1 egg**

3. Grease a pan and then pour the batter in—I use a 10-inch springform pan, but any 8–10-inch pan will work. Pour **1 cup of any fruit** (sliced or berries kept whole) on top of the batter. The pieces will sink in a little, but don't worry. Bake in a 350°F oven for 25–30 minutes. Test for doneness by inserting a toothpick into the center to see if it comes out clean.

## dawna's quick, any-shape cake

*Recipe provided courtesy of Dawna Fisher. Adapted from the 1989 edition of the* Better Homes and Gardens Cookbook. *Yields one large round or one 8-inch-square cake, or 6–8 cupcakes (you can double or triple the recipe to make more or larger cakes).*

One of my best friends shared this recipe with me. She's a totally hip mama of two girls, and her own mama, Mary, shared the frosting recipe that goes with it (and the piecrust recipe later in this section). This is the recipe Dawna pulls out when she realizes it's the day of the party and she hasn't left herself enough time to make an elaborate birthday cake. This recipe has been used to make a Godzilla attacking Tokyo, a Barbie driving a racecar, and a big hamburger (among many others).

1. Preheat oven to 350°F.
2. In a bowl, mix together the following:
   - **1⅓ cups flour**
   - **⅔ cup sugar**
   - **2 teaspoons baking powder**
3. Add the following to the dry ingredients and beat until smooth:
   - **1 stick of butter**, softened
   - **⅔ cup liquid** (milk, apple juice, orange juice, chocolate milk, etc.)
   - **1 large egg**
   - **1 teaspoon vanilla**
4. Grease a pan well and then add a couple tablespoons of flour to the pan. Shake it around to distribute the flour evenly; dump out any excess flour. Pour the batter in and bake at 350°F until a toothpick comes out clean. I always

start with 18 minutes for cupcakes and 25 minutes for any size cake pan.

## any-shape cake frosting

*Recipe provided courtesy of Mary Mauldin, Dawna's mom. Yields approximately 5 cups.*

This frosting works really well for cake decorating.

1. Mix **1 cup shortening** and **2 teaspoons vanilla extract** together.
2. Slowly add **4½ cups powdered sugar**, mixing constantly. Add **1 tablespoon milk** and continue to mix. If the consistency looks good for either piping or spreading, stop here. If not, continue to add milk in ½ tablespoon increments until the frosting looks and feels right. I usually add paste food coloring at this point.

## buttercream frosting

*Yields enough frosting for a 10-inch two-layer cake or 12–24 cupcakes, with more or less frosting per cupcake*

1. Set **2 sticks unsalted butter** out on the counter and allow to come to room temperature.
2. Combine butter with **3 cups sifted confectioners' sugar** and mix on low until sugar is fully incorporated. Bring mixer up to medium and add **1 teaspoon vanilla extract** and **1 tablespoon milk or cream** to achieve spreading consistency. Add additional milk/cream if frosting is still too stiff to spread.

204

3. Spread onto cake(s) immediately; refrigerate any left-overs (and allow frosting to return to room temperature before attempting to spread it again).

## cream cheese frosting

*Yields enough frosting for a 10-inch two-layer cake or 12–24 cupcakes, with more or less frosting per cupcake*

1. Set the following out on the counter one hour before making the frosting:
    - **2 packages cream cheese**
    - **1 stick unsalted butter**
2. Combine cream cheese and butter with the paddle attachment of a mixer and slowly add **2 cups sifted confectioners' sugar.** Add **1 teaspoon vanilla extract** (or flavored liqueur) or **1 teaspoon ground cinnamon** for flavor addition of choice.
3. Spread onto cake(s) immediately; refrigerate any left-overs (and allow frosting to return to room temperature before attempting to spread it again).

## mary's piecrust

*Recipe courtesy of Mary Mauldin. Yields two 9-inch crusts.*

Mary Mauldin's pies are beautiful and out-of-this-world tasty. She explained to me that this recipe evolved from years of trying various recipes; she could never get her mom's family recipe to roll out right. She encourages newbies to keep at it until you find the crust recipe and methods that work best for you. Many readers swear by adding vodka to their crust, the method touted by *Cooks Illustrated*.

1. Sift **3 cups flour** and **1 teaspoon salt** into a large mixing bowl. Add **1¼ cup shortening** and cut it into the flour with a pastry cutter or a fork to incorporate, until the flour-coated granules are about pea-sized. Form a hole in the center of the mixture and set aside.

2. Whisk together in a small bowl:
   - **1 large egg**
   - **5 tablespoons ice water**
   - **1 teaspoon white vinegar**

   Pour egg mixture into the hole in the dry ingredients mixture and combine with a fork until your dough ball comes together. Assess the dough; you want stays-together-when-pressed, but not sticky and gooey or the other extreme of too dry and crumbly. Add more ice water by the teaspoon if the dough balls aren't staying together. Use your hands to press the dough together and then divide the dough into two balls. (If it's too sticky, Mary suggests adding more flour only when you roll it out.) Try to avoid handling the dough too much, or the shortening will melt too soon and produce a tough crust. Freeze the extra ball if you're only making a bottom crust.

3. Sprinkle flour onto your countertop or a large piece of parchment paper and place one dough ball on it. Coat your rolling pin with flour and sprinkle the top of the dough ball with flour. Roll the dough out to 6–7 inches. Then pick up the dough disc, repeat the process of flouring the counter and the top of the dough, flip the dough disc over, and continue rolling to 8–9 inches. Repeat this process again, rolling the crust so it extends at least 2 inches beyond the edges of your pie plate. Avoid letting your hands touch the dough

too much here because they'll add heat, and this will toughen the crust.

4. Get the rolled dough off the countertop by setting your floured rolling pin onto the dough an inch from the edge. Peel the edge away from the counter and guide it onto the rolling pin. Curl up the crust by rolling the pin along the body of the crust as you feed more crust onto it. Unroll gently onto your pie plate. Settle the crust into the pie plate, working in sections, by picking up the edges and allowing the dough to sit down into the contours of the plate. Press it lightly into the plate with your fingers. If it breaks at any point, just pinch it back together with your fingers. Fold over onto the edge any sections hanging off the pie plate and flute the crust with your fingers or crimp with a fork.

5. Fill the crust, or prick the bottom with a fork and pre-bake according to the pie recipe you're following.

## resources

### books

- *Artisan Bread in Five Minutes a Day: The Discovery That Revolutionizes Home Baking* by Jeff Hertzberg and Zoe Francois
- *BakeWise: The Hows and Whys of Successful Baking with Over 200 Magnificent Recipes* by Shirley O. Corriher
- *The Bread Bible* and *The Cake Bible,* both by Rose Levy Beranbaum
- *The Gluten-Free Gourmet Bakes Bread: More Than 200 Wheat-Free Recipes* by Bette Hagman

- *Poor Girl Gourmet: Eat in Style on a Bare Bones Budget* by Amy McCoy
- *Ratio: The Simple Codes Behind the Craft of Everyday Cooking* by Michael Ruhlman
- *Ready for Dessert: My Best Recipes* and *The Perfect Scoop: Ice Creams, Sorbets, Granitas, and Sweet Accompaniments,* both by David Lebovitz
- *A Year of Pies: A Seasonal Tour of Home Baked Pies* by Ashley English

*web*

- Watch Hilah and me make gluten-free pumpkin pie on www.hilahcooking.com.
- I love Deb Perelman's dessert recipes (and friends swear by her yellow layer cake for birthday parties) on her blog, www.smittenkitchen.com.
- Visit www.baking911.com and look up their wedding cake baking time and batter amount information for a rundown on baking cakes and all the various pan sizes and how much icing you'll need.
- Visit localkitchenblog.com for Kaela's excellent tutorials on baking (and cooking) from scratch with locally sourced ingredients.
- Sean's blog, hedonia.seantimberlake.com, is an entertaining read where you'll find all sorts of baking, cooking, and taste-making posts.
- Beyond her expert canning advice on www.foodinjars .com, Marisa posts wonderful recipes for baking with homemade preserves and taking them to the next level.
- Julia's posts on baked goods and the seasonal-food lifestyle on whatjuliaate.blogspot.com are such a treat.

Part III

feeding others

entertaining and sharing

food with friends

chapter 7

# using stuff up

## preserving projects any beginner can handle

Preserving food doesn't have to be an all-day affair. Let's all agree that our modern lives are a whole lot different from the lives of our grandparents or great-grandparents. Our great-grandparents stocked their larders for long winters without access to fresh vegetables (and utilized every scrap of food).

We preserve food now for a number of reasons:

- Because it's empowering to know exactly what's in that jar of pickles and how to pronounce all the ingredients, as well as where the veggies grew and that non-GMO vinegar was used in the process.
- Because it's fun, and some of us, myself included, enjoy the art of "putting food by" (a sweet old-timey name for preserving). I look forward to the Zen experience of peeling peaches or skinning loquats for a unique pickling project.
- Because it's less expensive to make value-added components of meals than to buy them, and because shuffling bits and bobs from one cooking project into another is a leg up on self-sufficiency and living well with less.

This chapter is rooted deep in the heart of the Depression-era granny that inhabits my body. I certainly don't have an orchard at my disposal or under my care (thank goodness for my houseplants!), and purchasing large quantities of local, organic produce—not as seconds or via bulk purchasing deals (see page 71)—can be pricey and sometimes cost prohibitive for large-scale preserving projects.

My habit of making supersmall, single-jar versions of canning recipes is catching on. There's no rule that states that pickling must be done in large volume, which used to be the case out of necessity. Making and eating homemade jam doesn't mean you

212

have to lose an afternoon to blueberries and a canner pot (unless you want to!).

Not all preserving projects are for superfluous foods either. So you don't eat a lot of jam (neither do we, actually), but I bet you use mustard or sriracha sauce or kimchi periodically. Preserving is the art of extending the life of our ingredients in useful, delicious ways. Preserving allows us to turn a handful of spare radishes or an egg yolk into a value-added component of a current or future meal and can be adapted to any scale you feel comfortable with.

I've organized this chapter in a practical format, guiding you from a brief intro on general methods of food preservation to an ingredient-focused approach to doing so, that is, what to do when you have extra of something (veggies, fruit, milk, or herbs). As with the other chapters, the recipes for the projects are at the end of the chapter. I encourage you to extend your new ingredient-based cooking skills, the start-from-where-you-are approach discussed in Chapter 4, to preservation. You'll discover your project ideas pretty much take shape without you needing to purchase anything beyond your groceries for other kitchen projects. Using what you have seems like elementary advice (especially in this era of grocery store abundance), but once adopted and fully understood, it will shape the way your kitchen works.

## ways of preserving food

### *canning*

Canning food falls into two categories, water bath canning and pressure canning. Water bath canning encompasses putting up high-acid foods like fruits, jams, juices,

213

# why and how to sterilize jars

Many of the projects in this chapter and in Chapter 9 mention starting with a sterilized jar. By starting with a sterile jar, you help to ensure that infusions, preserves, and syrups will not be compromised due to ambient spoilage bacteria (see page 84) and will keep longer in the refrigerator. To sterilize a jar, boil it (completely submerged in water) for 10 minutes and do not dry. Use it immediately.

and all kinds of pickles (which are low-acid foods that have been acidified). The water bath method involves completely covering jars in water and processing them at 212°F. Pressure canning covers all other foods—stocks, sauces, meat, vegetables in water, and so on—and is done in a specific kind of pressure cooker, one that is designed for pressure canning, in order to process food to temperatures of 238°F–240°F. Generally speaking, a pressure cooker that can accommodate four quart-sized jars with space between and around the jars is suitable for pressure canning.

The difference between weighted-gauge and dial-gauge pressure canners is the method by which the level of pressure is indicated. The weighted-gauge canner allows processing at 10- and 15-pound increments and indicates correct pressure at those two weights by making a steady hissing noise with the gentle rocking of the weight gauge. The dial-gauge canner allows users to process food to exact pressures, which must be increased from the 10-pound sea-level baseline in 1-pound increments to various altitudes. Both types of pressure canners may also be used for water bath canning (by not adding the pressure regulators), and both come equipped with safety locks and overpressure release valves to ensure safety. Though the dial-gauge canner is more versatile, you'll need to have it checked once a year to make sure the gauge is calibrated correctly. Contact your local or surrounding area county Cooperative Extension service by visiting http://www.csrees.usda.gov/Extension/ and ask your agent for leads on where to have your canner tested, if not at their office. (The land-grant universities in every state provide extension services to help residents with things like food preservation, gardening, and urban agriculture.)

Both methods of canning produce sanitized, sealed jars that no longer have oxygen inside them. The processing time listed in the recipe ensures the contents of the jar reach either 212°F (water bath canning) or 240°F (pressure canning). Any processing time that is 10 minutes or longer will sterilize the jar. The best-by date for your sealed jars of home-canned goods is one year, unless it's a low- or no-sugar preserve, which should be eaten within 3–6 months or less. (Sugar plays a role in preserving color, texture, and some flavors, so your sealed jars of low- or no-sugar preserves will be more satisfying if eaten in a shorter time span, but they'll never be unsafe to eat.)

The kinds of things that you might water-bath can include:

*jams/sweet preserves*

- Jam
- Jelly
- Marmalade
- Conserve
- Fruit in syrup (or water)
- Fruit butters and no-sugar preserves. Fruit butters are good, lower-sugar alternatives to other sweet preserves. No-sugar preserves usually require a pectin product, since sugar helps achieve a set. Using honey or alternative sweeteners is fine for flavoring here, but they may darken the flavor of your preserve.

215

*savory preserves, a.k.a. condiments*

These goodies are somewhere between a jam and a pickle.

- ❧ Chutney
- ❧ Mustard
- ❧ Ketchup
- ❧ Hot sauce
- ❧ Relish
- ❧ Salsa

*pickling*

Vinegar serves two roles in a pickle jar: to acidify the low-acid vegetables (thus inhibiting microbial growth in the jar) and to help diffuse flavor from the brine into the produce. Also called fresh pickling, vinegar pickling works through osmosis where vegetables (and fruits!), which are mostly water when fresh, are put in a concentrated brine made from vinegar, salt, sometimes sugar, and spices. Over time, the brine draws out water from the produce and replaces it with the delicious flavors in your brine. Any canning recipe may be reduced and, rather than sealing the jars, you may place them in the fridge where they will infuse at the same rate as sealed jars and will last (if you keep them clean; see page 85) indefinitely. Brines for pickled vegetables include vinegar plus some portion of water plus a portion of sugar. The water and sugar cut the tangy bite of the vinegar.

Quick pickling, done only in the fridge, is a way of speeding up the infusion process by crushing spices, blanching the produce prior to submerging it in brine, and using higher concentrations of vinegar.

216

When I teach a canning class to a new round of students, their main concern is always not killing friends and family, which is certainly possible, though unlikely if you keep your improvisational acts confined to projects in other areas of preserving.

*Clostridium botulinum* is a normally harmless strain of bacteria found in our environment, but when exposed to heat, the inert bacteria forms spores that can bloom into a deadly nerve toxin if all the following conditions are present:

1. Low-acidity (the pH level inside a jar must be acidified to be below 4.6)
2. Room-temperature storage (beyond the 24-hour resting period for sealed jars)
3. Anaerobic environment (no oxygen)
4. Moisture

Although these conditions can realistically coexist in a sealed jar of your home-preserved food, they could also exist in a cooked baked potato wrapped in aluminum foil and left out all day at a barbecue; or in raw or even cooked garlic dropped in olive oil to infuse on the countertop (see safe ways to infuse oil on page 225). Don't scrap canning as unsafe; just learn the rules and gain an understanding of why you're not likely to kill friends and family with your jars of pickled beets!

Water bath canning does not kill botulism bacteria spores outright, but it eliminates the risk of the spores blooming by ensuring that the contents of a jar are a high-acid food (that's why you're not going to mess with acidity ratios in a recipe—e.g., the amounts of vinegar or lemon juice used per allotment of low-acid ingredients, like vegetables).

Besides water bath canning, there are other, non-USDA-approved ways of sealing jars, but processing at 212°F (the boiling temperature for water) for the processing time indicated by the recipe allows heat to fully permeate the contents of the jar and kill any fragile spoilers that could cause your jar to mold or spoil (in a less deadly way).

Pressure canning, on the other hand, reaches temperatures around 240°F, which is enough to kill spores, and it's a good thing because the conditions in the jar are exactly right for the spores to bloom (since you're sealing jars that have nonacidified, low-acid foods). Following processing times exactly and being precise in pressure canning is a must.

Fridge pickles, which are not canned (sealed to remove oxygen), have numerous spore-bloom negating factors, so march forth and pickle things without fear.

## fermenting/curing

Salting vegetables and meats is an age-old (literally) method of storing food and creating delicious things like charcuterie, sauerkraut, kimchi, and other fermented pickles. Curing involves the use of salt to halt the growth of microorganisms, and in the case of fermenting, salt facilitates the growth of specific types of microorganisms (*Lactobacillus acidophilus* primarily, a kind of probiotic) and prevents the growth of others.

## lacto-fermentation 101

Fermentation at a basic level is the controlled decomposition of food, where microbes are eating the things that cause it to rot and producing acidic conditions in their wake (which is exactly like pickling with vinegar except it's bacteria that performs the acidification process that halts spoilers from taking over in the jar, and as a result we end up with probiotic food, which is unlike vinegar pickles).

Fermentation's main control mechanism is salt, which inhibits the growth of undesirable bacteria and molds, the bad stuff, and allows very specific types of bacteria (*Lactobacillus*!) to grow and thrive. *Lactobacillus* does not contain dairy (it's the same bacteria that cultures dairy); you also don't have to use whey or other starter cultures to successfully ferment.

You do have to skim within the first week or mold will start to grow on the surface, where brine meets air (which you can confidently skim off and proceed with the fermenting). You also need to store finished ferments in the refrigerator after their two- to four-week countertop fermenting session.

Why consider eating fermented foods (besides the fact that they're pretty delicious)?

- **Predigestion factor.** *Lactobacillus* and its early-stage microbial predecessors do the handiwork of ingesting organic compounds, leaving you with more elemental forms of foods.

- **Nutrient-unlocking factor.** Thanks to predigestion, vitamins and minerals are more bioavailable to us than if we ate the vegetable raw. The most notable increase is in the amount of B vitamins, $B_1$, $B_2$, and $B_3$ (thiamine, riboflavin, and niacin), found in ferments versus raw.

- **Detox factor.** Fermentation produces compounds that in some cases, like cabbage ferments, have proven to serve as anticarcinogens. Just think of the unstudied and endlessly possible array of fermentation-induced compounds that might serve to benefit us. In today's world, where so many things are potentially carcinogenic, I'll gladly boost my immune system by including a few bites of kraut or kimchi on my plate.

→ **Live cultures factor.** The researched benefits of probiotics abound—though technically they only extend to those cultures that are grown in labs and sold commercially. Wild fermentation doesn't have big industry backers (seeing as all you need are salt, any vegetable or grain, and a glass jar or crock), hence there are no paid microbiologists going on the record to extend the same benefits to your home-cultured goods. The bacteria are the same (if not stronger and more diverse, seeing as it's coming from your local environment) and the benefits are the same. The thing about probiotics is, you don't eat yogurt or fermented pickles once and rest assured that your intestinal flora is restored forever. The probiotic benefit from eating fermented foods comes in eating them regularly in small servings—along the lines of a garnish or condiment in proportion to meals—to continue to introduce live cultures, which our bodies greet with good immune responses.

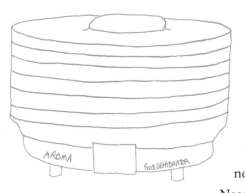

## drying/dehydrating

Dehydrating food is an excellent way to store foods at room temperature and can be done in open air, in ovens, and in a dehydrator. Ovens with low settings—150°F to 200°F—are ideal, but work-arounds for those of us with older, less technologically savvy equipment exist. Our lower-end Nesco-brand dehydrator sees a lot of action thanks to my discovery that the motor top sits nicely on our eight-quart stockpot and creates a no-fail incubator for homemade yogurt.

## 220

Consider going in on one with a friend or two who live nearby. Before the yogurt realization (game changer), I used my dehydrator about once or twice a month on average, which leaves plenty of opportunity to share it with someone else. I now use it once a week, and it has more than paid off the $90 investment.

## freezing

As I described in Chapter 3, the freezer is a fine place for storing foods, but it becomes a very expensive compost storage facility (or trash can) if you don't form a system for taking inventory of and using up frozen goodies while they're in their prime. Power outages can also leave you stuck, though an industrious friend, Kaela, behind the seasonal eating and preserving blog *Local Kitchen,* did rig up and run her freezer via her Volkswagen during Hurricane Sandy's long outages a couple years back.

A basic blanching for most veggies before freezing will leave you with convenient, ready-to-eat vegetables at any meal, and even less prep is usually necessary for freezing fruits.

## tool upgrades

- ⇥ Small and large sturdy, fine-mesh metal strainers for straining stocks, infusions, and other preserving projects.
- ⇥ Food mill, essential for pureeing sauces, butters, and leathers without having to peel the ingredient at hand.
- ⇥ Kitchen scale if you find yourself canning fruits and veggies or want to use a bake-by-weight process. I use my kitchen scale as a dual-purpose postal scale to calculate shipping online, too.

221

- 8- or 9-inch cake rack or other rack that fits in your eight-quart stockpot, so you can transform it into a water bath canning pot.

- Canning utensil kit, which includes a jar funnel, jar lifter, bubbler, and magnetic wand for lids.

- 16- to 23-quart pressure canner. There's no need to spend more than $80–$90; Presto brand is a great choice.

- Cheap coffee grinder. When you upgrade to a burr grinder for coffee beans, you can promote your old grinder to a position as spice grinder. You could also just buy one from a thrift store and run it a few times with kosher salt to clean the coffee out of it.

- Dehydrator, utility as mentioned above.

- Steam juicer. This is one of those major life event/gift/wedding registry kind of items. If you find yourself constantly with a full CSA box and not much time to preserve it for later consumption, having the option to juice your excess is fabulous. You want a slow-juicer, which causes the fruits/vegetables to be slowly tapped for their juices at a low temperature (to retain the most nutrients). Ours was a wedding acquisition, and my other half adores it and uses it almost daily. I appreciate it and love drinking her freshly juiced concoctions, but don't think it's essential. I've found it most helpful for juicing herb abundances and making sodas and syrups. We put the fiber (debris from carrots or beets mostly) that's removed upon juicing back into baked goods. You can't really taste it and your body will enjoy the nutrients.

# things to do with herbs and spices

*dry them*

I don't really discuss buying herbs in the spice stocking section (page 51) because buying fresh herbs, using them fresh, and then drying the excess yourself is so much better and involves a lot of tasty side projects.

## how to dry herbs

➻ **Low tech:** Form small bunches and tie at the base with kitchen twine or a twist tie and hang them from your hanging metal vegetable basket or a baker's rack, anywhere they will receive circulating air on all sides; keep out of direct sunlight if possible.

➻ **High tech:** Form single layers of herbs—still attached to branches or stems—on dehydrator racks and let the constant 95°F dry them out in a matter of hours. As with any dehydrator project, not all herbs will dehydrate at the same rate, so check on them periodically and shut off the dehydrator before leaving the house or going to bed if they're not quite done yet. Finishing them in the morning or whenever you get the chance is better than continuing to expose them to the drying heat.

Another option is to put them on a metal baking/cooling rack over a cookie sheet and stick this setup in your oven on its lowest setting (likely 200°F–250°F). Keep the oven door cracked open.

Store completely dried (think crunch, not bend) herbs in the same jars you store spices in (see page 51), removing large leafed things from their stems and leaving small leafed things, like thyme and rosemary, on the stems and storing them in larger or taller jars if necessary. Keep them out of direct sunlight for optimum flavor (I know you want to decorate with them, but the same goes here as for your spice jars—the less light they see, the better flavor they retain).

## *infuse stuff with herbs*

### salt

Use a ratio of ¼ cup coarse salt (sea salt, sel gris, or even kosher) to a half or quarter bundle of fresh herbs (which translates to about a cup of piled, unminced or ⅓ cup minced herbs). Clean and dry the herbs well and remove their stems as best you can. Mince and combine with salt. Spread flat and allow to air-dry for a few days, or stick in the dehydrator on the herbs setting (95°F). If you want a finely blended salt after it's finished drying, give it a whirl in your spice grinder.

To infuse salt with spices, use 1 teaspoon unground spice for every ¼ cup of salt. Generally speaking, roast whole dry spices in a dry skillet so they brown a bit or release a toasty smell, maybe a bit of smoke (though don't burn). Grind them with a mortar and pestle or spice grinder and combine them with the salt.

Store in a clean jar that seals tightly (we use a 4-ounce mason jar with a two-piece lid). Use herb- or spice-infused salts in place of the regular salt you'd add to finished food.

### sugar

Stick any dry spice or fresh herb you'd fancy as a flavored sugar directly into a jar of it and let it sit for a month; I particularly like using fresh herbs like rosemary or mint. More useful incarnations of this infusion include using a whole vanilla bean pod (or spent pod from making homemade vanilla ice cream), split cardamom pods, or a cinnamon stick. Use flavored sugars as a finishing sprinkle on baked goods or cocktail rims; herby sugars can also be used as a fun exfoliating scrub. Sift out infusion items that are small; leave in larger ones for presentation.

PURE CANE SUGAR
BIG BAG OF WHITE SUGAR

### oil

Skip the fancy bottles of infused oil (most commonly olive oils flavored with garlic, basil, or citrus) next time you're in the market for flavored oil. Infused oils are intended for fresh consumption (in applications like dipping bread, pouring over fresh, no-cook salads of all sorts, or as a finisher over a dish) because heat causes the flavor compound's tender aromatics to flit away. (If you want garlicky flavored oil to season your hot supper, then toss fresh garlic in the pan at the end of your sauté process to lock in flavor.)

To make infused oils, it's imperative to understand that commercially prepared oils use acidified vegetables, herbs, and flavor components to avoid the botulism bacteria's bloom under those ideal, oxygenless conditions (see page 217). On the home scale, the safest way to make your own oils is to use dried flavor components: dried garlic, peppers, fruits, or herbs. If you insist on using fresh components (that still retain their water composition and thus microbial flora), then infuse them in the refrigerator; don't attempt to acidify them yourself.

### flavored vinegar

Stick 3–5 sprigs (or ½ cup leaves, loosely packed) of clean fresh herbs into a pint's worth of just-simmered vinegar. White wine vinegar is ideal, but any kind will do. You can also substitute 3 tablespoons of dried herbs if necessary. Either keep it simple with the herbs or add things like peppercorns, a broken-up cinnamon stick, or the peel of one organic citrus fruit to spice things up. Start tasting the vinegar after three weeks and strain to remove aromatics within a month, so it doesn't become bitter. Bottle it into sterilized jars or bottles (see method on page 214) and cap tightly or cork. Store it at room temperature, out of direct sunlight, for up to three months (or for up to eight months in the refrigerator).

## simple syrup

Use a 1:1 ratio of sugar to water and make any herb-infused simple syrup. See the recipe on page 238.

## wine and cocktails

I have a prized old book, which my wife bought for me from a road-side street vendor in Williamsburg, Brooklyn, the day we married in New York City. It's called *The Book of Herb Cookery* (Gramercy Publishing Company, 1957), and in it author Irene Botsford Hoffmann describes a rosemary-infused white wine. The wine is made by chopping fresh rosemary sprigs, sprinkling them over any white wine, letting the concoction sit for a week in a tightly lidded jar, and then straining it. I like to make this and add it to sangria or fresh-squeezed orange juice or lemonade, which makes for a perfect summer evening or Sunday morning beverage. Experiment with leftover bits of wine and other herbs for another take on this recipe. There's no need to heat the wine, though starting with and straining into sterilized jars would be your best bet for successful infusions, so no residual microbes take over and cause the infusion to spoil.

Experiment and ramp up any cocktail with an herby zing by muddling a few sprigs of fresh herb (or a handful of leaves) with sugar or agave, adding the booze and other liquid, and then giving it a good shake. Strain through a wire mesh strainer if bits of floating herb are distracting or might clog your straw. Read more about cocktail basics in Chapter 8.

*Hip Trick*
Strain any of the liquid infusions through a coffee filter for clearest results.

## make herby butter

Start with one stick of softened, but not quite room temperature, butter. Employ the same method for preparing and amount of herbs prescribed for an herb salt—here you can also mix a few different herbs together if you'd like—and place the herbs, ¼ teaspoon salt, a few grinds of pepper, and the softened butter in a mixing bowl. It's best to begin with unsalted, but if you have to use salted butter, make sure to omit salt at this step. Drop butter onto its waxed paper wrapper or onto a piece of parchment paper and form into a roll. (If butter got too close to room temperature and is now oozy and oily, you can stick it in the fridge for a few minutes after incorporating the herbs and before you roll it.) Refrigerate for up to a week, or freeze for up to three months.

## frozen herby oils

Pouring olive oil over herbs in an ice cube tray is only a good idea for hearty herbs like rosemary, oregano, and thyme, because you throw them into a cooking pot early on and they cook for a long time, which usually causes more fragile herbs' flavor compounds to disappear, or worse, become bitter, and honestly, all three of those are easy to air-dry and stash in your spice drawer. You have

227

to use these cubes before they get freezer burn, too; otherwise, it would be much less expensive to just compost the excess herbs and buy a new bundle next time you need them.

*make herbtastic condiments, sauces, or spreads*

Each of these is flexible and adaptable depending on which herbs you use (yes, some are traditionally flavored, but it's your food; you get to decide what to put in it). Consult *The Flavor Bible* if you have any questions about what tastes good with "X," or just taste it and see. Most of these are based upon ingredients you probably already have in the fridge and/or pantry, and all of them are something you can whip up pretty fast.

- Herb vinaigrette (add 2 tablespoons of minced herbs to the basic vinaigrette on page 137)
- Herb mayonnaise (add 3 tablespoons minced herbs to one cup's worth of homemade [see page 163] or store-bought mayonnaise)
- Herb mustard (see page 251)

Look up recipes for these, which are herb-based sauces:

- Pesto
- Salsa verde
- Tzatziki

## things to do with vegetables

Beyond cooking them for dinner, here's a guide to what you might consider doing with an abundance of veggies. Abundance can mean as little as a pound or even a handful of something.

## pickle them

This is usually my first answer to any vegetable abundance scenario. Making a single jar of pickles is a great way to test out new flavor combos or vinegar/sugar ratios. Start with the method described at the end of the chapter (see page 239) and experiment away.

## ferment them

Yes, this is pickling too, but special pickling, so it deserves its own category. I trade kimchi (see page 248) and other ferments for haircuts. Having a few extra jars on hand never hurts. Make a single quart jar of veggies in a brine or shredded slaw or kraut-like ferment. Both are easy and delicious. Reserve shredding for veggies that keep their structure when shredded (think carrots, not cukes). Add dry or fresh herbs/spices and follow these salt ratios:

- ⇢ Salt brine veggies in liquid: 1½ tablespoons salt to 2 cups filtered water
- ⇢ Packed kraut/slaw: 2 teaspoons salt to 1 pound shredded vegetables

## infuse with them

### vinegar

Follow the methodology used for herb vinegars, but instead of herbs use 1–2 cups of roughly chopped vegetables such as shallots, onion, garlic, and deseeded peppers. Dropping a small handful of any of those directly in a small bowl of vinegar (white wine, red wine, or cider vinegars are the most flavorful, but distilled white will work) is a good call, too.

### booze

Deseeded peppers do good work inside a mason jar of vodka or tequila. Allow peppers to sit for 3–5 days, then strain into a sterilized jar (see page 214) and keep out of direct sunlight for preserving flavor best. Keeps indefinitely.

### make chips

Sliced thinly, tossed with olive oil, and baked, veggies become chips. Make sure veggies are completely dry before oiling and apply spices before you spread them out in a single layer and bake them at 400°F for 10–25 minutes. Consider experimenting with kale, sweet potatoes, beets, carrots, and parsnips.

### shred them

After shredding, either freeze for future use or reserve some for making muffins or bread in the coming days (see Chapter 6). Use excess shredded veggies in a slaw or kraut ferment.

## things to do with fruit

Fruit offers not only its tasty innards, but also its rinds, peels, and pits to savor. Here are my ideas for how to get the most mileage out of the fruits you buy.

### dehydrate/dry them

Cut fruit into ¼-inch-wide slices and line them on the dehydrator racks so they're not touching each other. Set the dehydrator to 135°F and check on them after three hours. Note that the exact time needed will vary with individual fruits' water content and structure. If you are dehydrating more than one kind of fruit at a time, rotating the trays and taking off the thinner, finished pieces will ensure great-quality snacks. Consult the book *Putting Food By* for good advice on drying fruit and testing for doneness.

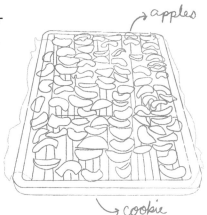

apples

cookie sheet

Another drying option is to put the fruit on a metal baking/cooling rack over a cookie sheet and stick this setup in your oven on its lowest setting (likely 200°F–250°F). Keep the door cracked open and let it sit for about two to six hours. This is a good project to do in a chilly fall house (you'll stand in front of the oven and catch the escaping heat); not a great project for a hot summer day when your house already feels impossibly warm.

## infuse stuff with fruit

### salt or sugar

Citrus peels or zest can be dried with salt or sugar in a similar fashion to the method used for making herb salts (see page 224). Both zest and peels need to fully dehydrate before you let them sit and infuse in a sealed jar. (Citrus peels also love to be candied—they're better than the best Sour Patch Kid you've ever had.)

### simple syrup or liqueur

My fruit-infused simple syrups tend to be less sugary than the herb versions, primarily because fruit has sweetness that it imparts, and I don't like cloyingly sweet syrup. A very sweet 1:1 ratio of sugar to water (or fruit juice) will keep for quite some time in the refrigerator (because sugar acts as a preservative), but I tend

**231**

to go with a 1:2 sugar to liquid ratio for my own flavor preferences. Situate yourself somewhere between the two for the best-tasting fruit syrups and be sure to use up lower-sugar syrups in three weeks or less. Make liqueurs with scraps or pits by reading up on the method on page 285.

vinegar

I rarely go to the trouble of infusing fruit vinegars with the level of ordeal surrounding veggie- or herb-infused vinegars, mainly because I put our fruit-infused vinegars immediately toward shrubs—delicious sweetened vinegar beverages that are always a hit at gatherings. Chopping roughly 1–2 cups fruit, dropping them in a jar of vinegar (white wine or cider vinegars are the tastiest, but any vinegar will work), and sticking the jar in the fridge to infuse for 5–7 days (or up to a month if I've forgotten it's there) is my preferred method. Pickling fruit and canning it also provides a stash of infused vinegar syrup, which is perfect for adding to drinks.

*ferment scraps into vinegars*

Follow the ratio of ¼ cup sugar to 1 quart of filtered water poured over any fruit scraps to cover them. See my apple-scrap vinegar recipe on page 244 and modify based on whatever scraps you have.

Suck down a tablespoon's worth every day to boost health. The researched benefits[*] include raw vinegar's effect on regulating blood sugar, promoting heart health, lowering the risk of cancer, and aiding in weight loss. (Most commercial vinegars are no lon-

---

* http://www.webmd.com/diet/apple-cider-vinegar?page=2.

ger raw since they've been pasteurized to halt fermentation.) Read about making shrubs, the drink mentioned above, with your raw, live vinegars in Chapter 8.

## puree them

If you have a food mill, this task will be much easier since you won't have to peel the fruit beforehand. You can freeze purees for future use, substitute them for sugar in baking recipes, make a fruit butter, and make fruit leather (see recipe on page 311).

## make jam

Making a supersmall batch of jam from any fruit is a fun project that takes about twenty minutes. Start by peeling, pitting, or coring and chopping your preferred fruit; cutting it into half-inch pieces will help your fruit cook down into jam. Skip peeling if you don't mind skin in your jam. However much prepped fruit you end up with, measure 60 percent of that volume and that's how much sugar you should add (e.g., if you end up with 2 cups prepped fruit, then you'd add 1¼ cups sugar). Squeeze a half or quarter of a lemon over it and either macerate (let sit overnight in the fridge) or put it in a wide, heavy-bottomed saucepan and start cooking on low heat until the sugar granules melt. Raise heat to medium-high and mash fruit pieces until they are the consistency you prefer (use an immersion blender for supersmooth, nonchunky jam). It will take about ten minutes for a jam with this sugar ratio to set (reach a gel). Use the frozen spoon test (see Appendix 2, page 315) to see if it's finished. Pour into a jar, let cool to room temperature on the counter, and then stick it in the fridge.

# 10 *whey cool* things to do with whey

Many of these ideas are provided courtesy of the *Hip Girl's Guide to Homemaking* Facebook page readers.

1. Freeze it in ice cube trays and add it to smoothies for a great textural and healthy addition to your morning beverage.

2. Juice an orange, and add a pinch of sea salt and a cup of whey for a natural electrolyte drink.

3. Add 4 tablespoons for every cup of water when soaking grains or before-bed oats to help break down the phytic acid that resides in the outer layer, or bran.

4. Culture mayonnaise or other condiments like salsa or even a cold soup like gazpacho by adding a

## things to do with dairy

If you haven't sworn off the kitchen based on information overload from the herb, veggie, and fruit ideas, here are some projects that originate from a gallon of milk. I tend to amass dairy by-products as opposed to dairy itself, things like whey and buttermilk, both of which I produce weekly from our stash of milk. Of course you can easily just buy all these things, but sometimes when you have extra milk on hand, it's fun to use it up in a future-useful way. I especially love the baked goods and other cooking projects that originate from having a spare cup of buttermilk on hand all the time.

Culturing dairy is a pretty simple process that involves either heating or not heating the milk, adding a starter culture (which can simply be an existing, store-bought product or more advanced heirloom starter cultures you can buy online), and letting it sit either in something that keeps it around 100°F or at room temperature.

I've moved up to an heirloom Greek yogurt starter culture, which means I can continuously culture new batches of yogurt from my previous batch. I have endlessly reusable cultures developed from a couple years of trying my hand at various culturing projects, from which I've discerned that yogurt and buttermilk are the projects I can handle every week. Note, though, that it's necessary to reculture every week to keep your culture healthy. That my foods require my attention once a week seems like a fair trade for the probiotic action and nourishment they impart. If you don't have an heirloom culture to care for yet, then your dairy datebook is open to whenever you feel like making your own goods.

## make yogurt

Make your own Greek yogurt with just an oven or a cooler with some hot-water-filled jars in it (no single-use machine required). See my method at the end of the chapter. Strain your yogurt after you make it and end up with thicker, Greek-style yogurt and whey for use in other projects.

## make something tangy

Culture milk with an existing buttermilk culture to get a new batch of buttermilk, or culture heavy cream with a buttermilk culture to make crème fraîche. Both can be made on the countertop and don't require creative incubation tactics as with yogurt.

## make ricotta

Acidify milk on the edge of drinkability to make cheese and whey. If you make ricotta by this method, it's technically called queso fresco. See the method on page 248.

tablespoon or two to your next batch and letting it sit at room temperature for 5–8 hours.

5. One reader, Emily, suggested adding to a cup of whey a squeeze of lemon juice, raw honey to taste, and some sparkling water, and then pouring it over ice—probiotic lemonade!

6. Soak nuts in whey to sprout them and then dehydrate them for the most perfectly crunchy (and fabulously digestible) nuts you've ever had.

7. Add whey instead of water or milk to baked goods, pizza, and bread doughs.

8. Blot some on a cotton ball and use it as a facial toner.

9. Give it to pets to keep them probiotically happy.

10. Water your garden with it every so often to give the plants a boost of vitamins and minerals.

**235**

## things to do with eggs

If you've exhausted your usual avenues for egg consumption—breakfast, lunch, and leftovers—hosted at least one brunch party, and made a custard-based ice cream (see page 192), then I suggest severing the perfect relationship between yolk and white. This breakup will position both components for effective storage and numerous (delicious) solo projects. For the things I don't discuss elsewhere in this book, I'll let you find a recipe that works for you.

### *hold on to those yolks, folks*

1. Mayonnaise (see page 163)
2. Homemade pasta
3. Citrus curd (see page 191)
4. Custard or pudding
5. Ice cream (see page 192)
6. Glazing baked goods (*pie!*—see page 188)
7. Frosting (German chocolate cake frosting)
8. Hollandaise sauce
9. Cakes and muffins that call for whole eggs plus extra yolks
10. Challah and rich breads
11. Classic Caesar dressing
12. Cocktails ending in "nog" or "flip"
13. Homemade paint
14. Combine with olive oil or avocado and apply to your hair for deep conditioning
15. Whip with castor oil and put it on your face

Egg whites, that is; see the Glossary to learn about folding egg whites and understanding stiff versus soft peaks.

Another Facebook query yielded these fine project ideas (and apropos subtitle courtesy of Kaela of the *Local Kitchen* blog):

1. Angel food cake
2. Forgotten cookies and meringues
3. French macarons
4. Friands
5. Pavlova
6. Lightening up omelets, scrambled eggs, or frittatas by whisking in extra whites to complement the other eggs, or going all-white for these projects
7. Crepes
8. Waffles, pancakes, or cakes that require stiff-beaten whites (though usually not out of proportion with the amount of egg yolks going into the cake)
9. Coating for breaded things
10. Frosting (Swiss meringue buttercream frosting)
11. Substitute for sugar in granola, or mix in with nuts before roasting to give them extra crunch
12. Glazing baked goods
13. Soufflé
14. Mexican sugar skulls for Día de los Muertos
15. Cocktails ending in "fizz" or "sour" (think gin fizz or pisco sour)

If, by chance, you end up with eggs or components of them after all this, then I suggest either of the following backup plans.

Extra hard-boiled eggs make a great protein-packed pickled snack. They turn pink if you drop them in a jar of pickled beet brine (or pickle them with beets)!

*freeze them*

Freeze eggs as separated components for future use in any of the preceding projects. Defrost by placing them in the refrigerator and then use as you would fresh ones.

## recipes

*parsley simple syrup*

*Yields about 1 pint*

1. Roughly chop **a bundle of parsley** (or whatever herb you're using), stems and all, and place in a medium-sized glass mixing bowl.
2. Simmer **2 cups sugar** and **2 cups water** over low to medium-low heat until all crystals are dissolved.
3. Remove the sugar liquid from the heat and pour it over the chopped parsley. Stir to incorporate the greens thoroughly. Let it cool on the counter (for an hour or so), and then cover the mixture and place it in the fridge overnight.
4. Strain the parsley chunks from the syrup the next day using a couple pieces of dampened cheesecloth set over a wire mesh strainer.

This syrup keeps safely in the fridge for about a week (before developing an interesting film of mysterious bacteria, yeasts, and/ or molds), so use it up!

*any vegetable vinegar pickles*

*Yields about 1 quart.*

Here's the formula for making fridge pickles.

1. Wash and cut up your **vegetables** and pack them into a clean jar. Use whatever veg you'll eat (or put into a martini): cucumbers, broccoli, cauliflower, brussels sprouts, carrots, onions, garlic, and so on. The weight of your starting produce will vary depending on what you're pickling—just eyeball it at the market, and if you end up with too little veg, you can always use a smaller jar (or make more brine to account for extra space in the jar).

   It's up to your palate how to prepare the veggies. I'm a fan of the raw pack method (putting the veg in the jar raw), but if you like a more tender, cooked texture, then you can use the hot pack method and blanch the veggies and/or cook them in the brine (step 3) for a bit to soften them up.

2. Add **spices, fresh or dried** to the jar. For a quart jar, use anywhere between ¼ and ½ teaspoon of whole dried spices like peppercorns, mustard seeds, fennel, cumin, coriander, dill, cloves, and celery seeds, or whatever else sounds delicious to you.

3. Combine in a medium saucepan and bring to a boil:
   - **1 cup any kind of vinegar**
   - **1 cup filtered water**
   - **1 tablespoon kosher or any noniodized salt**

   You can add sugar if you like a sweet pickle; the preceding is a standard tart pickle recipe. Try starting with **1 teaspoon sugar**; be sure to taste the brine to see if you like it.

4. Pour your just-boiled brine over the vegetables in the jar.

5. Wipe any vinegar spills from the rim with a clean towel or a paper towel and put on the lid. Consider reusing your already-used two-piece lids or recycle those single-piece screw lids that once capped salsa, tomato sauce, or peanut butter.

6. Now for the hard part. Hide the jar in the back of the fridge for at least a week. Two weeks is better, and three weeks is best. Your pickles will only continue to become more deliciously infused. But if you break into them early, I won't tell. They'll keep for what seems like forever—but if you have pickle experiments in there from more than six months back, it's probably time to do a fridge inventory.

## stella's pickled beets

*Yields 8 pints*

1. Wash **7 pounds of beets**, leaving the entire root tail and an inch of stem intact. Place them in a large pot, cover completely with water, and bring to a boil. Boil for 20–35 minutes, until they're tender enough to push the skin off. Test for tenderness by dropping the largest beet into a bowl of ice water and seeing if the skin pushes off easily. If it doesn't, continue to boil the beets; if it does, strain the rest of the beets and allow them to cool on the counter, or place them in an ice-water bath.

2. Combine in a large saucepan and bring to a simmer over medium-low heat:
   - **5 cups cider vinegar**
   - **1 cup filtered water**

- **3 cups sugar**
- **2 cinnamon sticks, broken in half**
- **2 teaspoons whole allspice berries**
- **8 whole cloves**
- **1 teaspoon pickling salt or 1½ teaspoons kosher salt**

3. While your brine is warming, place eight pint jars in your water bath canning pot, cover them to just below the rims with water, and bring the pot to a boil. Prepare your two-piece lids by placing them in a small saucepan with an inch of water. Don't turn them on to simmer just yet. Turn off the canning pot when it reaches a boil.

4. Peel the skins off your boiled beets and cut them into half-inch-thick pieces, any length you prefer. Mine are about two inches long, which is our preferred size for pulling out of the jar and eating. Place cut beets into the simmering brine and cook them over low heat for 8–10 minutes.

5. Remove cinnamon sticks from pot. Pull jars from canner pot and ladle beets into jars with a slotted spoon, distributing the spices evenly among the jars as you go. Now is a good time to turn on the heat and allow your lids to simmer (not boil) in the small saucepan.

6. Pour remaining brine into the jars over the beets, leaving a ½-inch headspace (the distance between the brine and the top of the rim). Use a chopstick or a bubbler to remove any air pockets from the bottom of the jar and adjust the headspace if necessary. Wipe rims with a damp paper towel. Seal with lids.

7. Process for 30 minutes in your canning pot.

*apple butter*

*Yields approximately 6 half pints*

You can do day one and day two on the same day, but I generally split it up to fit preserving into an after-work time frame or busy week's schedule.

day 1

1. Squeeze juice from **half a lemon** into a large saucepan and add enough water to cover the bottom of the pan. Core and quarter **5 pounds of apples**, skin on if you have a food mill or peeled if you plan to food process or use a blender to make the puree, and place them directly into the lemon water pan.
2. Bring apple pieces to a simmer, reduce heat to low, and cook covered until apples are tender enough to mash with a fork.
3. Strain apples and run through the medium screen of a food mill (or puree in a food processor/blender). For a finer butter, run through the fine screen of the food mill after the medium screen.

day 2

1. Measure the volume of your puree, which should be about 5 cups. Pour puree into a wide-based and heavy-bottomed pot and add:
    » **2 cups light brown sugar**
    » **½ cup sugar**
2. Bring mixture to a simmer over low heat, stirring frequently so sugar does not scorch the bottom of the pan. Once granules have dissolved, bring heat up to medium

or medium-high and cook down the puree. The mixture will need to cook for 20–40 minutes and you'll need to stir more frequently toward the end.

3. Stir well into the butter:
   - **½ teaspoon freshly ground allspice** (about 15 berries)
   - **¼ teaspoon freshly shaved nutmeg**
   - **1 teaspoon ground cinnamon** (changes the flavor, optional)

4. Now is a good time to place lids in a small saucepan with an inch of water over low heat, removing from heat once it reaches a simmer.

5. When the apple butter reaches a thicker, spreadable consistency, remove pan from heat. Taste your butter, and if desired, add a small splash of brandy or bourbon. Mix well to distribute evenly.

6. Ladle butter into hot jars (follow step 3 of the pickled beets recipe, page 241) and use a bubbler or wooden chopstick to release any air pockets trapped in the jar. Adjust volume in jars if necessary to leave a ½-inch headspace (the distance between the food and the top of the jar). Wipe rims clean and seal with two-piece lids. Process in a water bath canning pot for 10 minutes.

Allow jars to sit undisturbed for 12–24 hours, after which assess the seals by removing bands. If the lid is securely fastened to the jar (and can't be removed without the help of strong fingernails or a butter knife), the jar has successfully sealed. Place any jars that did not seal into the refrigerator and use them within three months. Clean jars with a rag dampened with warm water and a splash of vinegar to remove residue around the lid. Wash bands and store them separately to prevent rust. Label the contents and date on the lids.

## apple-scrap vinegar

*Yields 4½ cups*

1. Place **cores and peels of 5 medium-sized organic apples (or 3–4 cups of any kind of fruit scraps** or mushy but not moldy fruit) in a wide-based glass bowl. Avoid aluminum or galvanized steel. It's fine to freeze cores and peels until you have a large enough quantity to warrant a batch of vinegar.

2. Dissolve **6 tablespoons sugar** in **6 cups room-temperature, filtered water** and pour over scraps.

3. Cover bowl with cheesecloth or a thin dishcloth. Stir scraps daily to allow for bubbling, ensure even flavoring, and prevent surface mold from growing. After one week, strain cores and peels from apple liquid and pour liquid back into the same bowl. The liquid will smell like booze, which is totally normal and desirable.

4. Cover again and let sit for another two weeks, stirring every few days at first and then swirling the bowl gently as the "mother" forms on the surface of the liquid. The vinegar is finished when it smells and tastes like cider vinegar, which could take anywhere from three weeks to a month and a half (depending on temperature). Pour vinegar (and "mother") into a repurposed glass apple juice bottle or into smaller bottles and cap tightly. Store at room temperature; it will keep indefinitely.

*greek yogurt*

*Yields 1 quart*

1. Over medium heat, bring **6 cups milk** to 180°F. Do not use ultrapasteurized milk; you'll have trouble getting the bacteria to do its work.

2. Remove milk from heat and let cool in the pan. Allow it to return to 110°F (which takes about an hour).

3. Pour the 110°F milk into a glass bowl and, using a metal spoon, mix in **2 tablespoons active-cultured yogurt**. (Unless you bought an heirloom culture that can be reused, be sure to culture with a small container of new, store-bought plain yogurt.) Cover bowl with plastic wrap.

4. The ambient temperature in your oven needs to be between 85°F and 100°F for the bacteria in the yogurt to successfully populate the milk. Follow culturing directions below according to your oven type. Each method takes 8–10 hours.

   ⤷ **Gas oven:** Place bowl in your "off" oven.
   ⤷ **Electric oven:** Heat oven to 200°F, and then turn it off.* Wait five minutes and place bowl in oven.

   Or try one of these other incubator methods:

   ⤷ **Dehydrator.** Craft a yogurt incubator out of any size food dehydrator (see page 220).
   ⤷ **Cooler with hot jars.** Pour boiling water into quart-

---

\* For highly energy-efficient ovens, place another bowl in the oven during warming, and pour boiling water from your kettle into that bowl at least twice during the incubation process. This means you probably won't be doing it overnight.

sized mason jars that fit inside a cooler around the sides of your bowl of milk. Refresh the boiling jars midway through the process if needed.

5. When you take the yogurt out the next morning (or later that day), it should have firmed up to the consistency of a loose Jell-O. If it's still liquid, make ricotta and explore other incubation methods next time around. You can also reheat the milk and start over.

6. Strain your yogurt by placing a damp piece of clean cheesecloth (or a flour sack towel) inside a colander and allow the whey to drain for one hour. Use cheesecloth that's more muslinlike and less like a gauze bandage. The finer thread will help keep the liquid from leaving too fast. Check the texture periodically the first few times you strain to see how fast the liquid is leaving the yogurt. If you let it go too long, you might end up with a superthick yogurt cheese. Well-strained yogurt lasts in the fridge for three weeks (if you don't manage to gobble it up in the first couple days!).

## countertop buttermilk or crème fraîche

I have a stack of books that each have a recipe for home-fermented crème fraîche, and each of them varies on the specifics of how to do it. This method works for me, but if you find another you like, go for it.

Combine **1 pint organic heavy cream** (for crème fraîche) or **2 cups whole milk** (for buttermilk) with **1½ tablespoons organic sour cream or cultured buttermilk** in a clean pint-and-a-half-sized or quart-sized glass jar. Cap jar and allow dairy to sit at room temperature near your stove or in a warm place for 12 to 18 hours (up to 24 hours if your kitchen is cold and drafty). It's done fermenting when the cream/milk has thickened. Place jar in the refrigerator for up to three weeks.

Shake up your scones or dessert experience with the following tea-infused version.

## tea-infused crème fraîche

*Yields about 1 pint*

1. Bring **1 pint heavy cream** (slowly!) to 160°F in a medium-sized saucepan.
2. When it reaches the temperature, remove from heat and add **3 heaping teaspoons loose tea**. Cover and let steep for 30 minutes.
3. Wash and don't dry a quart-sized mason jar. Strain tea out of cream and pour cream into the quart jar. Allow the cream to cool to room temperature (no higher than 105°F).
4. Add **1½ tablespoons live-cultured buttermilk or sour cream** to jar and stir well to combine. Loosely cap jar and let sit in a warm place (80°F–85°F) for 12–18 hours, or up to 24 hours if temperature is lower. I set my jar near the stove and toaster oven with great success.
5. Once thickened, store in the refrigerator for up to three weeks.

## acidity-added ricotta, a.k.a. queso fresco

Heat any quantity of **milk** (can be soured, or about to go bad) to 180°F and remove from heat. For 1 quart or less milk, add **1 teaspoon distilled white vinegar or lemon juice**; for any amount over 1 quart, add 1 tablespoon. Curds and whey should begin separating immediately. Stir gently for a minute to facilitate congealing. Strain ricotta through dampened cheesecloth for 5 minutes, or up to 20 minutes if you want a superdry cheese.

## kimchi

*Yields 1 quart*

day 1

1. Cut a **1 pound savoy or napa cabbage** into 1½-inch squares, separating the layers as much as possible, and then toss them into a large glass or ceramic bowl.
2. Add to the bowl:
   - **1 medium carrot**, sliced thinly or grated
   - **3 inches of daikon** or a small handful of radishes, sliced thinly or grated
   - **2 scallions**, sliced in half lengthwise and chopped into 1- or 2-inch sections
3. Make a solution of **4 tablespoons pickling salt or fine sea salt** to **4 cups water** and pour over vegetables. Weight the veggies with a plate and let sit overnight.

1. Combine **1 tablespoon white rice flour** with **½ cup cold or room-temperature filtered water** in a small saucepan. Heat slurry, stirring constantly until it thickens, about 5–7 minutes. Remove from heat and set aside.

2. Grind into a paste, using either a food processor or mortar and pestle:
   - **4 cloves garlic**
   - **3 tablespoons grated fresh ginger**
   - **2 tablespoons red pepper powder/flakes** (The traditional Korean red pepper powder can be found in Asian markets. I use dried arbol or Anaheim chiles; any mild/medium heat red pepper will do, just avoid smoky peppers.)

   Add spice paste to your now room-temp rice slurry and combine well.

3. Drain weighted veggies, reserving at least 2 cups of brine. Taste for saltiness and rinse veggies if they're unpleasantly salty (they should taste salty, but not over the top). Mix rice and spice paste thoroughly into veggies. Don't worry if it's a thick paste.

4. Pack kimchi tightly into a wide-mouth quart jar. When completely packed, press down to force brine over the top of the kimchi. Add some of the reserved brine if necessary to completely cover veggies. Weight with an 8-ounce jelly jar or freezer bag filled with brine.

5. Let ferment for up to one week, tasting after a few days to see how the ferment is progressing and pushing the cabbage back down under the brine if necessary. Cap jar and place in the fridge when it's finished fermenting to your liking.

*dilled carrots or any brined veggie ferment*

*Yields 2 quarts*

1. Place into a clean, 2-quart or gallon jar:
   - **4 cloves garlic, smashed or halved**
   - **1 tablespoon dill seed or 1 fresh bunch dill** (or flowering dill heads if you can find them)
   - **10 black peppercorns**
   - **1 teaspoon cayenne or a fresh/dried hot pepper (optional)**
2. Quarter or halve **2 pounds carrots**, cutting crosswise to fit under the brine if necessary. Drop into jar over spices.
3. In a separate jar or container, combine **2–3 quarts filtered water** with **3 tablespoons pickling salt or fine sea salt** per quart (enough to completely cover the carrots with brine) and stir until salt dissolves. Pour salt brine over carrots.
4. Place a clean mason jar filled with water (for additional weight) inside the jar to weigh down the carrots in the brine. It's an excellent precaution to place the jar in a low dish or on a plate since the fermentation action causes bubbling and off-gassing, which could slosh the liquid over the edge of the jar if the brine is near the top.
5. Check on your pickles every day. In the first three to five days you'll notice bubbling and frothing around the rim. Do your best to skim excess foam off (without scooping out too many of the spices that have floated to the top). This keeps yeasts, molds, and less desirable bacteria from taking over in your jar. Rinse and clean the jar when you skim, too.

250

6. Your pickles are done when they aren't foaming any longer, they're not inherently salty, they taste and smell like pickles, and they're the same color throughout. You may try them at any time (they're not unsafe to eat at any point); just wash your hands before digging around in the jar with your fingers. Cap the jar loosely and place in the fridge when your pickles are done fermenting.

Mine are usually ready within 2–3 weeks in the early spring (cooler months) and as soon as a week and a half during warmer months. Fermenting time will vary with the temperature of your kitchen/house. They will keep in the refrigerator indefinitely, though they will slowly continue to ferment and sour.

## simple yellow mustard

*Makes one 8-ounce jar*

1. Bring **1 cup white wine vinegar** to a simmer in a small saucepan.
2. Whisk in the following:
    - **½ cup yellow mustard powder**
    - **¼ teaspoon salt**
    - **¼ teaspoon turmeric**
3. Continue whisking over low heat until the mustard thickens.

Increase the batch and water bath can this recipe, following the procedure outlined in step six of the apple butter recipe on page 243. Adjust headspace to ¼ inch and process for 10 minutes.

Make herb mustard by starting from an herb-infused vinegar or by adding one bunch of chopped herbs when simmering vinegar in step one. Remove pan from heat and allow vinegar to cool with herbs in the pan, covered. Strain herbs from vinegar and start again as described above.

## resources

### books

- *Ball Complete Book of Home Preserving: 400 Delicious and Creative Recipes for Today* edited by Judi Kingry and Lauren Devine
- *An Everlasting Meal: Cooking with Economy and Grace* by Tamar Adler
- *The Flavor Bible: The Essential Guide to Culinary Creativity, Based on the Wisdom of America's Most Imaginative Chefs* by Karen Page and Andrew Dornenburg
- *The Joy of Pickling: 250 Flavor-Packed Recipes for Vegetables and More from Garden or Market* and *The Joy of Jams, Jellies, and Other Sweet Preserves: 200 Classic and Contemporary Recipes Showcasing the Fabulous Flavors of Fresh Fruits*, both by Linda Ziedrich
- *Preserving by the Pint: Quick Seasonal Canning for Small Spaces* by Marisa McClellan
- *Put 'Em Up* by Sherri Brooks Vinton
- *Putting Food By* by Ruth Hertzberg, Janet Greene, and Beatrice Vaughan
- *So Easy to Preserve*, 5th edition, edited by Elizabeth L. Andress and Judy A. Harrison and Cooperative Extension/ The University of Georgia

- *Well-Preserved: Recipes and Techniques for Putting Up Small Batches of Seasonal Foods* by Eugenia Bone
- *Wild Fermentation: The Flavor, Nutrition, and Craft of Live-Culture Foods* by Sandor Ellix Katz

*web*

- For creative ideas for things to do with your ingredients at hand, visit my friends in Toronto who post at www.wellpreserved.ca.
- Find information about sprouting grains, culturing dairy, and including fermented foods in your diet at westonaprice.org.
- Find information on how to incorporate cultured foods into your diet, order heirloom starter cultures, and troubleshoot for yogurt-making at culturesforhealth.com.
- Check out edibleaustin.com for preserving projects and seasonal recipes featured in my quarterly column. Search for "hip girl" (including the quotation marks), and you'll find my archived columns.

*chapter 8*

# homemade entertaining

impressing your friends
(into trying it for themselves)

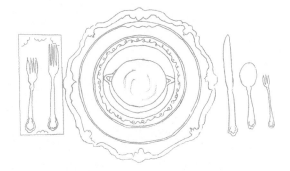

Having people over need not entail a day spent pulling your hair out and running around your kitchen like a chicken. The art of entertaining with ease is an acquired skill and requires practice. Expecting the first few gatherings you host to be a learning experience versus a perfect affair will set you up for future successes (and keep you from swearing off entertaining forever).

I'll start by addressing your concerns, as well as actual concerns from actual people and their actual experiences, and then go into some ideas for hosting different types of gatherings, from the simplest (a brunch potluck) to the more involved (a dinner party). The recipes section includes my favorite ideas for what to bring to parties or for simple, crowd-pleasing (and self-easing) things to make when you host your own gatherings.

Now is the time to host that gathering you've had in mind, not when you finally get around to painting the kitchen, when your bank account is flush, or when you've finally finished the ongoing remodeling process. If you wait for the perfect time, you're likely to be waiting indefinitely. Better to get a few practice sails

# five excellent reasons to have your friends over

1. You're broke, but you still want to enjoy good food and fine company.

2. You got a set of cloth napkins at the thrift store that are dying to make a cameo.

3. Your pal did something nice for you and you want to reciprocate.

4. You need to eat, and chances are your friends do too.

5. You made way too much of something and need peeps to come help you eat it.

under your belt before you launch your yacht of ideal entertaining, rife with visions of how it should be done, how your mother or Martha would do it. That ship will always be there; work your way toward it or invent your own way to cruise through a life of having friends over.

## tools to stock

- Cheesecloth, the kind that's more like a muslin bag when you buy it and less like a bandage (i.e., the holes are too big and don't strain out stuff).
- Shaker. Get a simple stainless steel one, no need for the full setup (the strainer that doesn't really work well and the removable cap; buy just the metal cup at the restaurant supply store, usually for less than $5). These come in 16- or 30-ounce sizes; the larger one is most versatile.
- Standard pint glass, the heavyweight glass that most beers are served in at the bar. Use this glass to muddle directly in and use with your metal shaker cup.
- Muddler. Get a wide-based, nonlacquered wooden muddler that's 7 to 9 inches long.
- Small strainer (or use your larger fine-mesh strainer with caution so cocktails don't end up on your countertop instead of in the glass).
- Jigger or small measuring cup that delineates 1-ounce markings.
- Ice bucket (or medium/small cooler for such purpose) and tongs or a scoop.
- 1 or 2 decent-sized pitchers, one for water and the other for tea or cocktails.

- 1 or 2 spare cases of 8-ounce mason jars; this is a handy way to avoid using disposable cups.
- A solid stash of thrift-store acquired flatware, enough to skip disposables.

## the entertaining lowdown

These are my thoughts on the play-by-play from the prep, through the actual event, to the cleanup. Hopefully they will clear up those but-everything-needs-to-be-perfect delusions and set you on the path to a lower-stress version of hosting friends and family.

Keep in mind your goals when dreaming up and planning a gathering:

*Goal 1: Feed lots of people something delicious without spending all your money.*

*Goal 2: Have fun with your friends, which means talking to them and not running around in a tizzy.*

## party logistics

*getting peeps to rsvp*

Common courtesy needs a revival. Let's start with you and me.

I try to dissuade friend-flake first off by sending a save-the-date e-mail in which I let peeps know they're lucky enough to be included and should go ahead and clear their calendars pronto. I'll request addresses if I'm feeling fancy and snail-maily, or just let them know the invite and an opportunity to RSVP is coming soon. This gets them ready and lets them flake on responding to the first note out of sheer e-mail habit if necessary.

Touch number two is where I'm counting on them to reply to me. I usually include it in the subject line. Don't do mass e-mail invites (unless you're down with bcc); it's too easy for e-mail-unsavvy people to "reply all" and annoy everyone involved. Give them a week if you can, and then reach out individually to people who haven't responded. Don't be passive-aggressive; just let them know you're planning quantities and arrangements and need to know if they'll be there.

Send a reminder e-mail the day before your event to those who said they'd be there. So much coaxing, I know, but it generally pays off and hopefully reminds people to be more courteous in the future.

## preparty cleaning

I did a call for entertaining stresses on the Facebook page and this area was by far everyone's top barrier to, or main stress surrounding, entertaining.

Do whatever level of cleaning your house actually needs. Now is not usually the time to do a massive deep clean (unless you're using entertaining as the sole excuse to do so). I think it's better to do deep cleans on nonmomentous occasions (well, besides in-laws' visits) because, clearly, we all associate the laborious task of house cleaning directly with entertaining, and as a result probably don't do either very often.

So long as your house is not gross, put your energy into the other prep work at hand and stop stressing over your not-impeccable house. Our pregathering (or prehouseguest) regime includes a complimentary sweep (and occasionally a mop) and a quick bathroom cleaning, you know, to get the toothpaste off the mirror.

## preparing for a party

*day before (or days before) duties*

Here's a handy list of what you should be thinking about the day before your party (so you're not thinking about it on the day of).

1. **Music.** If DJing is on your agenda, be sure to create your playlist way in advance of the gathering. Selecting music under the stress of a time crunch is not going to have the same effect on party ambience as you leisurely choosing songs—guests might end up listening to the Beastie Boys when you had more of a Nina Simone vibe in mind. Lots of music apps and sites feature playlists from friends or industry peeps that you can stream if you'd like to take this to-do off your list.

2. **Seating.** Count your chairs. If you don't have enough, call your neighbors. I like to pull out and set up the table, arrange the chairs around them, and sit in them—especially the ones in slightly compromised spots (in cracks where tables meet or corner-shoved-in seats). Make sure you could feasibly eat dinner and be comfortable in those spots before making your guests work with them.

3. **Eating essentials.** Assess the supplies situation—plates, cups, flatware, napkins, serving platters. Borrow what you're missing and save yourself from getting in a last-minute pinch or going out and buying anything.

4. **Clean.** Clean house the day before the party. Personally, I'm not worried about my not-spotless house. My friends aren't the sort to be paying attention to some dust lurk-

ing on my typewriter collection or the cobweb in the corner of the living room I've been meaning to swipe away.

5. **Menu planning/grocery shopping.** Don't count on grocery stores and their shelves for essentials at the last minute (says the person who went to three different stores for whipping cream because I waited till the last minute, proving my neighborhood to be a whipping cream desert).

6. **Prep.** Make or render components for desserts or dishes that can be made ahead.

## *day of*

1. **Set the table.**
2. **Select your outfit.** Do it first thing that day, not fifteen minutes prior to your guests arriving. Try to avoid putting yourself in the position of needing to answer the door when pesky on-timers show up while you're still judging the merits of seafoam tights with the pattern skirt or dark jeans and a flashy top. Having your complete outfit ready to wear will take a chunk of harried energy off the table.
3. **Ready the supplies.** Think through the equipment and serving needs for each course and do yourself a favor by prepping them in advance. It's much easier to grab a jar of spoons and a few stacks of little bowls than to scrounge around looking for the right number of spoons and adequate bowls during the serving of dessert. Same goes for glasses for different beverages you might be serving; for example, if it's a hot bev, have mugs nearby (and not in the cabinet across the kitchen). Whether you serve or guests serve themselves, make it easy for yourself

261

to not have to think about what you're doing while forming sentences (that make sense).

4. **Cook.** Shoot to have all the make-ahead things done an hour prior to your party. Best-case scenario: you get to do other last-minute things prior to guests' arrival. Worst-case scenario: it takes longer than you thought and you're in the kitchen praying for it to cook already while your guests are in the other room looking up pizza delivery numbers.

5. **Set out some appetizers and create a drink station.** A self-serve station for both these items will, in the words of Irma Rombauer in her early *Joy of Cooking* editions, "loosen tongues and unbutton the reserves of the socially diffident. Serve them by all means, preferably in the living room, and the sooner the better." She's really just referring to cocktails, but I extend it to snacks too.

## *run of show*

Make a detailed list with times and tasks for the day of your gathering. Be reasonable, if not overly generous, when projecting how long things will take. To-do list items always take longer when you are in a rush. Make sure your list has some areas that are nonessential or that can be parceled out to first-arriving guests or just plain get omitted. I always shoot for flowers, but they're something on my nonessential list that I have to drop on occasion for lack of time or insufficient trips to the garden/grocery, or I just forget them. (I have a Mexican sage bush and an oft-visited rosemary bush in proximity to our house and I've been known to pinch a few branches for table decor.)

# overcome your mental issues

*the cost-prohibitive nature of entertaining*

Any person who receives an invite to dine at your table will ask, "What can I bring?" at which point you request the things that will make hosting smoother and less expensive. We hosted a couple recently when our original plans to go over to another couple's house fell through. When our friends asked that question, we answered, "Gluten bread, wine, and cheese." They provided the appetizer and a round of drinks, which shaved off about $25 from our costs. If you apply your thrifty, cook-what-you-have tactics, then the things you provide on your end need not be a price gouge.

In the case of our dinner, since it was unexpected, I didn't really have time or funds to pick up anything fancy from the store or plan an elaborate meal (nor do I ever). Luckily, the night before's dinner was a slow-cooked pork shoulder with veggies and great northern beans, and its leftovers sufficed to feed three of us. The fourth was a vegetarian who begot an impromptu risotto using all the veggies I had in the fridge and a dried mushroom broth (see page 120).

Unnecessary costs for larger parties and gatherings are best hedged by borrowing stuff from neighbors and friends. Don't buy throwaway things, which are a waste of your money and suck for the environment. Read on to find my best beverage bets for entertaining on a budget.

## *let go*

Half the stuff you're really attached to (and that may or may not get done) will likely go unnoticed. Give yourself a break over not making the dinner rolls from scratch or that extra-fancy dessert you'd hoped to make. Your guests will appreciate your going to the trouble to host them. If it makes sense, have one of your early guests help with a project on the cut list instead of forgoing it entirely.

## planning the food

### *estimating how much to prepare*

This is a tricky area that won't have a single solution since recipes are each written differently with foggy estimations of servings. My first move is usually to identify portion sizes versus commonly accepted serving sizes. Portion sizes are vastly different from what restaurants tend to serve.

Here are some common object comparisons for what food labels mean when they say X ounces of something equals a portion (information provided courtesy of WebMD):

- Meat = deck of cards
- Fruit, vegetables, raw salad = baseball
- Bread = cassette tape (please tell me you've all seen one; unrelated: my first tape was Boyz II Men, and, yes, I was *that* cool)
- Baked potato = computer mouse
- Cooked grains or pasta = lightbulb
- Salad dressing = poker chip
- Ice cream = lightbulb

Clearly your guests would revolt if you served them a meal of these proportions, or would they? Paradoxically, places that offer dinners under $10 usually inflate servings to two to three times actual portion sizes (think supersize and the American love of "getting more for your money"), and places that tout dinners in the range of $18 and up tend to have closer-to-portion-suggestion-sized offerings. This is not always the case, of course, but this discrepancy points toward ingredient quality and ultimately why eating at home is where you're going to maximize quality and cost-effectiveness.

When determining serving sizes for your own gathering, you don't have to be the Soup Nazi, but there's certainly a compromise. Most recipes are written with a note of the amount of servings it provides, but a recipe that "serves four" might actually feed six if you stretch it right.

*ways to stretch more servings from meals*

1. **Cut it up.** When sausages are our protein, rather than serving the sausages whole, we cut them up into long slivers and stretch a couple extra servings' worth. Cook a whole chicken and carve it like a turkey; removing meat from the bones, even drumsticks, stretches four large servings into the six portions a chicken actually provides.

2. **Diversify your protein.** Include alternative proteins in the dish—like barley, beans, lentils, polenta, amaranth, farro, or quinoa—in addition to animal protein so guests feel full from less of one single protein. Cheese- or cream-based sauces also make dishes richer.

3. **Diversify the rest of the plate.** Cooking an additional vegetable side dish won't break the bank. Instead, it'll assist in filling the plate with an assortment of colorful and complementary items, effectively crowding out the gaping half-plate typically reserved for meat portions.

4. **Serve on smaller plates.** Our normal dinner plates

265

are antique-store-bought plates that used to suffice for dinner plates, that is, until dinner plates supersized (a 36 percent increase over the span of 1963–2007).* The mind is a powerful thing, especially when you have a full plate.

5. **Allow guests to serve themselves.** Bringing serving platters to the table (if you can) and dishing out family style helps people gauge what's there and how many people it must feed and allows guests to make a judicious allotment of their portions. Buffet-style dinners are fine, especially if your table doesn't have enough room for bowls and platters of food, though sometimes it's hard for guests to make calculations about what's there and how many people still need to get their servings. People in social situations tend to put less on their plates, which is great for ensuring there's enough of a recipe (that didn't seem like enough) to go around.

*accommodating food allergies and special diets*

This is an area where your guests should speak up (ahem, guests). I'm gluten-free and I always contact the host way in advance of the event to let him/her know my dietary issues and help troubleshoot the dinner plan. I always offer to bring something to supplement (bread, crackers, gluten-free pasta, etc.) and sometimes a host takes me up on it. I also always offer to bring a gluten-free dessert so hosts need not worry about accommodating me there, plus I want to eat dessert and what better way to ensure that's possible for me than to bring it myself!

If you're stumped for multiple-allergy accommodations, don't

---

* Study referenced in *American Wasteland* by Jonathan Bloom, p. 322.

hesitate to ask the person(s) who comes with the allergy for suggestions on what might work as a substitute. Hopefully you can try to avoid preparing completely separate meals by changing your assembly or prep so that the meat doesn't hit the dish until the vegetarians have received their portions, or by making two pots simultaneously—one free of gluten, dairy, or whatever the offending allergen is—which also happens to be the trick to upping recipe amounts.

## multiplying recipes

Marion Rombauer Becker notes in the 1975 edition of *The Joy of Cooking* the curious fact that many recipes are not to be scaled up infinitely, which is likely due to the necessity of cooking in your not-extralarge pots and pans. More food in the pan means more food to cook and likely less access to the heat source. Her advice: don't multiply a recipe by more than four; if you need more food, then cook it in batches.

This is the converse of the recipe reduction ratio discussed in Chapter 4, and usually it's infinitely easier to scale upward. Read up, though, on determining the master ratio on page 114 for instances when you end up with a decimal of an ingredient, and see Appendix 1, page 314, for common measuring equivalents when you need to recalculate based on your measuring equipment.

There's a great story behind *The Joy of Cooking,* which was originally authored and self-published by Irma Rombauer in 1931. In 1951, her daughter Marion joined the book's authorship. Read more about the history and evolution of this classic American cookbook in Anne Mendelson's book *Stand Facing the Stove: The Story of the Women Who Gave America* The Joy of Cooking.

## avoiding finicky foods

When planning your menu, stay away from things that require up-to-the-last-minute and more than "sprinkle with parsley to serve" finishing instructions, unless you have a friend or spouse on hand who has unbegrudgingly agreed to make those things happen. Steer clear of becoming the harried host by not making foods that will take you away from guests and enjoying the party all night.

Make-ahead things, like slow cooker roasts, soups, or other one-pot dishes that can be kept warm until ready to serve, are ideal for solo-hosting endeavors. Salads shoved in the fridge, sides warming in the oven, and vegetables basking at room temp in their postroast glory are also wonderful accompaniments.

## midparty management

### early peeps

People who arrive at parties early are just asking for a job. Put them to work and don't fret about how you're *so* not ready. It's annoying (ahem, guests take note), but try not to let your irritation engulf your welcoming spirit. They probably took strides to ensure they weren't late, so think of it that way and commend their thoughtfulness as you usher them into the kitchen or designated area to introduce them to the drinks station, or ask them to assemble it.

### late peeps

Remember all the times you were woefully late to something and try to give them a break. If, as your parties evolve, you discover particular friends are consistently late, then tell them the party starts earlier for occasions where timing matters.

Use your run of show to guess where things might take longer (and recruit help for those portions). Be conscious, though, that even meticulously planned coursing gets the occasional surprise, the "oh crap, the chicken's not all the way cooked" moments. Go with the flow and remember you're not a restaurant, and your friends hardly expect you to be.

# five fun things to do with mason jars

You've likely already gone Pinterest-wild, pinning every creative mason jar moment ever documented, but here are five fun things to do with mason jars at a party:

1. Fill wide-mouth pint or quart jars with predining breadsticks, lavash, or tall crackers for a unique cheese plate or snack station.

2. Make place markers. Clip name cards with a clothespin and set pinching-end-down in 4-ounce jelly jars filled with dry beans. Adjust so the card sits right in the middle.

3. Attach jelly jars to a strand of lights for a unique over-the-table lighting scenario (see the post on my blog for details) or drop tealights inside taller jars for a safe and wind-resistant candlelit atmosphere.

4. Stick flatware inside jars for casual or potluck events.

5. Make a series of small flower or herb bouquets in half-pint jars and line your table with those rather than having one large centerpiece that obstructs guests' vision.

*doing dishes*

When guests offer during a break between dinner and dessert, say yes. Pour yourself a cocktail, a cup of tea, or more wine and let them do as many as will fit in the dish rack or only the items that go in the dishwasher (see Appendix 1, page 316). Save the pots and pans for tomorrow.

If a natural break never occurs and it's clearly a disruptive, table-discussion-breakup activity, then clear the plates, assure guests it's not time to stop chatting, stack the dishes quietly (or set on the counter unstacked if you have the room), and return to the table pronto. The dishes will be there forever, your guests will not. None of this is applicable if you have children over the age of eight (who've been taught the rites of dishes), unless they're in bed.

A good meal will likely take two hours (if not longer) from sitting to standing up, so when you clear dishes during one of these affairs, it's a good idea to also stick any leftover food in the refrigerator—just shove it in there and don't worry about repackaging in better storage containers until after people leave. But then do make sure to do it; food poisoning is a crappy host gift to give yourself.

## beverage skills

The art of entertaining begins with offering someone something to drink. A beverage of any sort is the cornerstone of hospitality. I feel good about myself when I have multiple options to offer unexpected visitors. (I also don't sweat it when all that's on the impromptu drinks menu is milk and apple juice. It's a good reason to make tea or root around for cocktail fixings.)

## cold-brew and infused iced teas

Time and tea are the only things you need to cold brew. Experimentation is encouraged, if not required. Infuse your tea by way of fruity scraps from your kitchen like raw elements (cores and peels from an apple pie-making session), or postprocessed scraps from fruit butters or jelly making. Or just keep it simple and leave out additional flavors.

### cold-brew tea formula

The ratio is 1:1—you want one heaping teaspoon loose tea (or one intact teabag) for every 1 quart of water.

Add flavors when you add the tea and remember that if you plan to use the skins/peels in this or any continued way, consider buying organic (see page 76 for essential fruits to buy organic); pesticide tea is not likely a desirable part of your drink menu. Let it sit in the fridge, covered, for 24–48 hours (any longer and the tea will become bitter, which can be rectified by the addition of some honey plus sugar and/or water).

Strain with a fine sieve or a cheesecloth-lined colander and sip triumphantly.

# infusion smarts

- Heat extracts flavors faster, but also destroys tender flavors.

- Grinding spices means a faster infusion, but if left in over a longer period the flavors change, and possibly for the worse. It's best to keep spices whole if you are planning on keeping infusions for a longer time.

271

*other nonalcoholic favorites*

sodas

Homemade sodas are one of my main throw-together bevs for entertaining and they fall under two general categories:

1. Make a syrup/cordial/nectar (whatever the hell you want to call it) and add bubbly water.

    *or*

2. Go for a more involved (but well worth the occasional undertaking) kind of project, fermented sodas. Flavor water with fresh or dried ingredients, sweeten, and then carbonate with added yeast, either ale yeast or regular bread yeast.

shrubs, no longer just in the front yard

Your favorite swanky cocktail joint has likely featured a shrub or two on their drinks menu. In fact, as I was pitching this book, friends took us out to celebrate our recent marriage at Momofuku Ssäm bar in NYC, where I sipped a coconut shrub. Shrubs consist of a fruit component, a sweet component, and vinegar tang that are condensed into a syrup concentrate—and there are no less than ten ways to make it—which is then diluted with club soda. If you'd like to turn it into a nighttime affair, add a splash of brandy, bourbon, or homemade liqueur. See my shrub methodology on page 287.

## booze!

I'm not a mixologist by any means, but I do appreciate a fancy cocktail and have been known to happen on making them at home. As you're gathering your home-mixologist creds, I find it essential to go out in the world and taste great combos (oh, darn, another field trip!). When sipping cocktails, marvels of modern tastemaking and art they may be, don't forget to jot down components of those great drinks (so you might report back to your kitchen with new ideas to try).

Doing this all on a budget is where you get to play mad scientist. I stumbled upon boozy infusions after finding myself with a pile of perfect Meyer lemon rinds, and after I candied and zested and froze as many as I had patience for, I delighted in discovering that the answer to my remainder predicament was to pour alcohol over it and ignore it for two weeks. What's also reassuring is that with this project, besides its being easy, it is nearly impossible to kill anyone (the alcohol prevents bad stuff from growing), and you can't really mess it up. A long-forgotten rhubarb liqueur (left for six months in stage one, which I explain below) became an excellent candidate for rhubarb bitters.

### liquor

Most of us are not distilling whiskey or vodka in our garages—though I bet a few of us wish we were!—so your liquors are going to be the store-bought base

## quick chemistry primer

Alcohol is a good solvent and excels at penetrating cell membranes (thus extracting aroma and pigments from flavor component cells from solid ingredients like nuts, herbs, flowers, and fruit). A higher-proof alcohol is better at extracting and holding flavors.

273

of the cocktail. See pages 54–55 for my suggestions on the most useful things to stock when you're on a budget, and upgrade based on your budget as possible with ideas from this chapter.

*liqueurs*

Liqueurs are simple and undemanding projects to undertake; they involve only two stages. First, muddle and soak any type of fruit and flavor addition in a high-proof booze for a week or two, and second, strain and add a simple syrup and let sit for another couple weeks (or months) to develop flavor. The result is sippable on its own (though a bit too sweet for my liking) or a great component to add to beverages, baked goods, or ice cream. Common liqueurs

# bar smarts: vermouth 101

Vermouth is fortified wine (which means jazzed up with flavorful aromatics and made more alcoholic by the addition of spirits), and it comes in dry or sweet varieties. Dry vermouth is a martini staple; sweet vermouth is an essential for Manhattans and Negronis.

I suggest you only get vermouth if you can find it in the mini (2-ounce) or the 375-milliliter bottle. Buy the larger bottle and it is almost guaranteed to oxidize and lose its aromatic qualities during the two years you never use it. Store vermouth in the refrigerator to keep it fresh. Sweet vermouth has gone bad when it's cloyingly sweet and dry vermouth when it tastes like vinegar (neither of which make a dangerous-to-imbibe beverage, just not what you were intending to flavor your cocktails with). In a pinch, try substituting a sweet red or dry white wine (depending on the type of vermouth called for) and add a zingy bitters and spiced liqueur.

are citrus, amaretto (from stone fruit pits; see my recipe on page 285), and nocino. It's also fun to make them from rhubarb or any fruit you have on hand and feel like experimenting with.

## bitters

My bartender friend Meaghan told me the best answer to a too-sweet drink (many home-infused concoctions can quickly become just that): bitters.

Making bitters—traditionally medicinal tinctures flavored with roots, herbs, fruits, and spices—utilizes the same process as liqueurs, except that stage two involves adding only a little bit of a sugar syrup to stabilize the whole affair. Try making flavors like citrus, cherry, blackberry, rhubarb, peach, or anything that has a little tang in itself and might be great with zesty spices.

Keep a four-ounce bottle of Angostura bitters on hand to liven up cocktails and punches with this esteemed and secret combination of herbs and spices.

## cocktails and punches

In college, most of us learned that cocktails were 2 to 4 ounces of liquor topped off with some sort of sweet, fizzy flavored soda. Moving beyond the rum and coke or vodka tonics of our past, I'm taking the cocktail up a notch to emulate what we see on fancy cocktail menus. One of my favorite places to look for creative drink ideas is in old cookbooks (like *The Book of Herb Cookery* I mentioned in Chapter 7 and *The Joy of Cooking*'s 1950s and earlier editions). But when crafting under real-life, we-need-drinks-right-now-and-I-don't-want-to-flip-through-books kinds of moments, I fling open the pantry door and improvise from a standard base.

275

### cocktail formula

The ratio is 4:2:1, so you want 4 parts alcohol to 2 parts nonalcohol liquid to 1 part simple syrup or liqueur.

Use whatever measuring equipment suits you—a jigger (the official bartender's pouring measure), a tablespoon, or a Dixie cup. When making a special cocktail for party guests, do it by the pitcherful so you're actually sipping with guests and not making drinks all night long.

### ideas for nonalcohol and effervescent additions

- Fresh-squeezed citrus juice (lemon, lime, or grapefruit)
- Club soda
- Water (can be used to offset a sweet homemade liqueur)
- Tomato juice
- Ginger ale
- Tonic

bubbly bubbled
club soda

### alcohol-based ways to add some effervescence

- Sparkling sake
- Sparkling wine (don't spend more than $10 on a bottle you're using in cocktails or punch)

Beyond adding bitters, if your cocktails have taken a turn for the too sweet, my bar-maven friend Missy recommends muddling your potion with a peeled section of cucumber and straining to bring down the sweet.

276

## punch

Punch is a cocktail's less-finicky, more laid-back sister. My friend Missy is also the punch queen, and she schooled me on punch basics. Her favorite liquors for punch include clean, easy-to-manipulate spirits such as vodka, a "new world" gin (which means it has other flavors infused in it beyond the standard juniper berries), or 100 percent agave tequila. Using lemonade as the fruit juice makes a great base flavor for many punches. Be creative with your punches and think up complementary flavors and how to add them as components, like an infused liquor or delicious liqueur, or by adding fresh ingredients like herbs or cut-up fruit directly to the punch itself.

## punch formula

The ratio for a single pitcher that serves six to eight people is 1:1:1—1 part fruit juice, 1 part liquor, 1 part club soda, plus 6 ounces liqueur and any combination of herbs and fruit for visuals.

Serve with a bucket of ice and a strainer (either one intended for use inside the pitcher or any other strainer on the side of the pitcher) so guests actually strain as they pour it into their cups of ice. Punch is such a visual experience and Missy's comment that "people drink with their eyes first" makes a lot of sense here and in the art behind many a beverage's garnish. If making a punch for more than eight people at a time (or at a party where people will be drinking it throughout the evening), then make a punch concentrate by combining all the ingredients except for the soda and have guests decant the concentrate into glasses full of ice, filling it two-thirds full, and top it off with club soda.

**Word to the Wise**
It's best to tear fragile herbs like mint, cilantro, and basil so you don't run the risk of overmuddling them and making them bitter.

## margaritas

Yes, margaritas get their own category; I live in Texas and that's one of our finer points. As with nearly everything in the kitchen, there are a lot of conflicting opinions as to what constitutes a great margarita, and I'll leave it to you to ultimately decide for yourself.

### margarita formula

The ratio is 4:2:2, 4 parts tequila to 2 parts lime juice to 2 parts simple syrup and skip the liqueur.

Our friend Bob, a tequila connoisseur, believes this to be the best ratio to highlight decent tequila (which doesn't have to cost an arm and a leg; look for 100 percent agave tequilas). Have fun with it and make all sorts of margaritas with other citrus or tart juices.

My best advice to you as you set off on the exciting path of im-provised beverages: *always add the booze last.* That way, if your base somehow ends up undrinkable and appears unsalvageable, then your high-ticket item (the booze) isn't wasted.

## good drinks for the masses

These are my top choices for good places to start when plotting crowd-pleasers for the next time your house turns into the local watering hole.

### mimosa

No, I'm not going to tell you how to make a mimosa because that's ridiculous, but I'm going to remind you to never underestimate the power of (cheap) prosecco or dry champagne. Adding a couple teaspoons of homemade liqueur and fresh or preserved fruit or herbs to prosecco makes an instant fancy drink. Alternatively, you could pour a bottle into a big bowl and drop in a few scoops of homemade frozen yogurt and call it church punch.

## sangria

It's nearly impossible to mess up sangria, and even better news, the cheaper the base wine, the better. This makes for a low-cost way to feature excess fruit, fresh herbs, and homemade liqueurs. Sangria's winter cousin is mulled wine, which just involves you buying a box or large bottle of red wine and heating it up with mulling spices and maybe some apples.

## planning drinks by involvement on your end

- **None:** 6-pack of beer and a bottle of wine; don't forget about this option, especially if you're making something a little more complex for apps or dessert.
- **Up front:** Sangrias for any season, punch concentrate
- **Ongoing:** This includes making and shaking crafted cocktails for friends, which is fine if you are entertaining with a friend or two, but not if you're solo. Bump this into the up-front category by picking two specific drinks and making larger batches of them ahead of time. If you're worried about particular premade concoctions losing their fizz, then combine all ingredients except for the sparkling soda to make a concen-

trate. Make a little sign indicating guests should use the half-cup measure provided with the concentrate and fill the rest of their glass with the soda. Have a stirring spoon and a towel out for them and let the cocktails flow.

## the master plan

Enough hemming and hawing, let's do this thing. I hope to get you going on ideas for how to pull off entertaining without an extra paycheck or swearing off it entirely in the future. I grant you permission for early incarnations of any gatherings at your house to be charmingly imperfect and for you and your guests to appreciate and enjoy that.

# herbaceous pairing ideas

- **Rosemary:** in lemonade, spiked or not, or infused gin with Aperol (a bright orange, bittersweet aperitif related to Campari) or other herbal liqueurs

- **Mint:** in mojitos or fruit-forward cocktails

- **Sage:** muddled with a dark liquor and something acidic to balance

- **Cilantro:** in tequila drinks with lime and jalapeño

- **Basil:** in vodka drinks with ginger or in any fruit-forward drink

- **Thyme:** swirled in drinks with aquavit (a savory caraway spirit) or Aperol

Not hosting is the perfect step one to entertaining on your own. You get to see how things work without the stress of doing it yourself—score! Get yourself invited to as many friend-hosted gatherings as possible and pay special attention to the flow of parties you attend, taking note of things that worked well and (from a nonjudgmental, purely educational perspective) things that didn't work so well.

Here are some things to notice:

1. Where was the beverage station? Was it accessible, understandable as to how you might acquire a drink? Were all the necessary items easily found and/or placed nearby?
2. How was food served? Did it require a lot of organization or coordination on the part of the host?
3. What was the seating arrangement like? Did it work? For example, were you able to eat comfortably and chat with someone else while doing so?
4. Was there anything you needed during the party that gave you pause in finding it? A napkin, a cup, the trash or recycle bin?

*having a potluck?*

When you're the host, have a stash of serving spoons in your reserves because people rarely bring what's needed to serve their dishes, which is usually only a problem in larger party situations where flatware is at a premium.

Remember to ask yourself these things as you're planning and arranging for your own gatherings.

## Hip Trick

Make a yearly investment in stocking your wine rack by buying a case of wine; at many stores they'll give you a discount for buying more than six bottles at a time. It's helpful to have bottles on hand for impromptu entertaining or to take to a party.

### what to bring

While making cobblers, pies, and other potluck lookers might not be your thing, there are other foods your host will appreciate and not shove to the corner in the sea of chip/dip offerings. My signature potluck offering is a pickle platter, which consists of me loading up whatever ferments or fresh pickles I have in the fridge onto what looks like it might be technically a Japanese serving dish (with an array of cute bento-like ceramic components that fit inside a wooden frame). It's easy, travels fairly well, and always comes home empty.

You'll get extra kudos for putting protein on the table. Many potlucks can turn into a bread and chip and dessert fest in a matter of minutes, so bringing something that either is or forms a complete protein (see page 106) will fortify fellow guests in eating all the aforementioned items.

*cost-effective and extra welcome offerings*

- Deviled eggs, kept classic or dressed up into curried or avocado variations
- Quinoa or other grain salads, packed full of fruit, veggies, and nuts
- Salads, always a prize to find some balance on the potluck table
- Cheese served with homemade crackers
- Pizza, easy if you have a homemade crust in the freezer
- Beans, soup, or meatballs made in your slow cooker
- Fresh in-season fruit
- Vegetables and homemade hummus

*party 1:*
*brunch test-drive*

Hosting a brunch is an excellent way to dip your feet in the waters of casual entertaining. Much of the prep can be done in advance, and it's easier to be generous in times of a thin wallet with eggs than with good pork chops. Explore the libation situation described earlier and let yourself loose making breakfast for friends.

*menu ideas (based on your experience/desire level)*

**Easy:** Frittata.
**Medium:** Pancakes—make ahead and stash, covered, in the oven on a warm setting.
**Time to burn/spouse on the job:** Cinnamon rolls or quiche, frittata's more involved cousin.

*party 2:*
*the big dp (dinner party)*

For the record, entertaining is not normal life, so (until you've done it fifty times) you don't have to be good at it or feel relaxed. I've yet to bypass the frenzy prior to dinner party hosting. Don't be hard on yourself; after a few attempts, you'll invariably graduate to a less-stressy, more enjoyable version of hosting.

appetizers

Predinner snackage is the key to getting a dinner party off to a good start. You don't have to be formal about it or make yourself crazy coursing out the meal or even having people sit down for it.

*Hip Trick*

When traveling with a full slow cooker, wrap plastic or aluminum foil around the base of the rim to capture seepage. I always set a thin rag towel between the slow cooker base and the ceramic vessel to capture drips that manage to escape.

**Easy:** Radishes with sea salt and butter; chips and salsa; any jam, chutney, or apple butter with goat cheese and crackers or homemade bread.

**Medium:** Spiced nuts; fresh guacamole added to the chips and salsa platter.

**Time to burn/spouse on the job:** Anything in the "medium" category that you didn't prepare ahead of time.

### sides

**Easy:** Quick sautéed greens, roasted or steamed veggies (see steaming and roasting tips in Chapter 5).

**Medium:** Veggie casseroles (which are best made in advance, then covered and kept warm in the oven), mashed potatoes (which, if not made at the very end of the meal prep, can be kept covered in a warm oven so they don't get cold before serving them).

**Time to burn/spouse on the job:** Any side dish that demands waiting until the very last minute to assemble or prepare, like Great-Grandma Rose's Hot Bacon Cabbage Slaw (see page 289).

### mains

**Easy:** Soup (squash or white bean soup), slow cooker pork or beef shoulder roast, assemble-your-own tacos or big salads.

**Medium:** Risotto, lasagna, whole roasted chicken (which you then have to cut up judiciously into parts while hot).

**Time to burn/spouse on the job:** Grilling meats, cassoulet, anything you've never made before the night of your party.

## recipes

### *sangria*

Use **white or red wine** and for every standard-sized bottle have **at least three whole fruits** cut up, some of them hopefully citrus (including rind), **¼ cup of any liqueur** or aromatic/light liquor (gin, agave tequila, vodka, light rum), **¼ cup simple syrup**, and **1 quart club soda** (or omit simple syrup and use a quart of ginger beer). Macerate for 6–24 hours.

### *stone fruit liqueur*

*Makes about 3 cups*

1. Combine **1 cup stone fruit pits**, picked clean and left whole or lightly crushed (it's okay to freeze these as you eat peaches, plums, apricots, and nectarines and make a batch when you have enough pits), and **2 cups grain alcohol (Everclear) or a 100-plus-proof vodka** in a quart-sized jar. Seal and let sit for two weeks in a dark cabinet. Swirl it around every few days.

2. After two weeks, make a simple syrup by combining **⅔ cup sugar** and **½ cup water** in a small saucepan and dissolving the granules over medium-low heat. Raise the heat

Our good friends have us over often for something they call "big salads." They stretch a whole roasted chicken among six to eight people by pulling all the meat from the carcass in advance and then set the chicken out beside a giant bowl of salad greens. They prepare all sorts of fixings like hard-boiled egg crumbles, sunflower seeds, sliced veggies, any pickles I've brought them, croutons, shredded cheese, or whatever else they have on hand. We love this lighter, yet affordable and still-filling meal!

to medium-high to bring the syrup to a boil. Reduce the heat and simmer for 5 minutes.

3. Let cool completely before measuring and adding **1 cup syrup** to the pits/alcohol jar. Add **1 whole cinnamon stick** (optional). Seal the jar and let it sit for two more weeks.

4. Strain the solids from the liqueur and sip over ice or add to a cocktail for an almondy twist. Store liqueur either at room temperature or in the freezer, tightly sealed.

## *basic fruit bitters*

*Yields approximately 1 cup*

1. Combine the following in a quart-sized jar and lightly mash with a wooden spoon:
   - **1½ cups roughly chopped tart fruit** (blackberries, rhubarb, or rinds and white pith from grapefruit are my favorites)
   - **Rind, including white pith, from 1 organic lemon**, minced
   - **1 teaspoon whole allspice berries**
   - **2 teaspoons whole coriander seeds**
   - **5 white peppercorns**
   - **1 cup grain alcohol (Everclear) or a 100-plus-proof vodka**

2. Cap the jar and let the mixture sit in a dark, cool place for at least one week (or for up to a month).

3. The day before you plan to complete the bitters, make a syrup by combining **2 tablespoons sugar** and **1 table-spoon water** in a small saucepan. Bring the mixture to a boil and stir to keep the sugar from scorching. Reduce the heat and simmer for 3 minutes. Remove the syrup

from the heat and pour into a small jar with a lid. Let sugar syrup sit overnight at room temperature.

4. Strain out solids from the infusing jar first through a fine-mesh sieve, and again through a coffee filter. Add the simple syrup to the strained bitters, omitting any sugar crystals that formed overnight. Store the bitters at room temperature in a tightly sealed jar or bottle, where it will keep indefinitely.

### seasonal shrub concentrate

*Makes 3 cups*

1. Wash a quart-sized mason jar with hot, soapy water and do not dry. Chop **2 cups of any seasonal fruit** into roughly 1-inch pieces and drop directly into the jar. Pour **2 cups white vinegar** over fruit and cap the jar. Infuse the vinegar at room temperature for 1–3 days.

2. Strain fruit from vinegar (and use it as the base of a chutney or savory sauce). Wash the jar with hot soapy water again and do not dry.

3. Make simple syrup by combining **1½ cups water** and **1½ cups sugar** in a small saucepan and dissolving the granules over medium-low heat. Raise the heat to medium-high to bring the syrup to a boil. Reduce the heat and simmer for 5 minutes. Let cool completely.

4. Add cooled syrup to the strained vinegar in the jar. Store shrub concentrate in the refrigerator, where it will keep for up to six months. To make drinks, add 1–3 tablespoons of shrub concentrate to an 8- to 12-ounce glass of club soda or seltzer water.

*homemade root beer*

*Yields about 2 quarts*

1. Combine **4 cups filtered water** with the following in a large saucepan:
   - **⅓ cup dried sassafras root bark**
   - **8 teaspoons dried sarsaparilla root**
   - **2 teaspoons dried burdock or dandelion root**
   - **3-inch piece of vanilla bean**, split lengthwise (optional)
2. Bring to a boil, uncovered, and then reduce the heat to simmer for 15 minutes.
3. Strain out the solids and add **1 cup sugar** to the hot liquid.
4. Pour half of the concentrate into a one-quart-sized SodaStream bottle (or quart-sized plastic soda bottle), so you can gauge the carbonation. Pour the other half into a second bottle or—depending on what you have in your kitchen—a large swing-top glass bottle or quart-sized mason jar.
5. Pour **2 cups cold water** into each bottle.
6. Dissolve **⅛ teaspoon ale yeast** or active dry yeast in **2 tablespoons warm water** (no hotter than 110°F) and split that mixture between the bottles. Cap the bottles tightly and let them sit at room temperature. Check the carbonation level at 48 hours by squeezing the plastic bottle; it should be completely hard and the contents fizzy when opened. Place bottles in the refrigerator for up to three weeks.

## missy's moscow mule

*Makes two 6-ounce cups*

Cut off both ends of **one lime** and cut it into sections. Drop sections into a glass pint jar and muddle them until the juice is completely out of the limes. Add **4 ounces vodka** to the jar, fill with **ice**, and place metal shaker over the top. Shake vigorously. Pour evenly, including ice, into two 6- to 8-ounce glasses and top each off with **ginger beer**.

Make variations on this by switching out the vodka for tequila or gin and muddling with herbs to add flavor.

## great-grandma rose's hot bacon cabbage slaw

*Serves 8*

I grew up with this dish stinking up the house every holiday, positively despising it until I was in my twenties, at which point my taste buds (thankfully) shifted. While writing my first book and exploring solutions to our CSA cabbage abundance, I called up my dad to ask him how to make my German great-grandmother's side dish. It's an acquired taste, slightly tangy from the vinegar but perfectly balanced with the bacon and sugar. Cook this just before you dish up the meal to serve hot.

1. Finely shred **one small head (13 to 14 ounces) green cabbage** or use one 12-ounce bag of angel hair shredded cabbage (like my dad does). Place in a large bowl and dry the cabbage if necessary.
2. Thinly slice ¼ **sweet yellow onion** in long strips (see illustration on page 147) and mix with the cabbage.

289

**Salt and pepper** the cabbage and onion and let them come to room temperature before proceeding.

3. Cook **8 strips of bacon** in a large cast-iron skillet or stainless steel frying pan. Reserve 6 of the strips for the slaw and snack on the other two (like my dad and I do). Chop up the bacon for the slaw and add it to the cabbage and onion bowl.

4. Make the dressing by pouring off some of the bacon renderings, leaving about ¼ cup's worth in the skillet. Add ¼ cup water and put the skillet over medium-low heat to bring it to a boil. Add the following directly to the pan:
   - **2 tablespoons apple cider vinegar**
   - **½ teaspoon salt**
   - **¼ teaspoon sugar**
   - **3 grinds pepper**

5. Bring to a boil and carefully taste dressing, adjusting with more water, sugar, or salt to your flavor preference.

6. Pour dressing over the bowl of cabbage and onion and mix quickly to incorporate. Dump contents of the bowl directly into the skillet to soak up the remaining dressing and warm the cabbage with residual heat, but don't cook it.

   Serve immediately and don't plan to have leftovers (not entirely because it's so delicious, but because it doesn't transition gracefully from hot to cold).

*risotto*

*Serves 6*

My wife taught me how to make risotto. In fact, she coached me through this particular recipe on more than one occasion when I was a nanny in Brooklyn and responsible for making children's dinners happen from things I found in their pantry and fridge. There was usually a box of Arborio rice on hand, which makes a handy vehicle for sneaking veggies onto plates. If you don't have stock on hand, it's fine to use water. This is a hands-on project; once you add the rice to the pan, there's no stepping away to do anything else.

1. Bring **4 cups vegetable or chicken stock** to a boil in a small saucepan. Reduce heat to a simmer.
2. Cut up any combination of onions, carrots, celery, broccoli, cauliflower, mushrooms, green beans, or whatever firm vegetables you have on hand to yield **1–2 cups chopped veggies**.
3. Sauté veggies in a large saucepan or French oven for 3–5 minutes in a combination of **2 tablespoons olive oil** plus **1 tablespoon butter**.
4. Add **1½ cups dry rice** to the pan and stir to combine with the sautéed veggies. Let rice soak up the oil; sauté the mixture for two more minutes.
5. Add **½ cup dry white wine** (optional) to the pan and stir frequently to allow the rice to absorb the wine.
6. Add **1 cup simmering broth** to the pan and stir frequently to allow the rice to absorb the liquid. Add more of the simmering stock in ½-cup increments as the risotto continues to thicken and absorb the mois-

291

ture. Continue this process until you don't have any more stock.

7. Add **½ cup freshly grated Parmesan cheese** to the pan and stir to combine.

## *pot roast in the slow cooker*

*Serves 8–10*

1. Purchase a **3–4 pound roast cut** of either pork or beef. Beef cuts to look for in the butcher's case include chuck or rump roasts; pork shoulder will come bone-in or boneless (I prefer to buy bone-in so I can use the bones for stock). It will likely come tied together with twine so it forms a tight cylindrical shape; this ensures even cooking and creates more surface area for browning.

2. Cut up roughly **3 pounds of any combination of veggies** (carrots, onions, potatoes, other root veggies, cabbage wedges, etc.).

3. Season the meat with **kosher salt and freshly ground black pepper**. Use more salt than you think you should (about 1½ tablespoons on each surface—top, bottom, and sides).

4. Place meat in a hot, oiled skillet and brown the roast for three minutes on the top and bottom. Set roast into the bottom of a slow cooker, add a **bay leaf**, and scatter vegetables around the sides.

5. Pour **2 cups beef or other stock** into the hot skillet and bring to a boil to deglaze. Scrape the contents into the slow cooker over the roast and veggies.

6. Place lid on slow cooker and cook on 8- or 10-hour (low) setting. The roast is ready when the meat falls apart into shreds.

## resources

### books

- *American Wasteland: How America Throws Away Nearly Half of Its Food (and What We Can Do About It)* by Jonathan Bloom
- *Forking Fantastic!: Put the Party Back in Dinner Party* by Zora O'Neill and Tamara Reynolds
- *Homemade Root Beer, Soda & Pop* by Stephen Cresswell
- *Tipsy Texan: Spirits and Cocktails from the Lone Star State* by David Alan

### web

- The Kitchn has lots of great beverage roundups and cocktail recipes featuring seasonal ingredients and herbs at www.thekitchn.com.
- Check out great drink recipes at drinks.seriouseats.com.
- Scope out amazing supper clubbing by visiting www.thesundaynightdinner.com, my friend Tamara's website for the Sunday Night Dinner in Astoria.

chapter 9

# *better together*

### *edible gifts and*
### *food parties to host*

If you've played your cards right over the year by stashing away bits and pieces from the best of the seasons, the prospect of homemade kitchen gifts won't hit you up in December like an unexpected house-guest. Despite my meticulous stashing (borderline food hoarding), I'm inevitably not as prepared as I'd like come holiday time, or I decide upon an additional present project that involves some frenzy—what would the holidays be without it? Having a pantry full of in-case-that-project-doesn't-work-out presents is a real relief.

Of course, homemade foods make great gifts no matter the occasion—housewarming, new babies, birthday, or wedding celebrations. Handcrafted, edible food gift baskets and kits are superb presents because they take into account one of our most basic needs—to eat. They're also easy on the wallet. Beyond all this, my favorite reason to give homemade gifts is that they're a thoughtful and unique way to share a bit of you with friends and family.

## food gifting and packaging ideas

I teach a class every year called Gifts in Jars, and it covers how to make homemade holiday gifting easy. Yes, I know you still have to

# food gifting supplies
# to find at the craft store

- Little corks that fit inside standard soda bottles

- Small hole punch to make your own gift tags or jar labels

- Fancy twine (spiral spun colors)

# stuff to buy at the restaurant supply store

- Gift basket accessories (spoons, whisks, spatulas, etc.)

- Go for classic kitchen twine and get it in bulk here

- Assorted sizes of funnels for decanting your homemade goods into bottles

involve yourself in the process of making things, but it's probably much less traumatic than going to the mall anytime during the months of November or December. Here are a few gift set ideas to get you going.

## pull up a mug

One of our favorite holiday traditions is hot cocoa and marshmallows, both of which are extravagant when homemade and make excellent gifts! Friends and family anticipate our now signature holiday gift baskets, with homemade hot cocoa mix and big, deluxe marshmallows.

## pack it

Put cocoa in a mason jar and drop marshmallows in cello bags from the bakery supply store cinched with ribbon with a homemade tag attached (indicating how much and what kind of liquid to add). Include a few candy canes or a nice wooden spoon as an accessory if you'd like.

297

# diy
# gift tags

Spruce up holiday or birthday gifts with simple, sweet gift tags made from scraps of paper. Make the beveled shape by docking the corners and hole-punching between them, or trace around a canning jar lid and make circular tags. Use kitchen or other twine or spring for a roll of pretty, striped gift twine; fold twine in half and feed it through the hole. Feed the ends of the twine through that loop and voilà, gift wrap with some handmade flair!

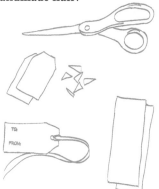

*just add an egg*

No, I'm not talking about sprucing up leftovers or a soup; I'm talking mixes. Extend to your friends some thoughtful convenience by making and packaging dry mixes for homemade pancakes, muffins, and breads. Dry mixes ship well and make perfect basket-mates with other home-canned goods or pantry-staple gift bundles.

*pack it*

If shipping, pack mixes in a new freezer bag and cinch out all air. Place the packet inside a cute paper box or crafty paper sack; anything opaque and sealed airtight will help your leaveners (baking soda/powder) keep their poofing power. If packaging for local friends, use mason jars and create wrap-around labels for the outside of the jar to block light from the mix. Create tags or include on your label or card directions for turning the mix into breakfast or dessert. As an upgrade, include any tools that might make the project smoother or more fun (a nice spatula, an apron for their kid, etc.).

*"there will be snacks, there will"*

The heading here is courtesy of one of my favorite Andrew Bird songs ("Tables and Chairs" on his 2005 album, *Andrew Bird & the Mysterious Production of Eggs*), best lyrics ever. I'm all about snacks and I'd be jazzed at anyone's thinking to give me some. Homemade teatime treats and midafternoon grabs like granola/granola bars, fruit leather, or crackers are relatively simple and such a fun gift.

I love making fruit leather with extra fruit puree (see page 311), which I usually have stashed away in the freezer. It's healthy and sweet and always gobbled right up. For my granola recipe, see page 158. Look up cracker recipes based on your ingredient preferences; I love the array of cracker recipes my friend Marisa has on her blog, foodinjars.com. Another idea for a homemade healthy snack is to craft a unique trail mix from bulk bin goods. Yes, you can go buy any of these easily and affordably, but their homemade versions are almost always superior.

*pack it*

Gift homemade snacks packed into a mason jar or cinched in a cello bag as described in the hot chocolate and marshmallow kit. Accessories that might be a neat addition are picnic blankets that fold into a bag, reusable snack pouches or cute containers for the recipients to refill, or a BPA-free tea pitcher they can use to make hot or cold tea with their snacks.

*condiment-ary*

Assemble homemade condiment baskets: mustard, tomato or other fruit ketchup, relish, infused vinegars, or herby salts and sugars. The great part of this project is that you can make the foods throughout the year (stock up on the main ingredients when they're in season) with a few extra jars' worth in mind for gifting. Holiday time can then be spent at parties with eggnog in hand rather than in your kitchen with a spatula and jar lifter.

## Hip Trick

If you missed making ketchup with summer tomatoes, cranberries are in season around holiday time and cranberry ketchup is a perfect candidate for your condiment gift bundle. I like the recipes for this in *Food in Jars* and the *Ball Complete Book of Home Preserving*, both included in the resources at the end of the chapter.

*pack it*

Buy interesting beverage bottles that come in four-packs with a carrier, and save the carriers. Have a party where the contents of the bottles will be put to good use and save those bottles for packing up infused vinegars, sriracha, or ketchups. Package your homemade condiments in the saved carriers. If your jars are too short and might get lost in a carrier, then head to the craft store and buy a few wooden craft or fruit baskets or hit up the organization store and grab a few metal baskets that are usually used for organizing your drawers (a functional addition to the gift, to boot!). I love including a little spoon, either vintage or new, with these kinds of kits.

## pantry stockings, hung from the mantle with care

A thoughtfully stocked (*not* overstocked) pantry is a prize; consider sharing these kinds of kitchen gifts with friends who will appreciate them.

The thought that goes into giving someone a stash of goods they can and might really enjoy using is what makes these gifts special, not the amount of money you spend. Think of things that are hard to find, more expensive than a normal grocery shop warrants, or generally nonessential but complementary to their kitchen style. Buy these items in bulk and dole them out among (yourself, of course, and) kitchen-savvy pals' gifts. You can never go wrong with tossing in a cute flour sack dishtowel or apron! (I know where you can find some pretty cool ones, too [wink, wink].)

*pantry gift ideas*

- ➥ Vanilla beans
- ➥ Locally milled flour or oats
- ➥ A good olive oil
- ➥ A bar of fancy baking chocolate
- ➥ Coffee beans from a local roaster
- ➥ Truffle oil
- ➥ Loose-leaf teas from a local purveyor

It's also fun to share the food love with items you enjoy, but don't think your friends would ever purchase for themselves. A gift of perishables can be wrapped up in the form of a coupon (you write an IOU on some cardstock or fashion some sort of empty package kind of thing) for things like farm-raised chickens, a gallon of local milk, or fancy artisan cheese. None of these things will cost more than a good present you'd have to go find (they might even be less) and they'll mean a lot to a recipient who loves food but feels restricted by a tight budget.

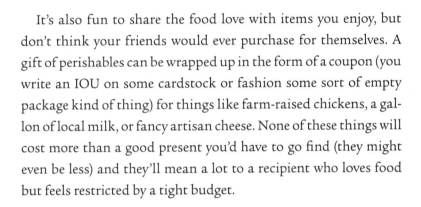

## sweet IOU ideas

- Make up coupons for a home-cooked dinner, where you'll go to a friend's house and cook him/her supper. (Added bonus: You get to eat, too!)

- Wrap up a canning utensil kit and include a coupon for the canning session of his or her choice.

- Buy a set of glass food storage containers and include a coupon for a picnic in the park. Everyone always needs more of these, and everyone loves picnics, right?

## three great ways to give thoughtful food-related gifts

1. Buy a subscription to *Cook's Illustrated, Lucky Peach, Bon Appétit, Food & Wine,* or any other food publication that feels fancy.
2. A gift card to your giftee's favorite grocery or specialty-food store is a simple, yet supremely useful present. It might inspire your giftee to purchase something he or she wouldn't normally purchase as a treat.
3. Make a donation in your friend's name to a pro-food nonprofit organization or hunger-fighting initiative.

## throwing food-making parties

You hopefully conquered your fear of entertaining and all around lowered your stress quotient in Chapter 8. The following types of gatherings are different from regular entertaining, primarily because they require cooperative action and lots of pairs of hands to fly. These parties are a fine way to share the work of all-day food making or any kind of food-making endeavor. I recommend finding a friend to cohost the party with you. Two brains, two sets of arms, two people on top of the supplies are much better than one.

### *pickle party*

I can't think of a good reason not to e-mail everyone you've been trying to make plans with and invite them over to pickle stuff. You don't have to turn this into a full-on canning party (the next party I discuss) because pickling can be done by the single jar (see page 239), and making a creative fridge pickle and maybe another jar of fermented goodness is a fine way to spend time with friends.

Buy an array of seasonal produce directly from the farmers' market and ask if you can get the wholesale discount since you're buying in bulk. Divvy up costs among the number of participants. If you have ten people, you'll need a case or two of jars, about 10–20 pounds of produce (since about 1 pound of vegetables fits in a quart/pint jar), and some vinegar, salt, sugar, and spices. (Roughly 2 pounds of shredded veggies fit into a quart-sized mason jar; double your number of jars if you're planning to make a slaw or kraut.)

Make an estimation about brine volume by using this calculation: you'll need roughly *half the volume of the total number of jars* you're hoping to fill. So with ten people each making a quart of fresh pickles in vinegar brine, you'll need 5 quarts of brine. I always up the brine volume by a bit just in case people don't pack their jars full of produce (and use more brine as a result). Running out of brine is the pits.

### canning party: two ways

I've hosted quite a few canning parties, and there are two general ways to make them work, depending on your desired outcome. Both parties benefit from counter space that's spread around the kitchen and a spare six-foot table if you have one.

If you want to socialize with friends over a cauldron of boiling water, then host a traditional canning party where you collectively go in on the costs and supplies—which usually works out to between $10 and $15 per share—and collectively share in the work. Everyone goes home with a couple jars of the day's projects. In this format you can usually only reasonably manage three projects (due to burner constraints and collective energy level as the afternoon marches on).

It's fun to get together and share the work of canning large volumes of things, like tomatoes, but I've found that if you're serious about putting up a year's worth of something, then splitting the bounty with the three or four friends who help out is not going to yield a pantry full of local tomatoes to eat through the winter months. I suggest hosting the other kind of canning party, which involves forming a very small collective and tag-teaming each other's canning projects, because the solution to the problem of how to end up with a ton of jars—doing it solo—is bleak, intense, and frankly no fun.

The team, which consists of three or four people, descends upon each person's house and rocks the hell out of tomatoes or whatever the harvest in question might be. Block out as many weekend days as there are team members, preferably not consecutive ones if your schedules and the seasonal produce will allow. The host (and beneficiary of the day's yield of jars) provides lunch, snacks, and bevs to keep the team motivated. After everyone on the team has knocked out each of the member's yearly canning needs, plan a dinner party using whatever you canned and share the work of making various dishes. If you managed canning together a few times, you've got a groove in the kitchen for sure!

*sausage-making party*

A party revolving around making sausages from scratch provides the perfect opportunity to gather a handful of friends, sip brunchy cocktails (like those mentioned in Chapter 8), grind up 15–20 pounds of meat, and make plenty of off-color comments and jokes. At the party I attended, we all chipped in and bought sustainably raised, local meats and the casings (which you can get from your local butcher or grocery meat counter) and went home with a couple pounds of sausage for our weekly tables for about $11 each. We made two kinds of sausage, a hot Italian pork and a mustard beef, using a KitchenAid grinder attachment, but for the more tendony beef we had to call in the big guns, a friend's Waring brand meat grinder. As host, you'll want to try and clean out your fridge and freezer a bit so you can store a big bowl or two medium bowls of meat chunks and fat (so it doesn't get too soft) prior to grinding.

### tamalada, a tamale-making party

A few years back my friend Megan, the blogger over at Stetted.com, hosted a tamalada, which is a holiday tradition in Texas. We took over her kitchen table, sipping bottles of Topo Chico, pumpkin beers, and Megan's frozen watermelon margaritas (a genius way to use up one of her last CSA melons), and made 480 tamales! We each brought three quarts of a filling, and she picked up the other essentials, which we then split between us—depending on your ingredients, it will cost between $10 and $15. I went home with five full bags of freezer-ready tamales that were popped out of frozen hibernation and steamed for no- or low-prep dinners for months to come. I also discovered that spreading masa (tamale dough) is one of my preferred forms of stress relief; with each husk splayed before me, the prospect of and accomplishment associated with making perfect spreads (or the chance to rectify the inevitably imperfect ones with the next husk) soothed my holiday frenzies.

Megan wrote a guest post on my blog with tips for first-time hosts. Here are a few of her recommendations:

- Purchase more masa, husks, and fat than you think you'll need. To make 480 tamales, we used 2 bags of instant masa, 2 bags of husks, and approximately 80 ounces of fat.
- Find local lard if you can get it. Yes, it's more expensive, but we all agreed that the flavor and texture of those

batches was superior. Use nonhydrogenated shortening or coconut oil for vegetarian tamales.

- ➻ Have a friend bring an electric mixer if you don't have one, and have friends bring extra mixer bowls so you can keep the batches rolling without having to do dishes each time.

- ➻ Switch roles, and thus make sure at least two people know how to do every step. Megan settled into a groove and got stationed at the mixer, where she became the sole mixer of every batch of the masa, while the rest of us assembling the tamales got to sit and hang out. Most people will likely want to trade tasks at some point, so it's good to spread out the skills and have a musical chairs moment or two throughout the day.

### kids' birthday parties

Incorporating food projects into birthday parties allows kitchen-curious kids to show off their skills among friends and gain a sense of confidence and communal work in the kitchen.

Younger kids might enjoy a playdough-making party. There are a few different ways to make playdough from scratch from things you likely already stock (well, except for cream of tartar). Look it up on instructables.com for both cooked and no-cook options.

Older kids might dig learning how to make bread, applesauce, or jam. Or maybe they want to be charged with baking or decorating a cake on their own with their friends. Younger kids might prefer to run around playing with bubbles, water balloons, and new Lego sets, but when you place a jar of heavy cream in their hands and tell them to shake it if they want whipped cream on their cake, they will. (Overzealous shakers will make butter, at which point you should make toast.)

Both older and younger kids might like combining flours and kneading bread dough. Also consider having the bread-making party as an outdoor event, to spare your kitchen from getting floured beyond repair.

## *cookie swap*

Another holiday favorite is the age-old cookie swap. There are a bunch of ways for this party to roll. My preferred method is pretty relaxed, in all aspects. Ask folks to bring two dozen cookies, something separate to put their take-home cookies in, and possibly a bottle of wine. Any more cookies than that and you and your friends may end up with too many—read: more work than you intended doing and not enough table space.

When it comes to questions of what kind to bring, I say viva variety! Don't limit or micromanage the types of cookies people bring. It's a wonderful feeling to have a homemade batch of your favorite kind. Is there such a thing as too many Christmas cut-outs or, heaven forbid, chocolate chip? If you invite gluten-free or vegan people, make sure there's a handful of other people who have the same dietary restrictions on your invite list so they'll have plenty of trading possibilities. (Don't be wary of trying gluten-free or vegan kinds yourself though—you may be surprised to find out that they can be as delicious as the kinds you're used to eating.) In addition to plenty of gluten-free choices, I took home a bunch of gluten cookies for friends from a swap I attended one year. I also hosted an exclusively gluten-free cookie swap another year, which was so excitingly inclusive for all of us GF attendees.

As host, make cookies if you want, but it's sufficient to focus on supplying cheese and other savory snackables to offset the truckloads of sugar your friends are bringing over. Hot beverages are a fine addition to the festivities, especially mulled wine or mulled cider (see page 279). Form a mingley open area out of wherever you are hosting the swap—maybe it's your kitchen and living room—and utilize every elevated flat space—bookshelves, mantels, coffee tables, and so on—as spots for people to set plates of cookies. Try to keep traffic flow in mind, not cramming tables or directing traffic into corners, because it's hard for more than a couple people to stand there at one time. It's also a good idea to have bags (paper lunch sacks or gallon-sized plastic bags) or boxes on hand so folks who didn't bring their own can pack up cookies to take home.

If you're feeling ambitious, you can ask friends to e-mail you their recipes or bring a copy that you can scan and share post-party with attendees. If you have a lot of time on your hands and money to drop on printer ink cartridges, you can make little recipe packets as party favors. (Cookies are perfectly suitable favors, too.)

## share your successes: swap!

It's not a new idea to gather friends and swap specific items like cookies, dinners, or soups, but in the past few years larger groups have formed across the country (and overseas!) as a way for people to share any kind of homemade goodies. Food swaps are a trend that builds a food community and connections and supports the sharing economy.

Swapping food need not be as involved as pulling together a formal gathering, such as those touted by foodswapnetwork.com. Keep your eyes out for opportunities to practice the neighborly trade, "You have X and I have Y, let's swap." Noticing when neighbors (or local Facebook friends) build chicken coops or take up beekeeping might score you the chance to trade for eggs or local honey. Expanding the one-on-one trades into small swap collectives is another way to diversify your pantry without making everything yourself.

### one-on-one

Reach out to friends who make or produce things you use regularly. I met a friend after returning to Austin who keeps chickens, rabbits, and ducks on her five-acre home just outside of town. She's a busy working lady and took me up on my idea to trade portions of homemade things from my kitchen for two dozen eggs each week.

Our weekly trade inspired me to explore new homemade projects (when it comes to using up those ingredients and by-products discussed in Chapter 7) and to create new sweet or savory preserves, breads, muffins, ferments, or custardy, ice creamy things to include in her bundle.

### small swap collectives

Form small groups and share things surrounding a theme, like fermented foods, paleo baked goods, vegan soups, or gluten-free holiday cookies. Inspired by a "culture club" in Indianapolis, I formed my own here in Austin.

Base your group size on how much making you can realistically wrap into your regular life. For instance, with our fermented food club I don't really have the capacity to make more than a gallon of something at one time, which means I'll end up with four quarts, one for me, three for the group. More people means more coordination (of schedules, items, etc.), so keep it simple.

**309**

## make it official

My friend Emily and I created a network for people to spread the swap love. Our site helps people find swaps near them or start a new food swap if there isn't one. The swapping community is growing, and only one swap since the inception of the website and model has been shut down by a city's health department based on a clause in the state's definition of food sales (saying that a "sale" is also defined as an "exchange," so the swap became subject to all the laws that pertain to food sales). I advise people to discreetly learn about the obscure rules and public safety threats surrounding sharing home-prepared food with people. Another city caught flack but passed out literature about food safety and preparations to avoid foodborne illness, which seemed to appease those concerned with this potluck model of sharing foods.

Hosts, plan your events and proactively ask participants to sign off on a waiver making clear their understanding that all foods that are brought to the swap are prepared in noncommercial kitchen facilities and could be dangerous and releasing you and the venue of liability for participation. Visit foodswapnetwork.com for information on how to host and how to attend, and for other frequently-asked questions surrounding food swapping.

WHO (your name):

WHAT (your item, how many if applicable):

NOTES (e.g. what's in it, how to eat it, what to pair it with, etc.):

_____

OFFERS ("Name/Item"):

_____    _____
_____    _____
_____    _____
_____    _____
_____    _____

*Use back of sheet for additional offers!*

# recipes

## *apple leather roll-ups*

*Yields approximately 9 individual fruit rolls*

1. Preheat oven to 175°F or your lowest setting (between 200°F and 250°F is fine too).

2. Combine in a medium saucepan:
   - **1 cup apple puree** (see method in apple butter recipe on page 242) or any unsweetened applesauce
   - **2 tablespoons sugar**

3. Warm over low heat until sugar granules are dissolved. Remove from heat and add **a pinch ground cinnamon**.

4. Tear off a piece of parchment paper large enough to cover an 11" x 17" walled cookie sheet. Use an icing tool to spread the apple mixture smoothly and evenly across the parchment paper. This is a patience-required kind of activity; breathe and Zen out over it, and just do your best.

5. Bake with door of oven cracked open (to facilitate dehydrating) for anywhere between 2 and 3 hours, until the puree has formed a sticky, but no longer tacky, leather (it doesn't come up on your finger when dabbed). Let cool. Or, if you have a dehydrator, line the tray with parchment paper (for round trays, lay paper over tray and cut out the raised hole in the middle with a knife) and spread as described in step 4. Use the 135°F setting for 1 to 3 hours and only do one tray at a time for best results.

6. Cut up and roll, either with or without parchment paper backing. Store in an airtight container for up to two months.

**311**

## resources

*books*

- *Ball Complete Book of Home Preserving: 400 Delicious and Creative Recipes for Today* edited by Judi Kingry and Lauren Devine
- *The Flavor Bible: The Essential Guide to Culinary Creativity, Based on the Wisdom of America's Most Imaginative Chefs* by Karen Page and Andrew Dornenburg
- *Food in Jars: Preserving in Small Batches Year-Round* by Marisa McClellan
- *The Homemade Pantry: 101 Foods You Can Stop Buying and Start Making* by Alana Chernila

## web

- Check out foodswapnetwork.com to find a swap in your area or get resources to help you host your first swap.
- Buy a stack of hand-drawn, screen-printed flour sack towels from my online shop at hipgirls.bigcartel.com.
- Read about hosting skill-share parties and see photos on my blog, hipgirlshome.com.
- Look for great kitchen gift add-ons at fishseddy.com.
- See homemade gift idea roundups at thekitchn.com.

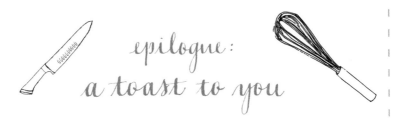

# epilogue: a toast to you

Congratulations on making friends with your kitchen, learning its limitations and defects (and proceeding anyway), and endeavoring to feed yourself, possibly feed others, and maybe make things you thought you'd never make. If we wait for the perfect house in which to cook elaborate meals and entertain with flair, or until we can afford that long-lusted-after dining room table that seats more than four people, we'll miss out on all sorts of opportunities to hone our abilities and test our new skills. I commend you for continuing to work out the kinks and confusions and keeping at it, for trying again after the failures, and for talking to as many kitchen-savvy people as you can find and asking them questions.

Welcoming the kitchen into your daily life is no small feat. Remember, this is a lifelong relationship that ebbs and flows alongside our human relationships, obligations in life, and career ambitions. Sometimes we just need a little refresher or reminder so we can pick up where we left off on the journey. The kitchen can mean so many things to different people, but, above all, I hope it brings you community, in one form or another.

# appendix 1
## my essential measures

### dry

1 tablespoon = 3 teaspoons

¼ cup = 4 level tablespoons

⅓ cup = 3 heaping tablespoons

### liquid

2 tablespoons = 1 ounce

1 cup = 8 ounces

2 cups = 1 pint

2 pints = 1 quart

4 quarts = 1 gallon

### weight

16 ounces = 1 pound

### butter

2 tablespoons = 1 ounce

1 stick = 8 tablespoons or ½ cup

4 sticks = 1 pound

### substituting butter for olive (or other) oil

*butter:olive oil*

1 teaspoon = ¾ teaspoon

1 tablespoon = 2¼ teaspoons

2 tablespoons = 1½ tablespoons

¼ cup = 3 tablespoons

⅓ cup = ¼ cup

½ cup = ¼ cup plus 2 tablespoons

⅔ cup = ½ cup

¾ cup = ½ cup plus 1 tablespoon

1 cup = ¾ cup

### temperatures for meats

You can follow the temperatures listed on your meat thermometer's sheath, but they're often higher than necessary. The temperatures shown below come from foodsafety.gov and represent the minimum internal temperature to which you should bring meats to make sure they are fully cooked. (You should still call your parents on occasion and pretend to ask them, though; it will make them feel good.)

| | |
|---|---|
| Poultry *(chicken, turkey, duck)* | 165°F |
| Beef or lamb | 145°F |
| *(steaks, roasts, chops)* | |
| Pork | 145°F |
| Ground meat and sausages | 165°F |
| *(chicken, turkey)* | |
| Ground meat and sausages | 160°F |
| *(beef, pork)* | |

**314**

**frozen spoon test:**
**how to tell whether your sweet**
**preserves have set**

Stick four or five metal teaspoons on a plate in the freezer before you start your jam or jelly.

When you think your preserves have reached a set, remove the pot from the heat. Grab your plate of spoons from the freezer and dip one of the spoons into the pot and scoop up a little of the preserves.

Place the spoon back on the plate and set the plate back in the freezer for a few minutes. Remove the plate again and observe the texture of the preserves when you tip the spoon over. This is what your preserves will be like at room temperature and in the fridge after you open the jar. If they are still runny or syrupy, return the pot to the heat and continue to cook them. Retest by repeating these steps.

**cleaning the kitchen**

Yes, you can stop using bleach in the kitchen (and everywhere else in your house). Yes, really. I described in detail in Chapter 5 of *The Hip Girl's Guide to Homemaking* how using chlorine bleach around your house creates a slew of dangerous compounds called organochlorines, which are toxic and persistent in the environment. Plus, I bet you didn't know that in order to actually disinfect, chlorine bleach–based sprays must be allowed to dry—no wiping them off. (It double sucks to use toxic

## homemade counter spray

Buy a heavy-duty spray bottle and fill it with half vinegar and half water. Add five to ten drops of your favorite essential oil to cut out the smell of vinegar; we use mint essential oil (be sure to get a pure oil, nothing that says "fragrance"), which makes our spray smell like Thin Mints!

**315**

chemicals and not actually achieve true disinfection all this time.)

When you need to disinfect, trade the persistent chemical spray for a botanical disinfectant like Seventh Generation's disinfecting product line (and follow their instructions for use). These products use an extract of thyme oil to achieve the same EPA-certified kill rate (99.9 percent) as chlorine bleach.

### how to load a dishwasher

Yes, I know that you are probably in charge of many moving parts at work; you command people, deadlines, and small circuses every day. Some people were never properly schooled in the art of loading a dishwasher, while for others it might be a fairly intuitive process. I will say that this task, no matter how easy it seems or how miraculous or expensive your dishwasher is, can still be messed up (and leave you with gross silverware or dishes that need to be rewashed).

If your dishwasher has particular design features or finicky behaviors, then consulting your manual might be a good place to start. No matter what the commercials say, no dishwasher gets residue off muffin tins without some presoaking action.

## hand wash only

- Anything made of wood or bamboo
- Knives you (should) sharpen
- Cast iron
- Nonstick pots and pans

1. **Prewash.** Like anything you wash, your dishes require a complementary rinse before being thrown into a hot and heavy dishwasher. To prewash, fill a bowl or pot (preferably one that's already dirty in the sink), or even one side of the sink if you have a divider, with water, and dip your scrubby pad or dishcloth in there to give those dirty dishes a swipe. Crusted-on things, or even just gooed on things, will not find magic redemption in the dishwasher; you'll just end up with bits of food on your rack or in the bottom, and heat-set, crusted-on food on your pots or plates.

    Growing up, it was hard for me to tell if the dishes in the dishwasher were dirty or clean because they went through a solid (nonsoapy) rinsing prior to their deep clean. While some may protest, this method means you get spotless and impeccably clean dishes every time, which is a claim I can't make for other approaches.

2. **Silverware: face up or face down? That is the question.** My answer is always up, unless it's a steak knife. Think of it this way: you might be attached to putting your flatware facedown so that when you unload it you don't touch it and get it dirty. Well, how about washing your hands before you unload the dishwasher (something you ought to do anyway), and then pulling the cutlery out carefully and trying not to handle them too much? Otherwise, when they are crammed into the basket they get a mediocre wash, with the part you're going to eat from receiving less cleaning action.

3. **Fill 'er up.** There should never be just a single layer on your dishwasher racks. Running the dishwasher uses a lot of water and energy, and we should maximize the value of those things each time we use it. My approach is to build layered structures, starting with

smaller dishes on the bottom and larger things surrounding them. (Make sure your layers don't cause one dish to completely block water and soap slosh from another.) You can always fit more items in there if you layer them well—e.g., a few bowls, funnels, or large utensils set over the top of a full rack of glasses. When building layer two, be sure that the items are secure and won't topple over when the dishwasher is filled midcycle with water—they'll require a rewash. (Avoid layering if you're not on board with the pre-wash philosophy.)

The top-rack dishwasher-safe icon looks like this:

If in doubt, hand wash.

## garbage disposal basics

I grew up with a garbage disposal, but then I went to college and lived in umpteen places without one. We have inched progressively over the years to a place where we now throw so little food in the actual trash can (thanks, compost!) that I can't see when we'd ever use one.

Honestly, I don't think disposals

Don't feel bad if you're not quite ready to part with disposaling. Here's a rundown on what should never go down the garbage disposal:

- Potato peels and other stringy, tough veggies like celery, asparagus, and oversize okra

- Rice and pasta

- Animal bones (you're using them for stock now, anyway [wink, wink])

- Grease (freeze it in a paper cup and throw it in the garbage)

should have a place in modern kitchens anymore. I urge you to spend your renovation dollars on something else—maybe prettier backsplash tiles or a fun sprayer faucet. I hope I've given you plenty of ideas for putting your disposal out of a job (or at least cutting his hours drastically). See Chapter 5 for ideas for cooking scraps into stocks and for inspiration toward actually eating those leftovers via the grand repurpose.

Clean and deodorize your garbage disposal by putting down the disposal half of an orange or lemon peel (roughly chopped) with two tablespoons of kosher salt. Grind with cold water, as usual, until there's no more grinding action; then pour a splash of vinegar down the drain while the cold water is running. Finish the whole ordeal off with a kettle full of boiling water.

If there's a persistent odor after this, try pouring a quarter- to a half-cup hydrogen peroxide down there and letting it sit for fifteen minutes. Repeat the boiling water rinse.

# glossary

**Blanch:** Method used prior to freezing foods; involves dipping vegetables in boiling water for a minute or two and then transferring them to an ice-water bath before packaging and sealing them for freezing. The boiling water deactivates enzymes that affect color (pigment) and the breakdown of vitamins, and the ice-water dip stops further cooking and damage to cell walls. Blanching thus helps keep foods true to their original colors and able to retain their nutritional value when frozen.

**Braise:** A cooking method in which food is seared at a high temperature and then cooked in liquid, covered, on low heat (200°F–300°F) for four to eight hours. Braising is an ideal way to cook tougher (a.k.a. less expensive) cuts of meat and can also be done in a slow cooker.

**Cassoulet:** Braised thick stew typically consisting of duck, pork sausage, and white beans; originated in a region of France.

**Chop (type of cut):** Cutting up vegetables, usually into half- to one-inch pieces. This word alone in a recipe's instructions usually means that large, uneven pieces will be fine.

**Consommé:** A clear soup known for its distinct flavors imparted into a well-strained broth; egg whites are typically used to strain out fat and sediment.

**Dash (measure):** An imprecise measure that's equivalent to roughly ⅛ teaspoon.

**Deglaze:** Removing browned food residue from a pan to make a sauce. This is achieved by pouring off most of the cooking fat and drippings, adding a few tablespoons of any liquid, bringing the mixture to a boil again for a few seconds, stirring vigorously, and then removing it from the heat. Use this liquid to make a sauce or gravy.

**Dice (type of cut):** Finely chopping food into small, evenly sized pieces.

**Dutch oven:** A nonenamel cast-iron pan with a lid (see illustration on page 6); must be seasoned.

**Folding (egg whites or whipped cream):** Technique used in baking to create a light and fluffy batter by using a spoon spatula to gently incorporate airy ingredients into an existing batter. To do this you should scoop and turn portions of the mixture over, turning the bowl slowly as you go; do not stir.

**French oven:** Enamel cast-iron pan with a lid commonly used for braising, cooking stews, or making jams and jellies (see illustration on page 6).

**Fry:** Food is either halfway submerged in cooking oil (shallow frying) or fully submerged (deep frying) and placed over high heat.

**Mince (type of cut):** Cutting as small as you possibly can; when mincing garlic, actually mashing and smearing it using the side of the blade of your knife will help you make it tiny.

**Mirepoix:** Flavor base of nearly all soups, stocks, and roasts; consists of onions, carrots, and celery sautéed in oil or other fat. *Mirepoix* is French; the Italian version is called *soffritto* and consists of onions, garlic, and celery.

**Monounsaturated fat:** These fatty acids come from vegetables, seeds, fruits, and certain animal fats. They are more stable under heat and exposure to the elements than polyun-saturated fats, but they are less stable than saturated fats. These fats are typically liquid at room temperature and solid when stored in the refrigerator; see a list of monounsaturated fats on page 103.

**Nonreactive:** Cookware or containers that will not react with salt and vinegar or other cooking acids; examples of nonreactive materials include glass, ceramic, stainless steel, and food-grade plastic. If a recipe calls for nonreactive materials, do not use aluminum, copper, or cast iron.

**Oxidize:** A chemical reaction that happens when chemicals in food are exposed to oxygen. Oxidation causes a loss of nutritional value and changes in chemical composition; in fats and oils, oxidation leads to rancidity, and in fruits and vegetables (like apples or potatoes), it creates discoloration and browning.

**Panfry:** Similar to sautéing but done with larger pieces of food (like a cut of meat) over a lower heat, so the exterior of the food doesn't burn while you're waiting for its interior to cook.

**Pinch (measure):** An imprecise measure that's equivalent to the amount of a dry ingredient you can pinch

320

between your thumb and forefinger, which is about 1/16 teaspoon, or half a dash.

**Polyunsaturated fat:** These fatty acids come from seeds, nuts, fish, and grains. They are the most susceptible to heat, oxygen, and light and go rancid faster than saturated and monounsaturated fats. These fats are typically liquid at both room temperature and in the refrigerator. See a list of polyunsaturated fats on page 103.

**Proof (alcohol):** Approximately double the percentage of alcohol. Forty proof is 20 percent alcohol and 80 percent water; in a bottle of spirits, 100 proof is 50 percent alcohol and 50 percent water.

**Proof (bread/baking):** Allowing the yeast to activate by giving it a snack, usually sugar and warm water (105°F–110°F). When it bubbles and foams up, you know your yeast is awake and ready for action. Yeast packets usually have a "use by" date on them, so there's no need to proof it to determine freshness (unless it's expired). Recipes will indicate whether you should proof in advance, so just follow their lead.

**Saturated fat:** The most chemically stable of the fats, which means a long shelf life and ability to hold up under high cooking temperatures. These fats are typically solid at room temperature. See a list of saturated fats on page 103.

**Sauté:** Panfrying small pieces of food in a small amount of some sort of fat (butter, oil, or other fat) over medium-high or high heat until they are browned on the outside and cooked through.

**Scant:** Imprecise measuring term indicating that you should fill the measuring utensil with just under the amount indicated. A scant one teaspoon means that the measuring spoon will be not quite filled to the top.

**Sear:** Placing food in a hot pan with some sort of fat and browning it on each side, usually for no longer than three minutes.

**Sift:** Using a fine-mesh strainer or sifter tool to separate dry ingredients like flour or confectioners' sugar into fine, evenly sized particles.

**Smidge or smidgen (measure):** An imprecise measurement that's approximately half of a pinch.

**Soft peaks (egg whites):** Term used for the look of egg whites when you

pick your whisk up out of the bowl and the whites are just starting to keep their shape, but the point falls back into the bowl after a second.

**Standard American Diet (SAD):** Stereotypical diet consisting mostly of refined carbohydrates, lots of processed meats, and calorie-dense but nutrient-deficient foods (like fast foods or processed food with added fats and sugars); fresh fruits and vegetables and whole grains are largely missing from the diet.

peak

**Stiff peaks (egg whites):** Term used for the look of egg whites when you pick your whisk up out of the bowl and the whites keep their shape, pointing up and not collapsing at all.

**Stir-fry:** Same method and theory as sautéing but done in a differently shaped pan (a wok or a larger pan that allows you to stir the food around to get it evenly heated).

**Tempering:** Method of introducing cold or room-temperature liquids to hot liquids by first mixing small amounts of hot liquid into the cold one, and then adding the warmed mixture to the rest of the hot mixture very slowly. This stabilizes the cold mixture and prevents it from curdling.

**Vinegar:** Composed of acetic acid, which is a good solvent because half of its molecule is more fatlike and the other half is waterlike. One end draws in flavors (which are fragile oils) and the other end passes those oils into things with a high water content, such as vegetables or syrups.

**Umami:** A savory flavor, one of the five basic flavors; the others are sweet, bitter, sour, and salty.

# acknowledgments

Thank you to Irma Rombauer, who opened up the kitchen to people like me.

Meredith Dawson started out as the agent who plucked me from the myriad of interweb domesticity dabblers and made my vision of a book a reality. When you ditched agenting to pursue illustration and graphic design, my heart sang. Thank you for illustrating so beautifully and with such grace. These images are perfect and make the book so lovely.

Alison Hanks found time amid being "Coco" to her daughter's newborn triplets to lend her stunning penmanship. I adore your style and appreciate your bending the calligraphy rules to make a perfectly imperfect cursive script for these books.

I've found a good friend in Julia Abramoff, my editor at HarperCollins, who catches and connects and polishes behind the scenes. I'm so lucky to have your brains and direction as a guide.

I'm still dazzled that Eugenia Bone responded to my e-mail

a handful of years ago, and I'm honored beyond words that she wrote the foreword to this book. Thank you for being a fabulous mentor in the business of writing and eating well.

Thank you to all the people who taught me how to do things in the kitchen. I am grateful for friends and family, including Wanalee, Rose, Stella, Mary, Dawna, Meaghan, Missy, Bob, Zora, Lottie, Emily, Lisa, Hilah, Megan, Tricia, Audra, Andy, Shae, Joel, Amy, Kim, Ernest, Andrew, and many more. And, no less important, thanks to Grandma Mannie, a.k.a. Bertha Burnham, for showing me how *not* to do things in the kitchen.

Thank you to the Kidz—you know who you are—for always listening and for all the "wind," both in person and in solidarity. Beyond the blessings of blog club, I'm doubly thankful to Sean, Kaela, Julia, Meg, Marisa, and Joel, pals that kick ass with gluten, for swooping in and saving the day. I love sharing your recipes in this book.

I am beyond grateful for Christina, my marketing coordinator and in-house illustrator. Thank you for all the gorgeous hand-drawn fliers, for learning fast, and for helping keep me sane.

My dad taught me how not to measure things. Watching him pinch and dash his way through my childhood of kitchen observation empowered me to understand that cooking is about making stuff taste good, and not making a fuss over precision. Thank you for giving me that power.

I wouldn't know how to problem-solve and think on my feet without the excellent example I have in my mama. You laid the foundation for all this culinary adventuring (even though you're not sure whose kid I am sometimes). Thank you for stepping out of your comfort zone and trying your hand at yogurt making (and then trying it over and over and over again) until it worked in your overly efficient oven.

This book exists because I met (and married) Jo Ann, who ended my manic relationship with the kitchen. I feel lucky to sit across from you every day and share the food we make. You teach me the art of patience, timing, and calm in the kitchen and beyond.

*index*

**327**